CHILDHOOD

PHASES OF

MATURITY

SEXUAL DEVELOPMENTAL PSYCHOLOGY

ERNEST BORNEMAN

INTRODUCTION BY VERN L. BULLOUGH
Translated by Michael A. Lombardi-Nash

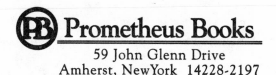
Prometheus Books
59 John Glenn Drive
Amherst, NewYork 14228-2197

Published 1994 by Prometheus Books

98 97 96 95 94   5 4 3 2 1

Library of Congress Cataloging-in-Publication Data

Borneman, Ernest, 1915–
    [Reifungsphasen der Kindheit. English]
    Childhood phases of maturity : sexual developmental
psychology / Ernest Borneman ; translated by Michael
Lombardi-Nash.
        p.   cm.
    Includes bibliographical references and index.
    ISBN 0-87975-895-3 (alk. paper)
    1. Children and sex. 2. Sexual disorders in children.
I. Title.
BF723.S4B6513   1994
155.4'18—dc20   94-18036
                                                      CIP

Printed in the United States of America on acid-free paper.

Dedicated to Prof. Dr. Hans Czermak

In their entire life, people never again learn so much in so short a time.

—René Spitz on the first months of a child

It is a basic error to assume that school-age children are asexual, and that when sexuality suddenly appears among them, it is abnormal. Exactly the opposite is the case.

—Tobias Brocher

We should condemn the sexual misconduct of our children only when we have done something to prevent it. To be sure, we can prevent it only through radical changes of the family and the state, but with more competent sex education in schools and at home, parents and teachers can perhaps temper the worst. But we should not accuse them of incompetence when they do not succeed. For, where were they supposed to have learned to educate their children?

—Wilhelm Reich

The moment of the first appearance of a specific mode of an infant's behavior is not important, because healthy children manifest different developmental tempi. The duration of a certain phase of behavior is also not essential, because it varies from child to child. The only important thing is the maturational sequence of the developmental steps, because from it alone one can recognize whether the child is healthy or ill. If one step is missing or if the succession of steps departs from the culturally specific sequence, then the child is abnormal according to the standards of this culture. Whether the child is biologically ill depends on the species-specific maturational sequence of developmental stages. But whether there is one such among people generally, we unfortunately still do not know according to today's position of comparative cultural anthropology.

—Bronislaw Malinowski

Contents

Foreword by Vern Bullough   **11**

Preface   **13**

Introduction   **19**

1. From Conception to Birth
   Prenatal and Perinatal Phase   **33**

2. First Month
   Newborn Age   **49**

3. Second to Sixth Month
   Early Infancy Age   **67**

4. Seventh to Twelfth Month
   Late Infancy Age   **89**

5. Second Year
   Toddler Age   **121**

 6. Third Year
    Beginning of the Toddler's Puberty   143

 7. Fourth Year
    Middle of the Toddler's Puberty   181

 8. Fifth Year
    End of the Toddler's Puberty   205

 9. Sixth Year
    Beginning of Childhood   231

10. Seventh Year
    Middle Childhood   253

11. Eighth Year
    End of Childhood   269

Afterword   277

Bibliography   283

Addendum: Translator's Note   321

Index   323

Foreword

Vern L. Bullough

This is a path-breaking book, the first comprehensive examination of sex in childhood development between conception and the end of the eighth year. Although the ages and stages of development have been popular topics for both parents and experts, left out in most previous discussions has been the accompanying psychosexual development. One of the reasons for this lack is simply that retroactive memory, a valuable source for constructing sexual histories, is not very valid for early childhood. Trying to overcome this lack of information has proved difficult because of public unwillingness to tolerate the kind of observations and testing in this area of childhood that it has permitted in others. Floyd Martinson, one of the few researchers to combine retrospective interviews with some observational data, found that even publishing such information met resistance, and to get the information out he had to publish it himself.[1] Alfred Kinsey relied on parental observations, and a few interviews in which children were accompanied by their parents. He also utilized detailed records kept by pedophiles, but usually again for older children. American researchers today, however, could not do what Kinsey did, because of the necessity of getting research projects through human-subjects

11

committees, something almost impossible to do because of the public anxieties over child abuse.

It is somewhat easier to do such studies in Europe, but even there it is difficult, and this is why Borneman's study is so important. He not only observed and collected data on some four thousand children eight years of age or younger over a twenty-year period, but developed a number of tests, including dream analysis, game experiment, longitudinal and cross-sectional examinations, and analysis of children's verses. Although this book is based on European children rather than American, his results should apply to American children in much the same way that the studies of Arnold Gessel, Jean Piaget, Erik Erikson, and others have managed to give us a portrait of different aspects of childhood that cross national boundaries.

Most important is Borneman's discussion of sex education as it should be for young children. Among other things he holds that the sex life of children is more complicated in earlier phases of development than later ones, that it has very much more in common with the adult sex life than with that of any animal model, that childhood sex is more than coitus, that actual sex contacts make up only a small part of the life of the child or of the adult, and that no aspect of adult sexual life can be understood without understanding that of the child. He might not be fully correct in some of his interpretations, but the burden is on those who disagree to furnish additional data.

In short, Borneman puts the study of childhood sexuality on a new plane and his book, as translated by Michael Lombardi-Nash, is a must for all of those who deal with children.

Note

1. Floyd N. Martinson, *Infant and Child Sexuality* (St. Peter, Minn., 1973).

Preface

The present book is the first work in which anyone has ever tried to set forth the sexual development of children in precise phases organized according to the stages of life.

This is the first of three volumes. The second concerns itself in the same way with the phases of sexual development of adolescents; the third, with those of adults.

At the conclusion of each chapter is a section entitled "Pathology" that deals with not only the age-specific sexual disorders of a given phase of development, but also the later results of fixations on or regressions to this phase. It is supposed to serve as instructions for physicians, parents, and schoolteachers and to make possible a preventive obstacle to such damages.

The educational discipline on which this book is based is sex pedology, the science of the sexual development of healthy children. Since there are no teaching chairs for sexual pedology in Germany, in Switzerland, or in Austria, this book serves as preparatory work for the establishment of such chairs.

In this sense the book follows on the textbook of my associate, Professor Tobias Brocher, M.D., *Psychosexuelle Grundlagen der Entwicklung* (Psychosexual fundamentals of development) (Opladen: Leske Verlag, 1971), published on commission for the Bund Ministry of Youth, Family, and Health of the Federal Center for Health Education. The book also follows the principles of the book of instructions for schoolteachers: *Gesundheitserziehung* (Health education) (Basel: Orell Füssli Verlag, 1964), published by order of the Swiss federal government and funded by the Pro Juventute Foundation.

This book is not a textbook of sex education, but it will be of use in the education of schoolteachers for academic sex education insofar as it presents age-specific standards for the sexual development of children and should help teachers to answer the questions of concerned parents whether their children are mature enough at a given age for certain sexual information.

In the final chapter the book certainly does cite a few of the psychical, psychosexual, and psychosomatic effects of incorrect education in schools and at home, but it does not pretend to prescribe some secret formula for the "proper" way to raise children. It is one of the acknowledged weaknesses of today's sex educators that they can certainly establish which failures in the sexual development of children can be traced to which type of wrongful parental or educational conduct, but they are not in the position to suggest forms of parental or schoolteaching behavior that could with certainty prevent the sexual developmental failure of children.

This is true to the same degree in pediatrics, child psychology, child psychiatry, and child psychoanalysis, because although these four specialities are not able to say to parents and teachers what they should *do* to raise healthy children, they can on the contrary, only say what they should *not* do. These colleagues also need a guidebook to the age-specific sexual development of children as an initial prophylactic resource against the sexual neglect of children. The present book attempts to supply this guide.

The sexual development of children is important, because it is the regulator of all other phases of development in childhood, and because it decisively influences the intellectual development of children. This realization can hardly be rated high enough in the academic field, because almost all of the Western countries have created laws that authorize or even make obligatory school sex education, yet few countries prepare instructors for these lessons.

In many countries teachers are thrown into the pool of sex education and have to sink or swim. They often founder, because they have neither received training in this function nor can refer to any authorized textbook. If they are assailed by worried parents who feel that teachers are undermining their parental custody rights, teachers find themselves supported by neither their own school boards nor even duly qualified governmental agencies, because there, too, the question of school sex education is controversial.

But why is it controversial? Because the sexual development of school-age children can only be understood as a result of the sexual development of infants and toddlers, and this only as a result of the sexual development of children in the mother's womb. A textbook of sexual development of school-age children that is not based on the preschool sexual development of children would be less than an unfinished work; it would be an absurdity. For this reason the present work does not begin with elementary school enrollment but with procreation.

In sex education we interpret "sex life" as life as a sexual being. In this sense children have a sex life not only from birth on, but also right from the time of conception. The principal difference between the sex life of humans and that of other mammals lies in humans' greater interest in fantasies and their lesser interest in the process of procreation. On the one hand, our sex life results in almost total independence from our procreation and, on the other hand, is determined more by desires and fears than by physical contacts. We are not conscious of these desires and fears. They run similarly in our dreams as in wakefulness. They are probably already created in rudimentary form by the incomplete nerve and brain apparatus in the unborn child. The opinion that children have no sex life only because they do not participate in coitus is, therefore, false. With regard to desires and fears, the sex life of children is more active than that of adults.

Yet, if the sex life of children occurs less in their sexual behavior than in their imagination, then how do we as adults know that it exists at all? As most people know, our sexual development is divided into three parts by two periods of intensive inhibition—infantile and pubertal amnesia—so that adults usually possess no recollection of their childhood sexual behavior, not to mention the sexual desires and fears of their childhood. This has made the research of child sexuality enormously more difficult, because it has debased one of the most important instruments of research, autobiographical notes.

A few other research methods remain: longitudinal research of one single child or of a small group of children over a number of years; cross-sectional examination of a larger group of children at a certain stage in their sexual development; the evaluation of the medical records of pediatricians, child psychologists, and child psychiatrists; the evaluation of the analyses noted by child analysts. As opposed to animal research, we should do only limited experiments with humans, and as opposed to the experimental sex research on adults, we should not do any sexual experiments at all on children. Even the questioning of children about their sexual notions and behavior is rejected by many parents and educational authorities. Therefore, we are confined to observation and to the evaluation of medical case histories, with one exception: children's dreams. There are approximately three thousand to four thousand children's dreams available in published or unpublished form—partly in the books by child analysts, partly in their unpublished notes. The author of this book consulted this material.

However, this book is based especially on the empirical work methods of Arnold Gesell, D. W. Winnicott, John Bowlby, René Spitz, Ernest Kris, and Margaret Mahler, and to a lesser extent on those of Jean Piaget, Henri Wallon, and René Zazzo. The works of the Austrian school (Charlotte Bühler, Hildegard Hetzer, Katharina Wolf) and of the French child analysts (O. Brunet, I. Lézine, S. Lebovici) have also had great influence on the form and content of the book. These researchers have undertaken both longitudinal and cross-sectional examinations to establish significantly and statistically at what age the appearance of a certain pattern of behavior can be viewed as normal. They have organized standard settings to establish how a large number of experimental persons react to the same experiment directive.

Between the years 1960 and 1980, my colleagues and I made use of dream analysis and game experiments in a prepared setting in addition to direct observation, longitudinal, and cross-sectional examinations, as well as a sixth research method I have explained in detail in the three volumes of my *Studien zur Befreiung des Kindes* (Studies on the liberation of children), in which I deal with the age-specific acceptance of traditional children's verses by individual children whose homes and parents' methods of upbringing we surveyed. Since every traditional children's verse most certainly contains sexual strong points, very clear conclusions about the strong points of their sexual development can be drawn from the age at which certain children admit a certain verse into their repertoire, as well as from the age at which they give it up and turn to another verse. Over a time span of twenty years we tested this method on approximately four thousand children. For it, see Ernst Borneman, *Die Umwelt des Kindes im Spiegel seiner "verbotenen" Reime, Verse und Rätsel* (The environment of children in the mirror of their "forbidden" rhymes, verses, and riddles) (Olten and Freiburg i. Br.: Walter Verlag, 1974; reprint, Berlin: Ullstein Taschenbuchverlag, 1980), pp. 369–74.

Introduction

This first volume of a textbook of sexual developmental psychology is entitled *Childhood Phases of Maturity*. The combination of the words "developmental," "maturity," and "phases" will prompt the critical reader to pose a number of questions: Was the basic concept of developmental psychology not revealed to be a biological one long ago? Has not the idea that human ontogeny proceeds in phases not been long out of date? Does the word "maturity" not carry traces of moral value, implications that are inadmissible in the value-free field of science?

Each of these protests is justified, but such great differences of opinion between the various schools of developmental psychology have made it hardly possible today to speak of one, unified developmental psychology. The founders of developmental psychology were conservative folk who, on the one hand, believed in an internal control over the psychical process of development. On the other hand, however, they stood with both feet so firmly planted in their own culture that all other forms of psychical development seemed "primitive" or even "abnormal" to them. That means: On the one hand, they were biologists, and on the other hand, Eurocentrists—maintaining two attitudes that are not

compatible with each other. Because if psychical development is biologically controlled, then it must run the same
course at all times in all societies, classes, and cultures. If
it does not run the same course at all times in all social
orders and strata, then external influences serve as a basis
for it, at least in part.

Today hardly any developmental psychologists of the
old school dispute every social, cultural, or historical influence on psychical ontogeny, but the extent of external
influences in comparison with the internal is still disputed
as before. Many European and American developmental
psychologists still believe that the timetables of maturity
and stages of development, which they derived from empirical observation of European and American children and
youth, are also valid for children and young people of other
cultures. Then, when it is proved to them that almost nothing
that we observed is valid in "countries that developed differently from ours" or even in the "underdeveloped" regions
of the world, these psychologists mostly become uncertain
to such an extent that they either doubt the observations
of the anthropologists or stubbornly continue to occupy themselves with their eurocentric scales and with the tables
determined by white American children.

Another childhood malady of Euro-American developmental psychology was its bias toward the somatic and the
measurable. Two dangers arose from this: first, the under-
estimation of unquantifiable psychical processes; second, the
inclination to view psychic developmental occurrences as
consequences of the somatic.

Psychical processes are certainly functions of somatic
organs, but they diverge in an extremely complicated, and
for the most part, unexplored manner from the processes
involved in bodily maturity and development. Physically
"mature" children do not need to be psychically "mature,"
and physically "developed" children do not necessarily show
an analogous psychical development. Whether there is any

somatic basis at all for psychical phases of development is unclear. Morphological, hormonal, and other perceivable somatic phases of sexual development—for example, pubarche, menarche, polluarche, and seminarche—in any case have no provable influence on the psychosexual processes of maturity. They can precede them, lag behind them, or run their course in a fully independent periodicity. Correlative and statistical comparative analyses between somatic and psychical development are often sometimes positive to be sure, yet they are seldom significant.

All individuals will naturally be controlled by their genetic hereditary factors, but the genes regulate only the *potential* behavior of the individual. If and to what extent organisms *realize* their genetic potential depends on their environment. And yet, since the beginning of the human species, hardly anything has changed in human biomorphosis and that of its determined sequence of phases. Since the early Stone Age, our phases of maturity have been meticulously programmed in the same genetic way down to the last hair. But the program is a *latent* one: if and to what extent it *manifests* itself depends on ecological and social influences to which individuals are exposed from conception until death.

In this fluctuation between the environment and individual, children for their part influence and change their environment to a great extent. Therefore, a broad picture of childhood phases of maturity should not be limited to those phases that the children experience with their own bodies, but must also indicate the influence they exert on their environment.

In any case, attempts to coordinate physical and mental developmental processes have proved to be unexpectedly difficult. For example, Paschlau and Paschlau (1963) studied 612 male and 612 female elementary school pupils in Stuttgart to prove that accelerated physical development went with good school performance, while delayed physical development, on the other hand, accompanied poor school achievement. The barely discernible problem of accelerated and delayed development in this case is based, at least in part, on the complication that both the somatic and psychical processes of development in humans do not process at a constant tempo, but rather advance in thrusts, phases, stages, or periods. (We are using these terms synonymously and interchangeably, as opposed to Busemann, who assigns different meanings to them.) This becomes most clear in the intermittent fluctuations in physical height and weight that present themselves as proportional shifts in the human body during childhood and adolescence. So, for example, head size decreases in degrees in proportion to the entire height of the body, while bone length increases in degrees in proportion to the height of the body.

Very similar phase problems also become apparent in the case of the development of the different sexes, and especially in the case of psychosexual development. Because these processes are enormously variable, any attempt at giving a binding statement about the age at which children go through a certain phase of development is destined to fail from the start. First, the developmental phases of boys and girls are not identical. Second, the individual variations within the sexes are widely compartmentalized. Third, enormous differences between children result from their different social histories. Fourth, there are observable differences between the different regions of each nation, but especially between city and country. Fifth, the parents' politics, religion, and world view play a major role in the sexual development of children. Sixth, the sexual maturity of children is determined by the attitudes toward sexuality held by those in charge of the children's upbringing. This last factor influences sexual development to a much higher degree than all of the other factors.

All together, these variables determine an approximately ± 20 percent difference of the respective age. When we use the word "age-specific" in the following, we therefore mean not a certain age, but rather a certain phase of development or, expressed in terms of age, a span of ± 20 percent around the mean age of this phase.

The expression "phase of maturity," must also be defined. Since 1946, the rule had developed in pedology that phases of maturity were no longer to be equated with phases of development. Rather the first expression was to be limited to phylogenetic and innate functions and ways of behavior, and the second reserved for those forms and ways of behavior and functions that result from an exchange between individuals and their environment. This distinction is legitimate and rational in the case of many developmental and maturational processes, but it is impractical in a textbook of sexual developmental psychology, because at every stage of development inherited sexual influences coincide with the learned; the phylogenetic influence coincides with the ontogenetic, and the innate sex influence coincides with the environmental.

Environmental influences already affect genetic makeup of the children during conception and pregnancy. Even the process of birth, too, is influenced by environmental conditions. They threaten the future life of children almost as much as those genetic and chromosomal malformations that we will discuss later. A slight loss of oxygen during birth can at once negate all the positive genetic material. In the face of these facts it is advisable to include, under the concept of "phases of maturity," all those nonbiological processes that Hartmann, Kris, Loewenstein (1946), and Spitz (1974) have called "phases of development." "Maturity" is in part a more stimulus-induced process. Without any stimulus, maturity becomes slowed down or checked. Sensual receptors that are blocked from stimulation at an early age lose a part of their ability to function. Children who are not encouraged to walk learn to walk later than do those whose caregivers encouraged their early attempts at walking. Children who become ill during the process of learning to walk and remain bedridden for a long period have greater difficulties in learning to walk than others.

All these influences affecting the processes of development and maturity from the outside make more difficult the establishment of a norm that can measure premature and retarded processes in the sexual development of individual children. European measurement during the first two postwar decades produced the following averages for children and youth:

1. Prenatal stages of development
   a. Blastogenesis (conception to day 15)
   b. Embryogenesis (days 16–84)
   c. Fetogenesis (day 85 until birth)

2. Postnatal development
   a. Sitting upright (end of year 1)
   b. First sexual awareness (years 3–5)
   c. First change in stature (year 6)
   d. First appearance of secondary sexual characteristics (years 7–8)
   e. Menarche (years 8–14); polluarche (years 9–15)
   f. Maturation of the secondary sexual characteristics (years 14–15)

However, for a long time these results have been called into question by the processes of acceleration and neoteny. *Acceleration* is the process of continual early-occuring physical maturity. *Neoteny* is the process of continually delayed mental maturity. When Julius Kollmann (1834–1918) coined the word "neoteny" in 1885, he meant by it the retention of infantile characteristics in certain primitive peoples, thus a prolongation of childhood until adulthood. Today we mean by it the evolutionarily caused prolongation of the learning phase of a given gender, i.e., an adjustment in adaptability to environment which can only be achieved through prolongation of the dependency relationship of the children to the adults. In terms of sex education this means that human reproductive maturity appears earlier from generation to generation; on the other hand, sexual maturity appears later from generation to generation. With that the traditional assumption that sexuality is the same as procreation (and sexual maturity the same as reproductive maturity) breaks down. Because, if human sexuality were only a phenomenon accompanying the "drive to procreate" or the "instinct to multiply" (and only if it serves these could it then be morally legitimate), then human sexual maturity would have to develop at the same time with reproductive maturity. But that does not occur.

Instead, we find ourselves confronted with the noteworthy phenomenon that the gaps between somatic and psychic sexual maturity became wider with the progress of so-called civilization. Ever since it has produced measurements of this kind, prenatal development has, indeed, been generally understood to be in a constant process of acceleration. Fetal length and weight measurements taken from year to year show earlier phases of development. The process of acceleration also continues after birth. Today, teething occurs in children months earlier than at the turn of the century. In the past, European children learned to walk at 13 to 14 months of age; today they start at 11 to 12 months of age. The number of children who have learned to walk at 8 months is increasing. At the time of Johann Sebastian Bach (1685–1750), the male voice began breaking at age 18; today it starts to change between ages 12 and 13.

Sex educator Carlfred B. Broderick, who carried out the most comprehensive research on the sexual development of children and adolescents, holds the opinion that menarche in the Western world occurs three to four months earlier every ten years. In 1875 it began approximately at age 16, in 1900 at 15, in 1925 at 14, in 1950 at age 13. Today, in the larger cities in Europe, the age of menarche has rolled back to 12.5 years. Centuries ago, polluarche often set in only at age 17; today, it is common at age 13. The same is true for pubarche and seminarche.

But, on the other hand, childhood diseases also appear earlier than in the past. Disorders in autonomic systems appear at a point in time at which they were unknown earlier. Angina, attention and concentration debilities, balance disorders, and headaches, which used to appear after the onset of puberty, are now already established in the first school years.

Whether the appearance of coitarche at steadily earlier ages is a healthy or unhealthy phenomenon depends largely on whether we judge it from the standpoint of acceleration or of neoteny. In terms of acceleration, it is a normal process that falls into the typology of the somatic phases that constantly appear earlier. On the other hand, from the standpoint of neoteny it is an abnormal process, because it widens the gap between somatic and psychic maturity.

Perhaps it will help to explain these contradictory ideas if we analyze them according to class. Until quite recently it was considered proven that the children of the Lumpenproletariat, the "uneducated" and "degenerated," are exposed to the "degenerate" influences of sexual precocity earlier than those of the educated, that puberty occurs later when the parents' educational level is higher. That was always in relationship to the strict discipline and the higher moral aims this class required. Today, certainly, the first sexual intercourse almost always occurs later in children of the middle class than in those of the unemployed, the uneducated, the full-time laborer, and temporary workers. Yet coitarche appears second earliest in children of high-income families, and third earliest in children of the highly educated. In children of farmers and industrial workers the age of coitarche is largely the same.

Acceleration and neoteny, therefore, are among other things also social, in part even class-specific, phenomena. No one knows how large the biological part is in both. Acceleration is probably based in part on improved nutrition, but also in part on a larger palette of gene mixture. Just as crossed (hybrid) grain is often larger and hardier than "pure," children of "mixed" marriages are mostly taller and stronger than those of ethnically similar parents. In biology this is called *heterosis* and the "luxuries of bastards."

On the other hand, neoteny is probably a product of the growing differentiation in society that began with the Industrial Revolution. People are not becoming more stupid, but the world is more complicated, so that it is becoming more difficult for each generation to assimilate the requisite quantum of knowledge in due time. The words "in due time" are many-layered, because they can mean three things: (1) at the entrance into professional life; (2) at the beginning of adulthood; (3) at the age of legal majority. But they can also mean at the beginning of puberty. And even there the effect of the constantly widening gap between psychical and somatic maturity appears especially clear.

On the other hand, we should also not allow ourselves to be misled by the shock effect of the acceleration to the assumption that coitarche necessarily has to follow this process. The discovery that during the first twenty years of the Federal Republic of Germany and the Second Republic of Austria, the age of coitarche in secondary school-age pupils and students has sunk from age twenty-one to age eighteen allows us to suppose that secondary school-age pupils during the Weimar Republic in Germany and the First Republic of Austria had begun to have sexual intercourse at a later age than in the intervening years, those of the "Third Reich." However, that is a false conclusion, because in the capitals of Berlin and Vienna in the early thirties, coitarche at age sixteen among secondary school-age pupils was common. That means coitarche is not controlled by a mysterious biological power by the name of acceleration, but rather by the social and political climate of the environment. Not biological, but rather social maturity regulates young peoples' behavior.

But how does it achieve that? With what stimuli? With what feedback mechanisms? With the action of social stresses on the psychical or with the influence of social crises on the emotional? Both of these theses have proved tenacious in the long history of developmental psychology. The one views the phases of maturity of childhood as "crises" and the periods of consolidation between them as "phases of calm." The other views the first as "phases of stress" and the second as phases of "rest." What it is that "stresses" or "rests" is certainly unclear. That conditions of stress (tone, turgor) have been ascertained in all bodily tissue, muscles, nerves, and blood vessels is certainly undisputed; it is even obvious that the fetus in the womb is plagued by phases of stress and relaxation. But to what extent are they reflections of external stresses and rest?

Of course, newborns react with displeasure at stress and almost certainly with pleasure at rest. This first exercise of pleasure and displeasure as a reaction to relaxation and stress is also no doubt the primitive form of that which will later occur in the sexual apparatus of the adult. Even infants try to free themselves of stress by thrashing about, sucking, spitting, belching, and urinating. They will soon look to overcome new stresses by grabbing, clinging, sneezing, coughing, and defecating. They do not know what is causing them the stress, and they are also not aware their behavior assists relaxation, but it is clear to any mother who looks at her children that their organisms oscillate between conditions of stress and relaxation.

Empirically it is hardly possible to verify or falsify whether such conditions of stress and relaxation recur in longer developmental phases of weeks, months, or even years. The alleged phases of stress are especially difficult to recognize because children in these phases alternate between forms of behavior that are contradictory to one another. This also has led opponents of the phase theory promptly to dispute the existence of the phases of development in general and to deny the phases of stress especially. Such a disregard of the obvious, however, can only occur to observers unschooled in dialectics, because the distinguishing mark of the phases of stress is precisely that children are torn between external and internal stresses. One can find a contradiction-free frame of mind only in phases of relaxation.

The numerous attempts to understand childhood behavior at a given age and to describe clearly the child's mentality at this stage of life are for that reason futile, mostly because of the nature of the matter: The child in our present Western social order is plainly just one thing or another only during phases of relaxtion. On the other hand, the one clear sign in phases of stress is the absence of a clear distinguishing mark or, if we may so express it, the presence of contradictions. Only a dialectical psychology, one that does not attempt to define passing conditions but rather understands them to be in flux, can manage these highly dynamic states.

Although we identify ourselves as little with the thesis of the phases of stress and recreation as with the analogous theory of the phases of crises and rest, it may make sense to make a comparison of both theories and later compare it to our own concepts of the phases of sexual development.

Age	Crises Theory	Stress Theory
Month 1	Newborn crisis	Postnatal phase of stress
Months 2–6	First resting phase	Postnatal phase of relaxation
Months 7–12	Infancy crisis	First phase of childhood stress
Year 2	Second resting phase	First phase of childhood relaxation
Year 3	Early childhood crisis	Second phase of childhood stress
Year 4	Third resting phase	Second phase of childhood relaxation
Year 5	Toddler's puberty crisis	Third phase of stress
Year 6	Fourth resting phase	Third phase of relaxation
Year 7	Childhood crisis	Fourth phase of stress
Year 8	Fifth resting phase	Fourth phase of relaxation

It certainly is meaningful (and also offers hope of rec-
onciliation of the present falling out among schools of developmental psychology) that the phases of age postulated
here are nearly equal to certain aspects of the theories of
phases by psychoanalysts and sex pedologists. Again we
should indicate that the given numerical ages have
orientational value only, and in practice express differences
of approximately ± 20 percent of the age. That means: Instead of 10 days of age in infancy, we can consider 8 to
12 days of age as a normal variant; correspondingly at an
older age, instead of 10 years of age, 8 to 12 years of age,
and in the case of 80 years of age a variation of 72 to 88
years of age. The older the person, the greater the range
of the absolute variant; the younger he or she is, the more
limited the range of the absolute variant.

In the following table, the predominant sexual educational phase divisions in this book are compared with the
psychoanalytic theory of libido phases:

Age	Sex Pedology	Psychoanalysis
Month 1	Newborn age	Oral phase
Months 2–6	Early infancy age	Oral phase
Months 7–12	Late infancy age	Oral phase
Year 2	Toddler age	Anal phase
Year 3	Beginning of toddler's puberty	Anal phase
Year 4	Middle of toddler's puberty	Anal phase
Year 5	End of toddler's puberty	Phallic/Oedipal phase
Year 6	Beginning of childhood	Latent phase
Year 7	Middle of childhood	Latent phase
Year 8	End of childhood	Latent phase

If we try to sum up in the following all that pedologists,
sexologists, and developmental psychologists of all the industrialized nations have ascertained about the sexual development of children and put into eleven prenatal and postnatal stages of development, then we will have to remember
again that these data here are taken from the year 1980 and

from the German-speaking region, and that an index of deviation of ± 20 percent is to be understood. This index allows for sex difference, for parental education, for social class membership, for residential region (country/city), and for individual variations inside of each and every age.

Flexibility is one distinctive characteristic of the phase theory of the sex pedologists represented here. It does not maintain that the individual phases are strictly separated from each other, but rather proposes that they overlap. It does not assert that each child enters into a given phase at the same age, but rather recognizes wide individual variations, which are decided in part by the child's hereditary material, but also in great part by the strictness or permissiveness, the receptiveness or unreceptiveness in the parents' home. This does not mean that the effects of a given phase end when a child passes into the next phase, but it does imply that until the end of their days people remain tied to a given stage to some greater or lesser degree or from time to time can even revert to several of them. On the other hand, the reason for almost all psychosexual disorders is represented by tenaciously staying at a stage of development already reached (*fixation*), just as well as the chronic reversion to a stage already overcome (*regression*). When the fixation or regression in adults manifests itself in acting out childhood desires and fears, we call it *perversion*. When it is repressed and operates seemingly illegally from the underground, it is called *neurosis* or *psychosis,* according to the extent of the loss of reality.

One of the diagnostic features of a neurosis imprinted by regression is the fact that, after patients resolve the anxieties that prevented them from progressing to the appropriate developmental stage and thereby caused their regression to an earlier stage, the childhood components of that stage to which they have regressed come quite clearly to light and therewith supply the proof of the precise age of origin.

Perversions are less dangerous than neuroses or psychoses, because they are at least in part subject to consciousness and so in part can be controlled by will power. On the other hand, neuroses and psychoses withdraw themselves from consciousness and therewith also from the will power of the patients, so they often resist the wish to be cured. When therapy is at all possible, then its first step consists in making conscious the unconscious. That means analyzing the repression and restoring the memory of repressed childhood desires and fears. In this sense the knowledge of the developmental stages of child sexuality is the most important prerequisite of adult psychotherapy. So, in the "Pathology" section found at the end of the description of each stage of development, the present textbook deals with the specific fixation or regression that originates in the described stage of development. That means: In opposition to all child psychiatry textbooks, this one orders sexual, psychosexual, and psychiatric childhood disorders not according to the age at which the symptom first appeared, but according to the age at which develop the roots of the later symptom.

1

From Conception to Birth
Prenatal and Perinatal Phase

The sex life of children begins even before birth. The pairing of the father's semen with the mother's egg determines the sexuality of the embryos. Their sex life begins with the attainment of their sexuality. Of course, their morphological sex form will first be recognizable in the sixth or seventh week after impregnation, but the genetic sex is determined even at the moment of fertilization.

Human hereditary material rests on twenty-two pairs of body chromosomes (*autosomes*) and two sex chromosomes (*gonosomes, heterosomes* or *gamosomes*)—XX in women, XY in men. The X chromosome can be considered as female, the Y chromosome, male. The child's sex depends on the father's sperm. If the father's X chromosome gets admitted into the female egg, a girl is generated. If his Y chromosome gets in, then a boy is formed. Fertilized egg cells (*zygotes*), that, because of a genetic disorder, contain several X chromosomes but no Y chromosomes are able to survive. Zygotes that contain several Y chromosomes but no X chromosomes die.

This discovery, paired with the alleged fact according to his genetic structure (XY) that a man is indeed a "half woman," has often been cited as the reason for the compulsive virile behavior of many men. Since a man is supposed to know he is really only "half" a man, his whole life long he is supposed to have to prove how "masculine" he is. On the other hand, women, or so this theory goes, never need to "prove" they are women, because they are already supposed to be fully feminine beings because of their genetic hereditary factors.

This theory, as well as all other psychosexual analogies derived from the somatic aspects of sexuality, is inadmissible. It is true that the Y chromosome is lighter than the X chromosome and possesses fewer genes, so that some of the X chromosomes do not have adequate partners (*alleles*) in the Y chromosomes. Result: Many X chromosomes are recessive, because the Y chromosomes do not possess the counterpart gene with the opposite effect.

If we assume that half of all human sperm contains female sex chromosomes and the other half male, then we would stand to expect that half of all fertilized egg cells would have to be of the female sex and the other of the male. However, this assumption is false, because in all of the cultures known to us more boys than girls are born. The enormously high rate of male intrauterine mortality leaves us to suppose that the original number of male zygotes is even much higher than the number of boys who are born.

We call the numerical ratio of male to female zygotes as the *primary proportion of the sexes.* The ratio of male births to female births is called the *secondary proportion of the sexes.* The ratio of surviving men to surviving women is called the *tertiary proportion of the sexes.* The primary proportion of the sexes is approximately 180:100; the secondary, 115:100; the tertiary, 80/90:100. The mortality of male children in the womb, therefore, is higher than that of the female. Boys' chances of being born are worse than those of girls. The childhood mortality of boys is higher than that of girls. Adult men die earlier than adult women. So, in the prenatal and postnatal stages, the female appears to be the sex more capable of surviving—at least in our present social order.

Nature neutralizes this advantage not only by producing more male than female zygotes, but also by allowing more males than females to enter the world as first-born children and by favoring younger parents with boy births. The younger the parents, the greater the probability their child will be male; the older the parents, the greater the probability it will be female.

The human egg cell has a diameter of 120–150 μm (0.0047–0.0059 in). Human sperm, on the other hand, is only 60 μm (0.0023 in) long. In contrast to the egg cell, however, sperm possess a mechanism for movement. Sperm normally contains 60 million to 120 million spermatozoa for every 1 ccm (0.061 cu in). So, through ejaculation, up to five hundred million spermatozoa can reach the vagina. From there they penetrate the uterus and continue to move themselves up to the oviduct, where fertilization can occur if one or more mature egg cells are present there. However, they are present there only on day twelve or thirteen of the menstruation cycle, because only then do they reach the oviduct from the ovary. They are capable of being fertilized in the oviduct for only six to twelve hours. The sperm cells also die within two to three days after coitus. Yet even at the time of ejaculation they are still not fully capable of fertilization, but only after being present in the female's body for several hours do the sperm, by means of female hormones, become capable of penetrating the egg cell.

If a sperm cell finds an egg cell, then it penetrates the egg cell with its head and in the process loses its tail, which up to this time moved it forward like the tail of a fish. As soon as this occurs, the egg cell contracts and prevents further penetration by other sperm cells. The sperm cells that were unsuccessful at fertilization die, while the fertilized egg cell, continuing to divide, reaches the uterus, where it attaches itself between days five and six.

Many sexologists have compared this process to the "battle for the woman," because only one sperm can be successful and the others have to resign and die. Also, the observation that sperm is mobile but the egg is stationary has led many ideologists in sex research to conclude that the wife is supposedly destined to be a "homemaker," but the husband is supposedly destined for "outside activity." These interpretations are just as inadmissible as those already cited. The behavior of cells and organs follows biological laws; that of the sexes, social laws. These laws are subject to a wide range of regional and historical variations.

Even in the apparently ideology-free world of anatomy, ideologies such as these have crept in. Up to the Second World War every medical student learned that the female's external sex organs were degenerate forms of the male's: the clitoris a stunted penis, the labia majora a split scrotum, the bulbs of the vagina an inferior model of the male bulbourethral glands. No one ever thought to explain the same aspects of the human sex organs in the opposite direction. So, one would be equally justified to argue that the penis was an overgrown clitoris, the scrotum was a shrunken form of the labia majora, the bulbourethral glands a later modification of the bulbs of the vagina.

All the same, whatever the genetic sex the embryo might be during the first seven weeks, its sex organs (both primary and secondary) are in any case of unmistakably feminine phenotype. During these first seven weeks, both sexes undergo similar changes defined by growth. While the male embryo experiences further sex changes in sexual heriditary factors from week eight until birth, the female embryo during this time is subject to nothing but a simple growth process that continually persists in the direction followed up to week seven.

Yet again, this led embryologists and morphologists with conscious or unconscious patriarchal logic to describe the original condition of the embryo not as feminine, but rather as "indifferent," "asexual," or "bisexual." This way of thinking is patriarchal because it implies that the sex that differentiates to a higher degree from the "indifferent" condition must be "higher," while the one that does little or no differentiation is by definition the "lower" and "more primitive" sex. "In the female sex the changes of the neutral hereditary factor in the formation of the external sex organs are so much more insignificant in nature that the indifferent condition for the most part remains" (Max Clara, *Entwicklungsgeschichte des Menschens* [History of human development], 6th ed. [Heidelberg, 1967], p. 348).

But if we agree that embryos are morphologically female, whatever their genetic sex may be, then this implies that the female sex is phylogenetically older. Now, how in the history of the species did the male sex differentiate itself from the female? How does the genetically male fetus differentiate itself from the morphologically female embryo? In answering this question, sexual research at first encountered contradictions that were difficult to overcome, because the development of the primary and secondary sex organs obviously did not obey the same laws. The primary are determined by the genes, the secondary, by the hormones.

It appeared that male sex chromosomes are certainly in the position to block the latent tendency to form female organs insofar as they prevent the formation of ovaries. But the influence of the Y chromosome is not strong enough to program the secondary male sex parts into the genetically male embryo without the help of certain glands. These are the so-called endocrine glands, whose secretions in week six of pregnancy imprint the male secondary organs upon what was until then a "female" embryo. If these glands are stunted before week six of pregnancy or if they are removed by operation, fetuses always develop secondary female sex organs, no matter if their genetic sex is male or female.

Expressed in other terms: If in the critical phase of its intrauterine development a genetically male embryo is deprived of androgen by an endocrine disorder, then female tissue—not male—develops, tissue that spreads into the central nervous system and feminizes the psychosexuality. This dominance of the female secondary sexual characteristics accounts for their not being dependent on the gonads of the female fetus, but rather being formed through the influence of the estrogen produced in the placenta. On the other hand, the male fetus is directed to the development of his secondary sexual characteristics exclusively at the androgen secretions of his *own* rudimentary gonads. We can conclude from this that the hormone economy of the mother regularly favors children of her own sex.

So, up to the sixth embryonic week, no further masculine morphological differentiation takes place in the later man. Only after that do the germ cells travel out of the endodermis, to the inner embryonic membrane of the yolk sack and the rear part of the digestive tract, into the gonadal core, the future testes. Settled there, they stimulate the production of a testicular inductor substance, which for its part promotes marrow development and refinement of the male hormone (androgen). Then the original female sexual predisposition is curtailed. Müller's canal, out of which the fallopian tube is formed in female development, and the gonad cortex, which would have become ovaries in forming a female, return to their original configuration. Instead of that, under the influence of androgen, the wolffian body shapes itself as the vas deferens of the embryo in the other part of the two-part canal system.

It is different in the woman. If the genetic sex remains female in week six thanks to the double-X chromosomes, then the germ cells travel to the gonadal cortex, form the ovaries, and stimulate the production of the cell core and the female hormone (estrogen). Significantly, estrogen is not necessary for the continuation of the feminization process, but provides only limited assistance, while androgen is undispensable for the masculinization of the embryo. Should estrogen production fail through some anatomical defect, a normal female individual is nevertheless produced. However, if for some reason the androgen supply ceases, complete feminization takes place. So, the norm for the embryo is the feminine. Only a healthy secretion of androgen will maintain the embryo on a masculine course. Hence, the statement that the woman is a failed man is erroneous, because the female organs counteract androgen very easily, while the male organs utilize estrogen extremely sparingly. The woman is hormone sensitive because her organism needs hardly any hormones. On the other hand, the man is sensitive to estrogen only because his organism excretes a large amount of androgen, which maintains his masculinity and neutralizes the estrogen.

That can be proven experimentally by three surgical operations. If the Wolffian canals are removed from the embryonic body and kept alive in vitro, they develop into Müller's canals, that is, into the beginning of the fallopian tube. If the embryonic gonads are removed before masculinization has occurred in week six, the embryo develops into a normal female individual in whom only the ovaries are missing, notwithstanding its genetic sex. The external genitals and the functions of the urogenital sinus derived from them reshape themselves according to the female model. The Müller's canal remains and continues to function normally while the wolffian canal re-forms itself. However, if one removes the beginnings of the ovaries from a female embryo, no analogous masculinization occurs. At the end of the normal period of pregnancy, castrated embryos of both sexes possess female genital systems that are morphologically fully formed and almost as well developed as those of normal women.

The differentiation of the testes begins in the seventh week, when the male embryo is approximately 13 mm (0.51 in) long; that of the ovaries in the eighth or ninth week, when the female embryo is approximately 18–20 mm (0.70–

0.78 in) long. When the embryo is approximately 27 mm (1.06 in) long, the development of the gonads in both sexes is complete. From the twelfth week on, when the embryo is 7.5-10 cm (2.95-3.93 in) long, the external sexual differentiation is clearly visible. The anal opening also is now fully formed. From this time on, one no longer calls the child an *embryo* (Greek: "that which is growing in the body"), but rather a *fetus* (Latin: "fruit of the womb"). So, the embryo is the germ from egg to final form, which is reached on day 85. The fetus is the child formed in the womb from day 86 to birth. From the twenty-eighth week of pregnancy (on days 190 to 196 of pregnancy), it is viable. It is then 35-40 cm (13.55-15.74 in) long and weighs at most 1 kg (2.2 lb). Furthermore, this is also the time at which the gonads of the male fetus descend into the scrotum.

Embryologists and fetologists calculate the period of pregnancy not in lunar months but rather in fetal months and estimate that it runs to ten fetal months of approximately 28 days (computed from the first day of the last normal menstruation). That is 273 to 282 days in practice.

At birth the child is 48-55 cm (18.89-21.65 in) tall and weighs 2.5-4.5 kg (5.5-9.9 lb). In the mature fetus the ovaries weigh approximately the same as the testes—around 0.2 g (0.00706 oz).

The last eleven to thirteen weeks before birth and the first week after can be combined into what is called the *perinatal phase* (from Greek *peri*: "around"). It is characterized by the fact that a few of the postnatal processes are already begun in the prenatal condition and that many of the prenatal conditions still continue into the first week of life.

Most laymen see the relationship between the parents and the unborn child as a one-sided relationship of the mother to the child. According to this opinion, neither father nor child plays an active role in the life of the three parties. However, in truth the embryo changes the lives of both parents from the moment when the parents decide to have children, i.e., from the moment the mother discovers that she is pregnant. Even prenatally, mothers' reactions to the needs of the children can influence the children's life positively or negatively.

This is also true for the sex life of the children, who can be affected until their death by the relationship of the parents during pregnancy. Severe psychical disorders of the mother, for example, offenses by the father, produce endocrine and neurohumoral products that flow from the mother's blood into the embryo and there influence the size of the body, the urogenital system, and the function of the adrenal glands.

So, it is not only the qualities inherited from the parents such as sensitivity, potency, and passion that decide the children's temperament, but it is also the mother's fears during pregnancy that, directly through the circulatory system, play a part in determining the children's preparedness for fear. On the other hand, too, the mother's joy in her sex life during pregnancy has results in the children's sexual vitality. In this sense the parents' sexual lifestyle during pregnancy determines a large part of their children's sexual destiny.

The parents' prenatal relationship to their children is also formed by their own childhood experiences, so that strong influences of the grandmother and grandfather contribute to the unborn children's psychosexual conditioning.

Otto Rank and Siegfried Bernfeld have designated birth as the primary human trauma—the original pain, the original fear, and the original separation—from which all later human fears derive and from which our feeling of undefinable loss originates. Bernfeld says,

> If birth took its course under psychical processes that are similar to our consciousness, or if we could remember it as we do some earlier experience, it certainly could be

described as a plunge into the depths, a thrust and pressure on the head and of the whole body at the passing through a narrow canal, an attack of suffocation, a scream, relief, a renewed attack of suffocation, weary relief, falling asleep; in addition to which would come a cold shower, noise, a flood of lights, a vigorous heartbeat and asthmalike breathing. It would be a complicated, serious state of fear. . . . In this sense, each (later) state of fear is psychically and physically a repeat of birth.

In fact, birth corresponds to fifteen minutes of oxygen deprivation and creates in the child all the known symptoms of hypoxia. Breathing is irregular or rapid, blood pressure is elevated; pulse is rapid or erratic; muscles are uncoordinated and show spasms, stiffness, or convulsions; vein pressure is high. If asked under hypnosis if they recall their birth, children or adults mention pericardial pain as with angina pectoris, sickness, nausea, vertigo. These are four of the best known symptoms of general hypoxia. Bernfeld sees in the trauma of birth not only the key to human fear, but also the sole possibility of understanding the physical forms of expressing all other human emotions. He points to the similarity of the somatic symptoms of contrasting polar emotions and asks if the explanation might not be in the fact that both pleasure and displeasure differentiate out of a common primal experience, perhaps the experience of birth. Now, since this experience affects the respiratory and circulatory systems above all, obviously both of these structures serve as the physical expression of our strongest emotions for our entire lives. So, fear would be the repetition of the birth experience, while pleasure represents the conquest of primal fear. "Then the emotions of pleasure would show in the foreground those components of the birth situation that correspond to the overcoming of the fear of birth, the symptoms of progress, heightened vital activity; the emotions of displeasure, on the other hand, would be understood to be regressive, a lower-life activity, allowing the components of the situation before birth to dominate" (Bernfeld).

Bernfeld's thesis was vehemently rejected by Sigmund Freud, the founder of psychoanalysis, but a few child analysts, for example, Phyllis Greenacre, have accepted it. Greenacre views birth as practice in all later fears and as a kind of vaccination against them. She says, "I consider the birth process as such to be the first important stage for preparation for becoming aware of separation; this occurs during birth through the considerable effect of pressure on the surface of the children's body and its stimulation and above all through the pronounced changes in the conditions of pressure and warmth that surround the children in their change from life within the womb to life without."

Many obstetricians and perinatologists today no longer reject the idea of a primal natal fear, but consider it very possible that the biblical legend of the banishment from paradise is a symbolic form of the story of birth. True paradise, they suggest, is the mother's body—the only place where people have always felt secure, free from fear, but also free from the necessity of having to take care of themselves and to assume responsibility for their own actions. The yearning of heterosexual men for the body of a woman then would be nothing but homesickness for the womb. Also, the desires for love of women and nonheterosexual men would be surrogate forms of the archaic quests for paradise lost; variants of the primal wish to return to the promised land; for a carefree existence; for freedom from the burdens of civilization, responsibility, and work.

These perinatologists readily interpret the "little death," the process of forgetting worries and at the moment of orgasm, as a temporary return to the prenatal status of freedom from care and from self: as proof that the origin of sexual intercourse in all individuals is to be found in the unconscious homesickness for a prenatal situation.

In most women, sexual appetite after delivery is suspended for approximately four weeks. Many men who have suffered under the abstinence their wives demanded during the later months of pregnancy feel that it is especially depressing that after the child's birth, their wives are not only disinterested in coitus (most men understand that it is necessary for physiological reasons), but also often reject oral, anal, or manual intercourse. Such a conflict throws a deep shadow over the child's sexual future. With that we arrive at the sexual pathology of this stage of life.

Sexual Pathology of the Prenatal and Perinatal Phases

In a textbook of childhood sexual development, symptomatology must be stood on its head. We cannot begin with the symptoms in the customary way and then explain the reasons, but we must bring the early childhood reasons of human sexual disorders before us in chronological order so that we can make it possible for parents, physicians, and schoolteachers to intervene in the etiology preventively and prophylactically even before the beginning of the disorder.

According to the knowledge of pedologists, almost all adult neurotic, psychosexual, and psychosomatic disturbances can be traced back, many into the prenatal period, to the child's relationship to the parents or caregiver. If these disorders with the characteristic time-delayed effects manifest their symptoms in adolescence or adulthood, they hardly respond to therapy. Up until recent times, the hopes for "curable" psychosexual disorders put forth by certain schools of psychotherapy have unfortunately proven to be all too optimistic. Today, we see the only possibility of enlightening parents and educators about the dangers in educating their children and of hoping that a more rational, enlightened attitude of adults in the home and in school will one day prevent the effects of incorrect education.

However, every stage of life, of course, has somatic sexual disorders that cannot be prevented by any prophylactic, for example, chromosomal and hormonal disorders of the prenatal phase. Nevertheless, somatosexual and psychosexual disorders have one thing in common: the earlier they appear, the more suspiciously they operate. Prepubescent disorders have greater consequences than postpubescent ones, childhood ones greater than pubescent ones, prenatal ones greater than postnatal ones. Since this appears as contrary to common sense to most laymen, who can imagine sexual disorders only as adult illnesses anyway, we would like to clarify the genetic disorders of the prenatal phase.

When we said at the beginning of this chapter that there are two sexes, one of which ("woman") is distinguished by two X gonosomes and the other ("man") by an X and a Y gonosome, we greatly simplified the true condition of the genetic definition of sex. In truth, there are people with the *karyotypes* (chromosomal structures) XO, XXX, XXXX, XXXXX, XYY, XYYY, XXY, XXYY, XXXYY, XXXY, XXXXY, and probably many, many more that we have not as yet discovered. People with a surplus of X chromosomes are called *surplus females*, those with a surplus of Y chromosomes *surplus males*. In between there are a number of hermaphrodite-like creatures with XO (*Ullrichs-Turner syndrome*), about whom for the time being we know very little. Many of them are physically healthy and mentally normal, but sexually sterile. Others are fertile, but have physical abnormalities (dwarfism, giantism, neck folds, neither man nor woman in shape). Many have fully developed external sex organs, but imperfectly developed inner ones. Others, such as the XO/XY-type of the *androgyne*, have the external and internal organs of both sexes.

Aberrations of the X chromosome are closely relationed to the age of the mother, because the mother's egg cells, which have combined with the father's semen cells, are indeed expelled in the middle of the last menstruation cycle, but they have not been produced at this time. They develop previously, in the mother's fetal period. This production process is completed in the mother's third year at the latest. After that, the egg cells are stored in the ovary until they— one after the other—will be retrived during the monthly egg release. The longer the storage, the greater the danger of damage by (for example) x-rays, atomic energy, or atomic weapons. More exactly stated: Under these conditions, in the final pairing of the "homologous" (belonging to each other) chromosomes, which represents the last stage of the maturity of the stored egg cells, it can happen that some of the chromosomes miss their "right" partner or that the "right" one has meanwhile died (nondisjunction).

This risk is obviously greater the older the mother is. So, today, in the third month of pregnancy, we attempt to take a sample of the amniotic fluid in the womb (amniocentesis), to test whether the child is chromosomally healthy. If not, an abortion can still be induced at this age without any difficulties. With this examination, moreover, we can also already discover the child's chromosomal sex.

Chromosome aberrations can befall the autosomes (mongolism, D-trisomy, E-trisomy) as well as the gonosomes (diplo-X-syndrome, poly-X-syndrome). Other numerical chromosomal aberrations arise from meiosis disorders in the maturity of sperm, by which sperm form with two or three Y chromosomes (diplo-Y-syndrome, poly-Y-syndrome).

Just as certain sexual disorders of the zygote can form through chromosomal aberrations even at the moment of fertilization, hormonal aberrations that develop postnatally into certain sexual disorders already begin in the embryonic stage. These newborns are genetically normal children of karyotype 46 XX or 46 XY who, however, exhibit hormonally caused changes of their sex parts and gonads, for example, penis and ovary in karyotype XX (hermaphroditus femininus), vagina and (undescended) testes in karyotype XY (hermaphroditus masculinus), fully developed vagina and fully developed penis with or without testes and ovary in karyotype XX or XY (*hermaphroditus verus*), penis or vagina with a testis on one side and an ovary on the other in karyotype XX or XY (*hermaphroditus verus lateralis*), penis or vagina with two bisexual gonads (mixture of testes and ovaries, so-called *ovotestes* or *testovaries*) in karyotype XX or XY (*hermaphroditus verus bilateralis*), penis or vagina with ovotestes on one side and testis or ovary on the other side in karyotype XX or XY (*hermaphroditus verus unilateralis*), or a vagina with stunted penis and stunted testes in karyotype XY (*testicular feminization*).

There are a great number of other sexual misdevelopments of the child in the womb, all of which exert the same effect on the parents or caregivers—and sometimes also on the midwives, obstetricians, and gynecologists—namely, those who classify the child by *phenotype* (the external appearance) into an incorrect, specific sexuality.

Defects of the urethra opening, which makes the penis look like a vagina (*anaspadia, epispadia, hypospadia perinealis*), and defects in the formation of the testes, which especially can lead to misclassification as a girl when the penis is underdeveloped (*penis hypotrophy, penis palmatus, anorchidy, cryptorchism, agonaditus, hermaphrodititus agonadalis*), belong to the congenital malformations that lead to such misclassifications. On the other hand, small girls can be all too easily classified as boys when they are born with imperfect vaginas (*aplasia vaginae*) or with too large a clitoris (*clitoris hypertrophy*).

The problem caused by sexual misclassifications is that of irreversibility. One would think that an erroneous sexual determination at the newborn stage could be revoked by re-education, but unfortunately that is not possible. Psychosexuality dominates over somatic sexual membership, and this process is regulated not only linguistically and on the way via conscious brain activity, but also begins even before children can speak and before their awareness is fully developed. Stated more precisely: The imprinted forms of human sexual conditioning do not develop with regard to consciousness and in the process of learning to speak, but distinguish themselves through the fact that they are controlled by socially established concepts of sex roles and sexual behavior, yet not—as is the case with other mammals—by sex-specific hereditary material.

Again: The imprinting part of this transmission process takes its course with regard to the unconscious, in adults as well as in children, and occurs not verbally but with the help of unconscious forms of body language. This explains why a boy who is treated as a girl in his infant and toddler stages remains psychosexually feminine up to his death. Likewise, a girl who in her childhood is dressed and raised as a boy remains masculine in her sexual identity and in her later choice of a partner. Such a girl should not also be classified as a lesbian, because the choice of a female or very effeminate mate is a normal one for her, just as the choice of a male partner is not a homosexual, but a heterosexual choice for a boy who in childhood was classified as a girl .

This dominance of emotional sexual membership over the somatic is a gender-specific human characteristic. It plays an especially large role in the child's sexual development and explains why we even have to speak of a child's *sex life* long before *coitarche* (the first sexual intercourse).

2

First Month
Newborn Age

The most important part of *biological* sexual differentiation is completed with the child's birth. Then beings the no less important process of *social* sexual differentiation. From the moment of birth on, numerous social influences act on the child to engender socially acceptable sexual behavior. In contrast to the theory of social learning (Albert Bandura and R. H. Walters, 1963), in no way may the child be understood as a passive derivative of social rewards and sanctions; rather the child must be understood even at newborn age as an active, just as impressing as impressionable member of society. Its character is not a purely cognitive one, as L. Kohlberg maintained even in 1966, but one motivated by a noncognitive psyche. In the operation of the unconscious character, identification with the female or male role model is the most important.

The newborn period, also described by many pedagogues as early infancy, is a time of difficult physical and psychical struggles. Therefore, it is called the *postnatal phase of stress* by advocates of the theory of stress/relaxation and *newborn crisis* by those of the crisis theory. Formerly, the phase was measured at seven to eleven days, corresponding to the second part of the *perinatal phase* (first part: from day 196 of pregnancy to birth). It is the time of adjustment to the extrauterine world, to life outside the womb. For, after birth, the child's body must change over to a new type of circulatory system and overcome the challenges of breathing, digestion, and temperature regulation.

The first week of life is also termed the *early neonatal period*. The World Health Organization has recommended extending the concept of *newborn age* from the first breath to the twenty-eighth day of life, since a few of the adjustment processes, especially the psychical, last up to the end of the first month. We have accepted this suggestion in our textbook. So, we define the newborn age as the first month of life.

As already stated, the weight of European newborns is currently 2.5 to 4.5 kg (average: 3.4 kg [7.4 lb]). As a rule, boys weigh a little more than girls. Because of the loss of postuterine fluids, weight during the first four to five days of life decreases 8 to 9 percent. By the end of the second week it is mostly restored.

An unusual side effect of our urban civilization is that Western Europeans have never seen a newborn until they are confronted with their own. Many young parents, whose ideas of a "newborn" baby are informed by commercial photographs (the infants are mostly two to three months of age), are startled at the first sight of their tiny, wet, sticky, and possibly red and wrinkled babies. . . . Many newborns—boys and girls—have enlarged breasts, which excrete a milky substance, so-called witches' milk (*Hexen-milch*), and, shortly before birth, many girls have a brief "menstruation." (L. Joseph Stone and Joseph Church, *Childhood and Adolescence* [*Kindheit und Jugend*, German trans., 1978], pp. 2–3)

Except for the genitals, which usually appear to most parents as unexpectedly large, newborn boys and girls hardly differ from each other in their body structure. The story of childhood and youth is, in a sexual-morphological view, then, partly a regular and partly a thrusting nullification of the original somatic similarity (between the sexes) and a corresponding polarization of the psychical into two distinguishable directions. From birth on, the physical proportions of the little girl look more like those of the adult woman, just as those of the little boy resemble those of the adult man. On the one hand, we could view this as meaning that here, too, the man differentiated from an original female physical structure or that the woman will mature earlier in physical structure than the man.

From birth on, girls also have higher pulse and lower breathing rates. That means their oxygen consumption at rest is less than that of boys. That gives the woman a higher chance of survival in many crisis situations.

> Shortly after birth, the child's vaginal epithelium, because of the effect of hormones produced by the placenta, shows the image corresponding to that of the sexually mature woman. It consists of sixty to ninety cell layers. During the second to third week it is reduced to five to six cell layers, only to become extremely dynamic again just before puberty. If the woman's hormonal production is absent (perchance by castration or by reversion of type of the ovaries at the time of menopause), the epithelium again is reduced to fewer layers of cells. (Karlheinz A. Rosenbauer, *Genitalorgane* [Reinbek, 1969])

In contrast to public opinion that every woman is born with a *hymen* ("maidenhead"), currently less than 10 percent of the young women in the European industrialized nations enter marriage as "virgins." At birth approximately 10 percent have no intact hymen. In approximately 15 percent, it is so thin that it tears by itself within the first year. In later years, in another 15 percent it tears without external means. More than 50 percent lose the hymen during pre-marital sexual intercourse.

Almost all male newborns even have penile erections, certainly shortly before urinating and usually after approximately a half-hour of deep sleep. The total picture of the newborn's sleep erections does not essentially differ from that of the adult man.

The child's chances of survival are slimmest during the first three days after birth. This period is called *trihemeron*. Approximately 80 percent of newborn mortalities occur within these three days.

At birth, a mature European child weighs around 2.5 kg (5.5 lb) and is at least 48 cm (1.59 ft) tall. The newborn's brain has a mass of approximately 350 cc (21.37 cu in). All nerve centers are fully present at birth, even if they are not totally mature. At birth even the vestibular apparatus in the inner ear is actively functioning, although the newborn's muscular and nervous systems are still unable to correct faulty physical coordination. When a newborn is held high, cradled, or swung, it immediately shows clear signs of pleasure. But not only is positive vestibular excitation obviously working here—which has to do with the sense of balance—but also positive excitation of the skin, as in the case of being caressed and stroked.

On the other hand, the newborn is immediately sensitive to negative stimuli to the greatest extent. Unpleasant odors, loud noises, bright light, extreme differences in temperature (heat, cold) are perceived as stressful. Children seek to decrease stresses by crying and by making temporary yet extensive uncoordinated body movements. Although newborns are controlled, above all, by sleep and a state of semi-consciousness, they awaken if they become aware of pain, hunger, or even emotional hunger. They then cry and fall asleep again provided a caregiver calms them.

Naturally, newborns are just as little conscious of the signal effect of their crying as they are of the fact that another person is reacting to their crying. Yet, as soon as they discover that their crying somehow frees them of their displeasure, they develop the illusion of absolute power. The newborn's experiences obviously have the function of focusing perceptual and memorized experiences on the caregiver. Newborns can be calmed as well as upset by their caregivers' words without understanding what is being said.

Up until the eighth month, however, the most important communication takes place through body language, and it is true for both sides, children and their caregivers. The only difference consists in the adults' having to struggle through learning the children's body language, while children are born with the ability of understanding the adults' body language. This ability fades when children learn to speak, but until age three children can understand many aspects of their elders' body language even better than their parents can understand the children's. We will repeatedly return to this point in the course of this book.

Children, who were continuously protected in the womb against cold, shaking, noises, light, and other disturbances, are enormously endangered during and after birth and so are supplied with a kind of psychical shield that protects their organism from many disturbances invading from the environment. During the first days of life, this shield reduces the perception of environmental stimuli. So, René Spitz says that perceptions such as these are limited to the "enteroceptive" and "proprioceptive" systems up to the end of the first month. *Enteroceptors* are the body's internal receiving and sending apparatuses that serve the vegetative nervous system. Bodily irritation stimulates enteroceptors there, and they then serve as controls of numerous physical functions by bringing about secretions or motor responses via the thalamus and sensory pathways. *Proprioceptors* are the nervous receiving and sending organs that serve muscular functions. They respond to changes in the condition of the motor system—thus, the muscle and tendon pivots, joint coverings, periosteum, and the inner ear—and they bring about the sensation of movement and of the position of the body in relationship to gravity.

According to Spitz, infants' reactions are only responses to perceptions of needs sent on with the help of this system. External stimuli then are only perceived when the degree of their intensity is higher than the threshold of sensation. They then break through the barrier to irritation and disturb the newborns' state of rest, whereupon infants react with great displeasure.

Spitz now maintains that you certainly can observe reactions of displeasure from birth on, but of pleasure, not before the end of the first month. This coincides neither with more recent observations (including my own and those of my associates), nor with the same idea brought forth by Spitz himself on the dominance of enteroceptive and proprioceptive apparatuses in the first month of life. For both apparatuses are thoroughly capable of facilitating pleasurable sensations. If Spitz maintains that both apparatuses function from birth on, he also has to admit that the infant can feel pleasure from birth on.

On the other hand, it is certainly correct that newborns cannot distinguish between the pleasant or unpleasant type of stimuli that act from the outside of their body from those that originate inside their body. Newborns certainly experience pleasure and displeasure, but perceive both only as stirrings of their inner world. Even the need-gratifying, nourishment-dispensing, warm, and elastic mother's breast, and the mother's or caregiver's warm hands that rock and stroke the children are also in no way perceived by the infants as parts of the external world; but newborns view both exactly as they did in the fetal stage: as a part of themselves.

They "love" the mother's warm arm, they "love" the mother's breast, they "love" the nipples, and they "love" the mother's warm milk. But they are not aware of the fact that all these beloved things are parts of another person.

We call this state of self-love and self-deception *narcissism*, after the psychologist Paul Näcke. He took the word from the Greek saga of the handsome demigod Narcissus, who fell in love with his own image. From Näcke's basic thought, Sigmund Freud developed the concept of two narcissistic phases. The first month is considered the *primary narcissism* phase. With the second month the period of *secondary narcissism* begins. Since both phases—primary and secondary narcissism—leave lifelong traces behind in the adult's sex life, we can also define narcissism as auto-erotism. If autoerotic activity serves as *foreplay* to coitus, sex researchers categorize it as *primary narcissistic* activity. If it serves as a voluntary *substitute* for coitus, they define it as *secondary narcissistic* behavior.

Although newborns live in a narcissistic, autoerotic state, their manual skills are still too poor to carry out autoerotic behavior with their genitals. But they absolutely can obtain autoerotic satisfaction by thumb sucking and by touching other parts of their body. Because no erogenous zones have formed at that age, the entire skin surface of newborns reacts in exactly the same way to sensory stimuli—no matter if they produce it themselves or if another person does it. For that reason, many years ago my colleagues and I had already designated this phase as the *cutaneous phase* (from Greek *kytos*, Latin *cutis*: "skin").

You can compare the undifferentiated state of neonatal skin eroticism very well with a prehistoric tribe, one not yet divided up into the ruling and the ruled classes. Just as you can see progressive social development on the one hand as a process of differentiation of society, on the other hand as the process of establishing evermore complicated relationships with other tribes, families, peoples, and nations, the child's sexual development can be viewed, on the one hand, as the progressive division of the body surface into erogenous zones, and on the other hand as entering into relationships with the parents and other adults that steadily become more complex. The first process is a more limited one: it leads from an undifferentiated state to an ever more narrowly differentiated state and brings with it the domination of a certain zone on the body over all others. The second is an expanding process: it leads from the first "beloved," the caregiver, to an ever-larger circle of potential love partners. We call the differentiation process of erogenous zones *libido development* or *ontogenesis of the libido stage*. The development of relationships to other people we call *ontogenesis of the object relationships*.

The words *ontogenesis, libido,* and *object* have to be defined. *Ontogenesis* (from Greek *onto:* "individual"; *genesis:* "origin") is the life history of the individual (as opposed to *phylogenesis*—Greek *phylos:* "tribe"—the life history of a people, race, class, or family). Albert Moll, pioneer of sex education who wrote the first book on our theme (*Das Sexualleben des Kindes* [The sexual life of children] [Berlin, 1909]), derived the concept *libido* (Latin for "desire") from the then still early research on electricity. Exactly as electricity can be measured according to its potential in voltage as well as its performance in wattage, Moll postulated the libido as a form of sexual energy that must be understood both qualitatively as well as quantitatively.

We call the persons, things, and ideas toward which the libido directs itself *objects*. In contrast to the devalued meaning that the concept "object" possesses in many contexts in everyday speech (for example, "objects of desire"), sex educators use the word in a grammatical, thus value-free, sense, by reason of the difference between *subject* and *object*, yet without distinguishing between inanimate and animate objects.

The first love object of newborn subjects is their caregiver or attendant. By that we mean those persons on whom children depend during their period of physical and psychical dependence. If the mother dies during delivery, the father may become the attendant. According to recent research, there are no innate qualifications, ones that only the living mother or only a woman might possess for taking care of children. Child care requires great empathy. Many men possess such a gift for empathy; many women do not. The ability to understand and to care for a child depends on neither the caregivers' sex nor their blood relationship, but on the readiness for sympathetic understanding in a filial spirit.

While the mother or caregiver cleans, washes, and changes newborns, certain zones of the skin, especially the genital and anal regions, are released from the "primal communism" of the undifferentiated neonatal skin eroticism and changed into erogenous zones by daily stimulation. The opinion supported by psychoanalysts is no doubt correct: that the mouth is the first erogenous zone, because from the first suckle on, infants' lips, gums, and tongue are sensitized by the desire for receiving nourishment. Yet, before the so-called *oral phase* in psychoanalysis children experience that preoral stage we have called the *cutaneous phase*.

The notion prevails among many European mothers that newborns neither need immediate nourishment nor could digest it, and that the colostrum, the milky substance discharged from the mother's breast before the first mother's milk (18–24 hours after delivery), is harmful—the severe colic that occurs in many newborns between the second and third weeks is caused by consumption of the colostrum or the "early" enjoyment of mother's milk. Both ideas are false. If you place a newborn beside its mother's undressed body, it turns toward the warmth of its mother's body. If children are placed on their mothers' bodies, the infants begin to search for the nipples very soon. Both reactions are naturally inborn. René Spitz dubbed this behavior *rooting* ("search behavior"). Since his pioneering work in the forties and fifties, it has been established that "rooting" is not only a searching for warmth and nourishment, but also an exploration of the mother's entire body.

Obviously this first exploratory activity of the child involves the senses of smell, taste, and touch especially, less so the eyes and ears.

The films made by Frédéric Leboyer and other advocates of a "soft" approach to obstetrics show, in an impressive manner, how curious newborns are and how unmistakably "erotic" their devotion to their mother's body is. On the other hand, the films made by Spitz and his colleagues show how the mother's hands secure an immense number of tactile stimuli for newborns and how these delights move children to practice their own orientation and to strengthen their power of perception. Through delightful stimulation mothers entice children to try out their own skin eroticism, their deep sensibility, and their sense of balance.

The investigations by Spitz brought about another, previously unnoted, observation—of the intelligence-producing value of skin contact at the newborn stage, namely, that breast-fed children make eye contact with the mother or caregiver much earlier than bottle-fed children. Most breast-fed children do not stare at the breast, but at the mother's face, until they fall asleep at the breast. Therefore, bottle-fed children first recognize their attendant later than breast-fed children, so they mature more slowly. In the first four weeks of life breast-fed children store the first trace of a memory of the caregiver's face; bottle-fed children establish this recollection only in the sixth week at the earliest.

Newborns' eyes can focus steadily to approximately 18–20 cm (7.08–7.87 in). That almost corresponds to the height of the mother's head or the distance between her nipples. As soon as newborns are regularly suckled, depth perception increases approximately 10 cm (3.94 in) and now corresponds to the distance between the infants' eyes and those of their mothers while nursing.

While being fed, newborns make certain motions that correspond to the kicking movements of suckling small animals. These stirrings include the sequence of orientation movements, followed by grasping the nipples with the lips, sucking, and swallowing. At the same time, children make squeezing finger and hand movements, as if they wanted to milk the mother. These hand motions are accompanied by arm and leg movements whose intensity depends on the degree of fullness of the stomach (René Spitz). All these movements are repeated in adult sexual intercourse. Therefore, they not only serve the taking of nourishment, but also the practice of our sensuality, which means testing our sense organs and preparing for our role in adult sexual intercourse.

The Klein school of child analysis (Melanie Klein, 1882–1960) infers from the proven fact that newborns dream (one recognizes that by the sleeping child's rapid eye movement [REM] among other things), the hypothesis of a precedence of the inner world over the external world. It postulates that fantasy emerges before the experience of reality, and that children's psychical process of maturity is not defined by the influence of reality on the psyche, as empiricists believe, but by the children's attempt to bring postnatal reality into harmony with their prenatal notions. This process is supposed to be a thoroughly difficult, conflict-filled, and painful one. In no way does it make the experiences of the first year of life into a paradise—which many child psychologists see in the fact of being served, the being free of all cares, and the childish illusion of omnipotence—but into a kind of hell that overshadows the whole of later life.

This image of early childhood is disputed and deviates from that of most sex pedologists, above all because the newborn's retina is still not yet fully developed, and so can hardly produce dream "images" in the strict sense of the word. But empirical child psychologists also now have hardly any doubt that from birth on (and possibly even before then), people possess a prototype for mental potential, the capacity of a certain psychical activity, which certainly is not yet to be equated with the act of thinking, but evidently originates from the archipallium, the oldest part of the cerebral cortex and exerts a stimulating effect on those cortical regions, those parts of the cortex in which sensory stimuli are formed. If that is so, then it in fact means that internal stimuli develop before sensual influences from the environment begin to have an effect on the newborn's psyche.

On the other hand, extrauterine influences do not naturally quash the intrauterine, and finally from the fetus's standpoint the womb represents a real environment. So, one could also argue that even these earliest proto-mental activities of the fetus are not independent psychical activities, but reflexive responses to uterine environment.

Contrary to the popular belief that sexuality is injurious to thinking and learning, but also contrary to psychoanalytical dogma that certain antitheses between sexuality and culture exist that allow themselves to be overcome only by "sublimation" (the change of sexual into cultural energies), sex pedologists are of the opinion that healthy sexuality promotes learning and thinking even at the newborn stage. The newborn suffers from an inborn lack of balanced tonicity. It exhibits dominant hypertonic states in the limbs and torso. Yet, when it is stroked, kissed, and cuddled, the lower limbs relax. Hypertonicity yields to relaxation. The experience of delight decreases hypertonic conditions and makes possible the voluntary muscular activity of the next phase of development. The erect carriage of the head and torso, the sitting position, the activities of holding and walking are not possible before postnatal hypertonic conditions disappear. So, children learn especially through sensual receptor gratifications. The passage from the first to the second stage of development takes place with the help of the tenderness children receive from their caregiver. If this affection is lacking, progress to the next phase of development is either delayed or does not happen at all.

Sexual Pathology of the Newborn Stage

Shortly after the moment of birth, when the child's morphological sex becomes known to the adults, they attribute to the child all of those qualities that are considered characteristic and typical for this sex in their social order. Most children take on these characteristics even in early childhood and behave as if they were born with them.

In that way, the illusion begins, in adults just the same as in children, that the characteristics that a respective social order views as "typically feminine" and "typically masculine" are in fact characteristics of women and men.

In truth, however, there are enormous variations among the ideas each cultural circle creates concerning sexual traits. In any case, human psychosexuality does not allow itself to classify the concepts "active" and "passive," as our parents and grandparents believed. For in many cultures women are the active and men the passive sex. Their whole life long, boys and girls who grow up in such a social order will understand masculinity as passivity, femininity, on the other hand, as activity. So, as difficult as it may be for us, we must accept that masculinity and femininity, as we understand them in our culture, are not attributes of man and woman, but rather culture-specific forms of thought, feeling and behavior.

Children's future attitude toward their sex partner arises neither by *instinct* nor by *drive,* but is determined by the parents' and caregivers' attitudes toward sexuality. If the child receives love, then it will later be in the position to give love. If it receives tenderness, it will later be able to give tenderness. The drive for body contact with a later sex partner is imprinted from the parents' drive for body contact with each other and with their child. A morally divided attitude on the part of the parents toward their own bodies, those of their spouses, and those of their child conceals great danger for all three, but especially for the child.

If the mother does not fulfill her marital "duties" out of love, but begrudgingly and without love, the child takes in this lovelessness even at the newborn stage and brings it into later life. If the father feels his sexuality is a curse and vacillates between compulsive drive and deep regret, he can never develop unconditional love and give it to his child. The children of such parents as these form no stable, resistant, independent personality and never in their lives learn to offer another person unconditional love, not physically or emotionally. The signals of this psychosexual derailment are already set at the newborn stage.

On the other hand, children have to disengage themselves from their parents, attendant, or caregiver to find their own sex partner, and this process of detaching does not first begin at puberty or upon leaving the parents' home, but at birth. Just as learning to love occurs in stages, learning to separate is accomplished in a number of phases. If the first one fails, then all later ones will most likely fail. But if, on the other hand, the first one is successful, learning later lessons will become easier with each phase.

In this sense the problems of the first days, weeks, and months of life are much more difficult for boys than for girls. Just as in the course of intrauterine life the fetus's morphological masculinity has to differentiate from the embryo's feminine condition, so from the moment of birth on the boy's psychical masculinity has to differentiate from the mother's feminine psyche. The female body that had served as his home for nine months, has, during this impressionable period, conditioned the female line in not only his body, but also his brain and his central nervous system. Before boys develop into individuals they are a part of their mother—up until birth, even organically part of her body—but for a long time after that still a psychical part of the person attending to them. Since in our present social order the caregiver is still mostly a female individual, boys must first of all release themselves from ostensible femininity to build up their masculinity. So, in our case masculinity is something acquired, in contrast to femininity, which is inborn, and certainly in boys exactly as in girls.

In opposition to Freud's idea that a girl first acquires her femininity in a roundabout way from her childhood love for her father, femininity is congenital, is a part of her physical and emotional oneness with her mother. In comparison, boys need to make an enormous effort to struggle through to masculinity. The more lovingly the mother or caregiver treats the children at the newborn age, the easier the children make the separation from the attendants.

It is impossible to "overindulge" a newborn. Gentle skin contact is indispensable. If a child at this age is treated unkindly, it develops behavioral disorders. They do not begin immediately, but appear after a delay of weeks, months, or even years. In spite of this, the etiological reasons are clearly fixed in position in the first months of life.

If children do not feel warmly received by their mother or caregiver, they react with a kind of cold disposition that can set in years later. People who are fixated at this phase or who regress to it suffer all their lives from the coldness of the environment and seek love above all as a source of warmth. Only when they have received a certain form of nest warmth do they begin to thaw.

There is a close relationship between the caregiver's lack of tenderness in the cutaneous phase and certain skin disorders (*dermatitis exfoliativa neonatorum*). The delayed reaction to this cutaneous deficiency extends into the second half of the first year ("infant eczema") and sometimes even appears to be the origin of "nervous" skin disorders in adulthood.

If the mother or caregiver immediately rejects the child right at birth, it reacts with coma, extreme pallor, and reduced breathing. One can see from such children that they are in a state of shock. If such a child is placed at its mother's breast, it does not drink. Here it becomes unmistakably clear to what great extent even newborns understand adults' body language, for example, how intensively they react to the mother's behavioral physical rejection when even she is unaware of it. But one can also observe from the physical behavior of such a mother that she treats the child not as a living being but as a lifeless object.

This is often the reaction of mothers who reject the children's fathers or who are rejected by them, and who now project this rejection onto the child. To save these children one has to keep them alive with salt enemas, intravenous glucose injections, or blood transfusions. As soon as they have recovered one has to teach them to suckle by constantly, patiently stimulating the mouth parts. But at best this only helps to keep the child from starvation. It does not help to teach it confidence and trust.

A change of caregiver at this age (for example, because of the mother's illness or death) has severely traumatic effects. On the other hand, children who from birth on have been attended to by several, but not too many, caregivers, mostly escape traumas such as these. For that reason, children raised in large families or in communal households are often more stable than individual children of small families and suffer less from fixations and regressions. We repeat the explanation of this concept: We speak of *fixation* when a part of the child's libido clings to a certain stage of development and impedes the transition to the next stage. We speak of *regression* when the child, adolescent, or adult reverts to a certain childhood phase during a mental crisis. Also, many "normal" adults think back on some childhood phases with a kind of homesickness and now and then develop involuntary ways of behavior that actually belong in childhood. All so-called *perversions* are relapses into childhood stages of sexual development. Therefore, in sex pedology there is a guiding principle that the general public may think is paradoxical—"Perversion is normal in children." We will return to this point again and again.

There is an as yet unproven theory advocated especially by Melanie Klein and her school that says that newborns experience displeasure as aggression and divide their bodies into "good" and "bad," exactly like the entire, not-yet-perceived-as-such, social surroundings. Pleasant stimuli are "good," unpleasant ones are "bad." So, the mother or caregiver who is not yet recognized as an individual, not yet as a part of the external world, is already considered by the newborn as "good" when she is there, and as "bad" when she is away. All motherly actions that benefit the children are "good," all that hurt them "bad." So, from the newborn's point of view there is no totally "good" or totally "bad" mother. This *ambivalent* (forked) behavior of children from birth on toward their first "beloved" for that reason also imprints our lifelong ambivalence toward our parents and our sex partners, according to the Klein school.

It can be stated with certainty that caregivers can influence the later choice of a partner exactly because in these earliest periods in children's lives caregivers are not yet perceived as such. At that time, the caregivers' influence is vital for newborns (if attendants do not feed the infants, they die), but on the other hand, since the imprint originates from the deepest and as yet unconscious levels of memory, it exerts an almost irresistible influence on the adults' later life. We can resist only those influences of which we are conscious. We are powerless against unconscious influences. The ways in which the mother or caregiver behaves when faced with newborns are, therefore, in the sense of life history, of great significance to the children's later sex life. Caregivers determine not only the unconscious reasons for the choice of a partner later on, but also a large part of the sexual practices the adults will accept or reject in later life. This is the reason for our opinion that what is "normal" for small children (for example, finding pleasure in sucking milk from a woman's breast) is "perverse" in adulthood, while what is "normal" in adulthood (for example, coitus) is perverse in childhood.

3

Second to Sixth Month
Early Infancy Age

Near the end of the first month, boys and girls are approximately the same height (around 52 cm [1.7 ft]) and also
have the same weight (around 3.7 kg [8.15 lb]). Thereafter
physical size and weight increase proportionally according
to sex.

Toward the end of the second month the girl weighs
4.6 kg (10.14 lb), the boy 4.7 kg (10.36 lb). She is 55 cm
(1.8 ft) tall, he 56 cm (1.83 ft). One month later she is 59 cm
(1.93 ft) tall, he 61 cm (2.0 ft). She weighs 5.6 kg (12.34 lb),
he 6.2 kg (13.66 lb). Near the end of the fourth month, she
weighs 6.4 kg (14.1 lb), he 6.8 kg (14.99 lb). She is 62 cm
(2.03 ft) tall, he 63 cm (2.06 ft).

Four weeks later the girl is 64 cm (2.09 ft) tall, the boy
65 cm (2.13 ft). She weighs 6.7 kg (14.77 lb), he 7.1 kg
(15.65 lb). In many children the birth weight doubles within
the first five months. At the end of the early infancy period
the girl weighs approximately 7.1 kg (15.65 lb), the boy
approximately 7.7 kg (16.97 lb). She is 65 cm (2.13 ft) tall,
he 67 cm (2.19 ft).

Early infancy age is a time of rest and consolidation.

The trauma of birth and the succeeding processes of conversion from intrauterine to extrauterine life are completed. A phase of peaceful practicing of important life processes now begins. Above all, the relationship to the environment and to the caretakers especially must now be stabilized. What happens now between children and their mother or caregiver will one day determine the relationship between the children who have matured to adulthood and their sex partner.

Early infancy age is the time of awakenings from the sleeplike state of the first month of life to the beginning understanding of social surroundings. Of course, already toward the end of the first week children have reacted to certain signals, but these reactions were undifferentiated and nonspecific. Brunet, in fact, has maintained that even in the first month it is possible to induce children to stick out their tongues by showing them one's own tongue, but this observation has never been confirmed by other pedologists. Between the fifth and seventh weeks infants first begin to recognize certain things, but even then only a quite limited number of forms. For example, they cannot discern whether what they see involves two- or three-dimensional objects.

After the eighth week, infants now show that they can distinguish between two- and three-dimensional objects. They can now also distinguish between movements that lead toward them and those that lead away from them. One week later many infants can already visually perceive another person, certainly only at feeding time, i.e., when they are hungry. So, visual learning develops from the gratification of the desire for nourishment.

Approximately one month later, most infants succeed in following their mother or caregiver not only with their eyes, but also with their head. One week later, children can already react in a similar way to the *voice* of their attendant. From the fourth month on, they exhibit ways of behavior in which the desire for this person expresses itself independently of the infants' physical needs.

From the third or fourth month on, most infants clearly show libidinous skin reactions. They giggle, laugh, and radiate sensual gratification when you tickle, bathe, or caress them. At this age children also begin to rub toys and other objects against their own body with an unmistakable expression of joy. People used to think children did this to get rid of the objects, because at this age they can certainly close their hands to grasp an object, but cannot willfully open their hands to place the object aside. Therefore, people thought children used their body as a kind of rubbing surface to slip off the objects from their hands. That may also be true. But the obvious joyousness with which the behavior is carried on allows us to suppose that at the same time here is a kind of self-gratification or at least a stimulation of certain zones of the body.

Infants soon begin to inspect their fingers. They feel one hand with the other, stick each finger in their mouth, check the fingers' taste, their skin structure, their hardness or softness. This is an unqualified sensual process. In spite of this, people who see infants in their cradle playing with their own limbs do not have the impression that here a *conscious* activity occurs or that children experiment on *aiming* to give themselves pleasure. They make gurgling sounds and follow their hand and foot movements with their eyes. They appear not to recognize that these are parts of their own bodies and that they move them themselves. The same is true for children's play with their genitals. One does not have the impression that the children are trying to excite themselves, but that they are trying in turn whatever they can undertake with their limbs. But whether infants know that these limbs belong to them, themselves, is questionable.

For that reason, for the infants the genitals are endowed with no greater importance than any other zone of the body, for example, the mouth, thumbs, the navel, toes, or earlobes. It is mostly the parents' or caregivers' excessive reaction to the childish playing around with their genitals that in general gives infants the first impression that these zones are somehow more significant than all others. Also the by-pass of the genitals during parental caressing and coddling makes children aware that here is a bodily zone that is "different" from all the rest. So, it is mostly the parents' fear of childish masturbation that puts into children's heads the idea that there is something forbidden there and for that reason something interesting to do.

Infant masturbation is obviously good for the acquisition of sensory experience. In this sense it does not differ measurably from the earlier ecstasy of sucking or from later rocking, hopping, jumping, or tickling. When children smell and lick all their toys; when they later place their ear next to a shell, a clock, or to the neck of a purring cat; when they make soap bubbles, egg slop, and do other childish things, then, according to their age-specific scale, they are doing exactly the same as when they play with their limbs: they are learning. And since certain learning processes function only when they are fun, children learn all the more when learning is made more fun for them.

Between 1961 and 1980 we repeatedly confirmed that children who had shown themselves to be especially agile as infant masturbators developed all other motor abilities, especially manipulation, earlier and more efficiently than nonmasturbators. Now, we do not know whether it is so that motor-intelligent children masturbate earlier and more efficiently than less intelligent ones, or whether masturbation developmentally and biologically is good for the training of manual dexterity. However, the one probably furthers the other.

The actual erogenous zone of infancy age is not the genital, but the mouth. For infants suckle, and through sucking not only take nourishment, but also provide themselves the age-specific form of pleasure and satisfaction. They do not suck only on the mother's breast, but on every other bodily part, every other object at their disposal. In the third month they grasp their feet with their hands and stick one toe after the other into their mouth. They sometimes bite so hard with their toothless gums that they startle themselves, because at this age they are probably still not aware of the difference between I and You, between cause and effect.

Their own finger or thumb, but also every toy within reach, each piece of cloth, every corner of the bed is introduced into and tested in the mouth. This phase of *oral exploration,* testing with the mouth (Latin *os,* genitive, *oris:* "mouth"), lasts up to the middle of the second year of life. Whatever escapes the as yet imperfectly functioning hands and fingers will sooner or later be captured orally, with the mouth. People are not perceived as people, things not as things, but rather both only insofar as they cause or satisfy hunger, can or cannot be placed into the mouth, procure oral delight or produce oral displeasure.

Children sometimes suck the mother's breast with such intensity that one would believe they wanted to suck themselves into the mother's body. So, many pedologists also believe sucking is a cannibalistic process, an attempt to eat up the mother. Therefore, they designate the infancy period as the *cannibalistic phase.* Others think that sucking is an attempt to return to the womb, to open a tunnel through the breast into the uterus. Still others believe children want to fuse with their mother, want to be one with her.

That is not surprising, because "breast-fed children are very much the ectoparasites of the mother, just as in the fetal period they are endoparasitic, they live on her" (Sandor Ferenczi). The only strange thing is that the matter appears exactly in reverse from the children's perspective. They do not view themselves as part of the mother, but rather their mother as part of them. While they ingest her in tiny sips they become one with her. The primitive knowledge of mammals clearly says to them that the only possibility of never losing their mother, of carrying her with them always, exists in incorporating her. On the same perception rests the universal religious yearning for a magical communion in which people become one with a deity, whose body and soul the people symbolically ingest.

In the infants' relatively immature motor system the sucking apparatus is the only one that makes possible an adequate rapport with the environment. The mouth cavity with all its equipment—tongue, lips, cheeks, and the sinuses—is, in the opinion of many pedologists (for example, René Spitz), the first erogenous zone used for tactile perceptions and explorations. It is well suited for this purpose because the senses of taste, smell, temperature, and pain are prominently represented in it. Even depth perception, which we already described as one of the most important of early life, is mobilized by the act of swallowing. On the other hand, the perception that is established through the mouth is still a form of close-up. It is distinguished age-specifically from the perceptions of distance such as seeing and hearing that develop later.

This has great significance not only for the development of object relationships, but also for that of the sense of reality. Children learn that pangs of hunger can be reduced by taking nourishment. Inner tensions can be released by introducing a substance coming from the outside. From now on, this knowledge becomes a model for conquering reality. People test whether something is "real" by sticking it into their mouth. If it can be eaten, it is "real." If you have to spit it out, it is "not real." So, the attempted ingesting is the first active reaction not only to objects in general—therefore, to the environment—but also to reality, to the distinction between what is imagined and what is "real."

One of the first signs of this process is that children can now find the breast nipples without the searching rotations of their head. On the other hand, they still cannot find the nipple on a bottle if a person does not stick it into their mouth. So, bottle-fed children develop the age-specific reactions later than breast-fed children. If bottle-fed children are at least held in the arms so that they feel the mother's or caregivers' body heat, make body contact, and can maintain eye contact with her, then the retardation of maturity in relation to breast-fed children is not as great. However, if children are strapped down and fed through a bottle holder, this last sensory contact between children and caregivers also gets lost. Infants raised in such a way are predictably hostile to sensuality in adulthood in addition to the expected losses of potency and capacity for devotion.

If in the second month children are smiled at and spoken to, they react with their tongue. The disinterested mother says, "It's slobbering." But in reality something significant is occurring here: When children at the age of one month react to the breast or to the bottle by sticking out their tongue, they now do the same as a reaction to a much more abstract, no longer physical, but psychically gratification-producing signal.

Near the end of the second month infants suddenly begin to interrupt their sucking to smile at their caregiver. They sometimes continue to suckle only to stop a second time and smile at the caregiver. When they are satisfied they no longer immediately fall asleep, but rather begin a kind of dialogue with the caregiver's face, which now obviously becomes more important to them than nourishment. René Spitz believes that this dialogue and this smiling (he calls it the *three-month's smile*) is still no proof of a genuine object relationship of the children to their caregivers, but rather is the motor perception of visual signals: images of another person's forehead, eyes, and of the nose in a certain emotional state, namely, that of smiling. He calls these signals *object precursors* and therefore designates the entire phase as *preobjectal*. According to him, the actual object phase is arrived at only when children begin to recognize their mother or caregiver as individual beings.

The children's first unmistakable recognition of their

mothers or caregivers is for both one of the most joyful moments in life. The process of mutual gratification that begins with this event stabilizes the children and furthers their development. That this, among others, is also a sexual experience follows from the Bible, in which coitus is often described as mutual "recognition" ("to know"). However, many mothers deny themselves this recognition so thoroughly that the children suffer under the mother's incomprehensible rejection. We discovered in our own observations that those mothers who refuse to recognize the erotic aspects of motherly and childish love got into special difficulties when, while feeding, they have orgasms against their will and to their horror.

One must then explain to such difficult mothers that in this case a purely organic process is occurring that is beyond good and evil. It has nothing to do with incest. Nipples become erect once stimulated no matter from whom the stimulus might come. They are stimulated by the infant's mouth as the penis is by the vagina. The milk of many mothers shoots out with ejaculatory pressure. These processes are not voluntary and many mothers cannot willfully suppress them. On the other hand, we cannot be silent about the fact that the mother's delight in her child is closely related to her readiness for sexual pleasure and that the preparedness to be "known" by the child is greater and more enjoyable in the case of mothers who revel in their bodily sensuality than in ones who are hostile toward the body.

Ever so great as the delight of many mothers while they are feeding, however, is the delight of many infants while they are being fed. That infants suck not only for the sake of nourishment follows from the fact that when they are diverted from drinking by some disturbance, they do not return to take nourishment by themselves, but first of all have to be orally stimulated: "Long-lasting oral stimulation is necessary to motivate infants again to return their attentions to the nourishment they are crying for, and which had already been at their disposal the whole time" (René Spitz).

Another piece of evidence that the sucking is pleasurable as such is to be found in the *ecstasy of sucking* already mentioned as a method of exploration, by which the vernacular very correctly designates as "ecstasy" the act of *sucking* and not that of *drinking*. This pleasurable sucking without swallowing has a very characteristic rhythm. And since pleasurable activities almost always possess a rhythmic structure, here, too, we can see a form of the practice of later enjoyable activities (masturbation, coitus, dancing, playing music). The facial expressions and body language of infants while sucking in ecstasy are similar to adults' during sexual intercourse. Among many suckling infants— even those younger than six months—we find muscle tension in the abdomen, hips, and back; then sudden release with convulsions and congestion; finally blissful falling asleep with flushed cheeks. Anna Freud's investigations have shown that infants at this age can bear the most difficult loss of childhood, that of the mother or caregiver, if only they receive enough oral satisfaction.

For all these reasons the infant age has also been designated the *oral phase*. This phase breaks down into two stages, of which the first especially is determined by the desire *to suck*, while the second (from the seventh month on, approximately) is determined by the cutting of the first teeth and by the desire *to bite*. Under favorable conditions the initial stage of the oral phase can be the happiest part of life. Never again do so many auspicious, satisfactory elements converge. Children do not need to trouble themselves with either work or earning money; are fed when hungry; are dried when they wet themselves; are embraced, rocked, kissed (at least they should be). Skin, muscle, oral, and manual stimulations are secured simultaneously.

On the other hand, even at this age children have a few painful experiences, for example, when they are hungry and are *not* fed, when they wet themselves and are *not* dried, when they cry and are *not* consoled, but also because their dull fantasies about incorporating the mother and the environment cannot be realized, and because being stuck in this stage or a later relapse into such fantasies can have profound consequences in the adults' sex life.

In any case, a sign of this developmental stage is the irregular back and forth between ravenous hunger and refusal of nourishment. This is unavoidable and belongs to the normal rhythm of this phase. Quiet and "good" infants are often anything but healthy and need a greater amount of care than "bad" or "crying" ones. If children are especially "good," the reason may be found in the fact that the postnatal stimulus buffer we discussed in the previous chapter is still not as yet developed, and that the children cannot at all perceive the greater part of internal and external sensory perceptions. Electroencephalographic investigations have revealed that the last remains of postnatal boundaries of sensation in healthy children are demolished by the third to fourth months. From this time on, children begin a period of *symbiosis* with their mothers or caregivers, the illusion of a perfect *dyad*. Margaret Mahler also calls this developmental stage the *symbiotic phase*. Its time span, its origins, and its effects are identical to those of Spitz's preobjectal phase.

Since most infants at this age still have the illusion of absolute power, Ferenczi calls the same period (the second to sixth months) the *stage of hallucinatory omnipotence*. This stage is marked by the fact that infants certainly learn to identify a growing number of stimuli and signals that stream in to them from the external world, but they still always believe they come from the symbiotic unity with their mother or caregiver. Since their ability to love grows steadily, they now begin to put a growing amount of libido on their caregiver. However, since what the infants invest with love is not an individual, but first of all only a kind of appendage of their still not clearly outlined, still not clearly defined selves. In spite of this, the libidinous investiture of the caregiver is the ground-laying psychical achievement of this age.

Near the end of the symbiotic phase, the primary narcissism that originated in the newborn stage decreases and gradually makes room for secondary narcissism. Now children begin to view not only their own body, but also that of the mother as an autoerotic object. That sounds paradoxical, but is explained by the fact that infants can break out of the primitive self-love stage in which they spent their first four months of life only when they draw their mother or caregiver, who for them is certainly a part of themselves, into their self-love. If they then discover that the beloved person is not a part of themselves and also is not in symbiosis with their own body, this self-love becomes *object love,* the ability to love *another* person.

Sexual Pathology of Early Infancy

The most important sign of early infancy is the inordinate desire, the wish, for acquisition, for incorporation, for introjection. Orally conditioned adults manifest the same behavior in their sex lives as infants in their behavior toward their mother or caregiver. They want to swallow up their sex partner; they cannot get enough love; they are always hungry for more.

Since these persons during their oral-developmental phase have divided all objects into "good," what can be eaten, and "bad," what has to be spat out, they relate in the same way toward their love object in later sex life: They consider those who allow themselves to be "gobbled up" as "good," and those who refuse as "bad." They "spit out" every partner who is not prepared for total self-surrender.

On the other hand, the trauma of the early infancy period is the fear of the loss of the mother's breast. In adulthood it is expressed as fear of the loss of sex partners or their affection. The experience infants have during feeding deter-mines their behavior toward the social surroundings in general and to their later sex partner in particular. If they are fed often enough, even in adulthood their trust in the environment can hardly be shaken. If the mother has too little milk, if she is inept at feeding or allows the child's hunger signals to go unnoticed (for example, because she thinks children have to learn to bear privation), the children's primal trust is destroyed. Until the end of their days they will remain suspicious and consider their contemporaries untrustworthy. That mistrust will also precipitate into their sexual relationships as adults and make life difficult for their sex partners.

One can sometimes recognize these people in the infant stage by the dogged intensity with which they suck their fingers. Excessive finger- or thumb-sucking always indicates that children are not fed enough or that the mother changed them over from long to short drinking periods too early. It is almost always the expression of an unfulfilled need for close body contact, care, and tenderness. The proof is that habitual thumbsuckers always do this before falling asleep, when the need for attention, consolation, and tender-ness is greatest.

The insatiable greed of the initial oral phase in oral-regressive people is often marked by the inclination to suck other people dry and to exploit them without at the same time being burdened with a bad conscience, because the needs originating from this phase are indeed totally free of those destructive impulses that appear during the second oral stage, thanks to the development of the teeth. The more undis-turbed, the more joyfully the infancy period of these persons passes, the more convinced they are as adults that their sex partner is supposed to gratify them as their mother or caregiver had done during the first six months of life.

In many oral-regressive people another variant of re-gression often appears. Since they live under the illusion that the entire world is their mother, they never bother about a sex partner and expect the other to take the first step. In the infancy age they were so well cared for that they believed the mother's milk would flow forever for them. They certainly do not have any great conflict with their sex partners, but also no real passion, because in general they do not perceive other people as emotional objects.

People should not underestimate the evils of a delayed weaning. Today among enlightened and progressive parents there exists such opposition to premature weaning that many mothers now slip back into the opposite and feed their children much too long. However, delayed weaning is at least just as risky as premature and often means that mothers feed for their own satisfaction and not for that of their children. The result may be either that lifelong inhibition of sexual initiative just mentioned, which can manifest itself nonsexually as a paralysis of the will to live, to strive, and of the ability to succeed, or in the other previously described syndrome—the unprincipled appropriation of other people's affections. Those who are not familiar with the effects of ambivalence may have difficulties being able to trace back two such different forms of sexual behavior to the same developmental phase. However, clinical experience leaves no doubt that in both cases it is a question of the same origin.

In addition, a third syndrome can be traced back to analogous causes—the flaunting of their potency by many men. This often is an overcompensatory regression to the passive oral state of infants, who want only to be fed, caressed, and coddled. Extremely active sexual behavior in men points mostly to suppressed desire for sexual passivity.

The clinging to their sex partner of many orally damaged adults suggests that at the initial oral stage the fear of losing the mother's breast was especially great and later led to the above-mentioned "swallowing up" of the sex partner.

The forms of voracious appetite ("pubescent voracity") and of refusing food ("pubescent thinness–mania") often manifested in puberty are regressions from the genital to the oral phase. The fear of the responsibilities of sexuality and of partner choice then expresses itself in a desperate return to the lesser fears of the infancy period: genitality is regressively transformed into orality.

If children in the age of infancy are especially seriously frustrated, their unsatisfied desire for nourishment can also be transformed into a desire that allows itself to be satisfied with the help of one of the other senses. Many of the so-called perversions of adulthood go back to this syndrome. Persons such as these strive for the gratification of the senses of seeing (voyeurism), hearing (audiophilia), smelling, or touching instead of genital gratification. The incorporation they strived for is no longer possible by mouth, but through the eyes, nose, ears, or skin.

Since language is an oral activity, oral frustrations also often result in later speech disorders. Many deviances of the adult stage expressed in speech and writing—obscene phone calls and letters, the compulsive expression of "forbidden" words, and similar "perversions"—in many cases originate in oral damages in the infancy age.

Of the neuroses, the manic-depressive ones are mostly due to the fixations on the oral phase. The manic-depressive cycle originates in the cycle of hunger and satisfaction. In the manic phase persons fixated in the oral phase behave like euphoric, intoxicated, fully satisfied infants. In contrast, in the depressive phase they behave like infants who refuse the breast because it had been denied them the last time (refusal of nourishment is an accompanying symptom of almost all depression). The etiology of manic-depressive disorders always points to great frustration in the initial oral phase (more exactly: during the symbiotic phase). Frustration such as this is not only painful for the infant's body, but it also destroys the illusion of motherly omnipotence, which during this period is experienced as the infant's own omnipotence.

To compensate later for the mother's inadequacy that they have experienced, such children develop an especially rigid conscience that places all too great and unreasonable demands on their own behavior and thereby leads to a constant alternation between depression and euphoria—euphoria whenever they succeed in adapting their own behavior to the norm they are striving for, depression whenever they do not succeed in doing so.

If parents by their own behavior cause their children to make an especially drastic regression to the children's initial oral stage, the children's methods of defense often remain archaic and immature. Paradoxically, the danger is all the greater the stronger the children's ego-core is, because they then can certainly succeed with resistance against overpoweringly strong needs; however, they are unable to follow up this success with mature defensive measures. The result can be a compulsive neurosis. Certain forms of schizophrenia and catatonic stupor probably originate in oral fixations. Such schizophrenics frequently see all sense organs and even many aspects of the environment as formed "like a mouth," functioning like a mouth, dangerous like a mouth ("swallowing up"). The vagina is also considered as threatening and "devouring" by such people (both women as well as men).

When children have the daydream typical for the initial oral phase, they devour their environment and thereby suffer rejection by their caregivers, so they promptly fantasize being swallowed up by the caregiver. In this way fantastic fears of physical destruction arise that can destroy the children's entire future sex life. The most important one is the fear of castration, which is stirred up by a parental prohibition of masturbation during "toddler's puberty" (the fourth year).

We have already said that attentive, intelligent infants masturbate more frequently than retarded ones. Here should be added, as a characteristic of the relationship between masturbation and sense of reality, that autistic children masturbate only rarely or not at all. It is also obviously such that nature puts a premium on sensual gratification so that children will be motivated to exercise flexibility and the sense of reality. Now, if parents out of misunderstood morality forbid children sensual gratification, they also prevent thinking and learning processes that are tied to the gratification.

This is shown rather convincingly by the observation that children whose hands are restrained to prevent masturbation sometimes suffer from diminished motility their whole life long. Similarly, just as learning to walk is delayed in orphanages, where children have to be left in their cots for longer periods of time because of the lack of personnel, so is delayed the sexual development of all children who through wrappings, diapers, or prohibition have been prevented from masturbation. Every human organ that is one day supposed to function efficiently must be exercised as early as possible. That goes for our genitals as well as for our brain and our nervous system.

Experiments with sensory deprivation have revealed that adult subjects suffer psychical damages when they are deprived of normal sensory contact with their environment for some time. However, exactly this deprivation occurs at the level of sexuality in most Western families when parents already prevent children in infancy from the age-specific exercise of sensory and motile apparatuses and at later stages of sexual maturity forbid them the necessary gratification.

Nature did not shape us as sexual beings without reason. Our sexual needs are useful to the acquisition of physical abilities. The satisfaction of these needs assists the production of harmonious relationships in psychical life. Every interference in this healthy process results in health disorders and leads to retardation of all related maturity processes.

That which is healthy and normal in childhood, nevertheless, becomes dangerous in adulthood whenever it is the result of regressive behavior. So, it is a diagnostic indication of sexual infantilism whenever adults still seek gratification from their own bodies. This is not only in reference to masturbation, but also to the numerous other variants of psychosexual autoeroticism—all those ways of behavior that regard one's own gratification as primary and that of the other as secondary or irrelevant. Of course, narcissistically fixated persons can be thoroughly satisfying sex partners under certain conditions. Just such men and women often attempt to gratify their partner with especial perseverance and skill. But they do not do this out of alloerotic motives, thus for genuine object love, but only to prove to themselves how efficient they are in the practice of sexual techniques. If they are not sufficiently praised, loved, and pampered for it, their confidence shatters immediately. Then the uncovered autoeroticism appears from beneath the alloerotic mask: self-love stands behind the object love. A symptom of such narcissistically socialized persons is that as adults they cannot bear anything unpleasant and collapse under the slightest psychical pressure.

Such people not only demand to be loved, but they also cannot bear a situation in which they are *not* loved. They fall into depression whenever they feel that someone, toward whom they feel totally indifferent, is returning their feelings of indifference. Their fear of the loss of love is so great that they even dread losing affection they never possessed in the first place.

Many of these disorders of adult sex life can be identified as direct results of incorrect parental behavior in the infancy stage of the person involved, for example, as a result of the parental fear of destroying the children's illusions of omnipotence. However, if these illusions are not dispelled at the right time, children regress from normal activity to total passivity when they grow up. Such adults then treat their sex partners as if they were their caregivers. They consider themselves as omnipotent and their partners as motherly executive assistants. They are horrified when their sex partner does not engage in this game. They then consider themselves as betrayed and abandoned, as motherless children from whom one has willfully and groundlessly robbed their right to love.

If infants again fall into ideas of omnipotence after they have already recognized the mother or caregiver as such, the danger exists of a fixation in this stage or a regression into secondary narcissism. Expressed in the professional jargon: *primary narcissism* is the subjective pre-stage of object love; *secondary narcissism* is the regression of object love into the subjective stage. If the libido occupies the subject, we speak of *narcissistic libido*. When comparing the symbiotic and the narcissistic aspects of this phase, it has to be pointed out that the narcissistic fusion, the confusion of the boundaries between ego (child) and nonego (caregiver), is an etiologically different phenomenon from the symbiotic illusion of finding oneself in a dyad with the caregiver. Either way, no matter how much infants would like to fuse with their mother during the symbiotic phase, near the end of the phase, in a state of panic, they also will develop *fears of fusion*. That means, as soon as they have become aware of their separateness, they again develop a deep fear of losing the newly acquired independence.

In anticipation of the next chapter, we would like to add here that by the time they have taken the first steps into genuine independence in the fifth to tenth months, infants develop deep *fears of separation*, panicky fears of their own independence. But hardly have they overcome the psychical separation from the mother (near the end of the third year), when the *fear of symbiosis* begins, a fear of renewed symbiosis with the mother.

So, the process of the psychical separation from the mother or caregiver is a very painful and lengthy one that is threatened by many obstacles and contradictions. It begins in the fourth month, after the bond between mother and child has become especially established. For a separation can occur only when a bond has been made in the first place, and the bond can occur only after the child has recognized the mother or caregiver as an independent, autonomous, and self-reliant personality.

To recognize these characteristics, children at this age begin to explore the mother's face and body carefully and systematically, and certainly all the more carefully the less clothing she is wearing. Mothers and caregivers who are free of sexual scruples confirm that, when allowed, children between the fourth and seventh months will visually and manually inspect every part of the attendant's body—with special curiosity about their genitals.

As soon as children have discovered with their five senses what kind of body it is that has taken care of them until now, they are prepared to undertake their initial steps into independence. The more the parents behave with hostility toward and denial of the body, the later the process of separation begins and the longer it takes. It should begin in the fourth month at the earliest, in the tenth month at the latest. One can recognize the beginning of it when children lean their bodies away from the mother or caregiver more often—not in annoyance or protest, but as if they only wanted to see how their caregivers looks from a distance. In the fact that children maintain eye contact with their caregiver we notice that this is a good-natured act of testing a new, distant state of affairs. With it begins not only actual childhood, but perhaps also the first separation from it.

From now on children can bear an increasing amount of physical frustration as long as they may at least be permitted to maintain eye contact with their attendant. However, conversely, they react with rage and tears whenever they lose the possibility of eye contact with the attendant—even then when all their physical needs are fulfilled by another person.

So, here again something specifically human appears—the primacy of certain psychical over certain physical needs. The more children are assured of the love and reliability of their attendant, the earlier they succeed in separation as well as individuation. The less parents and caregivers love their children (but also: the more they spoil and browbeat them), the slower, more difficult, and more painful is the process of separation and of finding oneself.

That creates certain problems of fixation on and regression to periods before the separation and finding of oneself. They can lead to those serious disorders that Margaret Mahler and Bertram Goslinger called "symbiotic psychosis" between 1952 and 1955. But milder cases of regression to this phase in adulthood can also appear as disorders of the sex life. Since infants during this time live with the symbiotic illusion that everything the mother or caregiver does for them they have done for themselves, if they are fixated in this phase or regress to it as adults, they will also retain the illusion that everything their sex partner does for them is done by themselves. Such persons sometimes appear to live in a perfect dyad with their spouse, yet the dyad functions only as long as the spouses bear the entire burden of care and never rob the "omnipotent" ones of their illusion of omnipotence.

The most prevalent form of symbiotic fixation is the already mentioned fear of fusion that is developed in the earlier stages of the separation phase—just when children develop the initial core of their ego and achieve the initial awareness of their own identity. As we have seen, in this phase children often exhibit panicky fears of newly won independence. They do not want to fuse with their caregiver again, but they find themselves in a terrible dilemma, because at the same time those carefree, blissful times of symbiosis also entice the children to return: the *longing for symbiosis*.

In our social order, the all-too-widespread man's fear of a woman's dominance over his physical and emotional autonomy probably goes back to this phase. The permanent defensive measures such men take against every woman who threatens to penetrate their "private sphere" are often more effective than the sexual charms of women.

So, the fear of fusion is the small child's fear of merging with the mother, which in adulthood manifests itself as the fear of fusion with the sex partner. The result is a sequence of neurotic forms of behavior, frigidity, potency disorders, and deviance. R. J. Stoller goes so far as to designate sexual deviations simply as "fissures resulting from the alternation between the wish for fusion and the wish for separation." According to him, these fissures may be healed in non-perverse persons, be healed in neurotics only with difficulty, and be open wounds in those with perversions. However, in all three cases it reaches down deeply into identity and requires lifelong care against renewed opening of the wounds.

Stoller characterizes transsexuality—the lifelong feeling of having been provided with the wrong sex organs by the parents—as the specific deviation of the symbiotic phase and believes that even transsexual women—persons with somatically female and psychically male sexuality—are products of incorrect parental behavior during the symbiotic phase. Male transsexuality, then, would be nothing but a son's incomplete separation from the mother. In contrast, female transsexuality would be the product of excessive fears of fusion caused by the mother's incorrect behavior. According to Stoller, in the process of separation such daughters distance themselves so intensively from their mothers that they take on the contrary psychosexuality: that of the man. Their somatic sexuality remains female; in the process of separation, their psychical sexuality changes into a male one.

4

Seventh to Twelfth Month
Late Infancy Age

Late infancy age, the time of teething, weaning, crawling, learning to walk, and separating in stages from the mother, is a period of serious crisis and a high degree of emotional stress. Therefore, many developmental psychologists also call it the *weaning crisis*. Others call that time when children can sit but not yet crawl, the *sitting age*, and the time when they can creep or crawl but not walk, the *creeping age* or the *crawling age*. Advocates of the infant's stomach position consider "sitting age" an unnatural concept and report that their pupils can already stand when those infants brought up in a back position still cannot even sit.

In the seventh month a girl weighs about 7.2 kg (15.87 lb) and is approximately 66 cm (2.1 ft) tall. At the same age, a boy weighs about 8.2 kg (18.07 lb) and is 69 cm (2.26 ft) tall. A month later the girl weighs 7.7 kg (16.97 lb), the boy 8.6 kg (18.95 lb). She is 68 cm (2.23 ft) tall, he 70.5 cm (2.31 ft). In the ninth month she weighs 8.1 kg (17.85 lb), he 8.9 kg (19.62 lb). She is 70 cm (2.29 ft) tall, he 72 cm (2.36 ft). In the tenth month the girl reaches the imposing height of 72 cm (2.36 ft); the boy, however, is still about

2 cm (.75 in) ahead of her. She weighs 8.8 kg (19.4 lb), he 9.4 kg (20.7 lb). A month later she is 74 cm (2.42 ft) tall, he 75.5 cm (2.47 ft). She weighs 9.1 kg (20.06 lb), he 9.8 kg (21.6 lb). Near the end of the year she has grown approximately 24 cm (9.44 in) since birth, he 25.5 cm (10.03 in). The weight of both of them has tripled. The brain, at 750 ccm (45.75 cu in), has more than doubled since birth from 350 ccm (21.35 cu in).

Just as the second stage of the infants' sensual development goes back to teething and its psychical effects, at this age the children's relationship to the caregiver rests upon the growing control over their arms and legs, but also over their back. When they first begin to creep, then to crawl, and finally learn to walk, children become independent of their mother or caregiver and now strive to get out of the symbiosis with her that had dominated the second to sixth months. Margaret Mahler therefore called this phase that of *separation and individuation*. René Spitz speaks of the *phase of object development*.

Children learn to creep, stand, and walk in three significant stages of development. Standing is important because it allows better opportunity for visually discovering one's own body. At this age many children consciously look at their genitals for the first time. We will soon return to the significance of this discovery. It is reinforced when children become accustomed to holding their body upright. While learning to walk, many boys notice through the rubbing and tossing of the penis and testicles against the upper thigh that they have a limb there with which they can do much. For those children, too, who have already for months carried on so-called infant masturbation, this is an important discovery, because it is indeed a sign of primary **masturbation**, that it is an unconscious act and in this **sense may** not be classified as aimed at self-gratification.

In this period of rapid expansion of **psychical** horizons, children also learn to understand complicated matters; to distinguish what is suitable from what is not; to recognize what goes with what; to string objects, put them together, and take them apart; to hand toys to other children and to take them back. They learn to waddle, to raise themselves, and to climb. That means: Using many techniques, they learn to distance themselves from the mother or caregiver.

The more mobile children become, naturally, the greater the risks are that they will hurt themselves, break breakable things, upset things that overturn, pull down things that can be torn down, and throw the entire household into chaos. So, at this age parents are forced to break into the children's world with prohibitions for the first time.

The first word infants learn from their parents, besides "mama" and "papa," is often the word "no." René Spitz supposes that the headshaking of parents saying "no" is the first gesture children assume from their parents. At the same time it is also the "first objectivation of genuine abstract thinking in the child's emotional life" (Franco Fornari).

With mastery over the forbidding headshaking gesture and the word "no," children move from the smelling, tasting, and touching proximate experience to distance communication with the aid of their eyes and ears. At the same time, children also proceed with the ability to say no to their social surroundings in their first *obstinate phase,* which begins near the end of the first year of life and, after an abatement in the second year, finds its high point in the third year (*obstinate age, first adolescence*). The first indications of this phase appear around the eleventh month, when children begin to harass their parents again and again by throwing their playthings (and sometimes also the adults' breakable possessions) as far as the children's muscle power and skill will allow.

For these and other reasons already mentioned, the final weeks of the first year are often a period of annoyance, rage, and jealousy. Making the body grow rigid or limp, kicking, biting, and scratching appear according to the progress the children have made in their motor abilities up until then. Within the transitional period to the second year, when their vocabulary grows just as their dexterity does, parents sometimes try to help them with especially difficult tasks. The answer parents get mostly is a furious cry, "me." On the other hand, love, affection, tenderness, joy in living, and pride also belong to the contradictory profile of this phase of stress. Children not only rejoice in the expressions of love they receive, but also respond to them with warm embraces and hearty kisses.

René Spitz, who had an especially good eye for the rhythm and periodicity of human developmental phases, compared the attempts of one-year-olds to come to terms with their environment with those of infants who, in their first months of life, try to acquire some pattern and behavioral style for their motor abilities. Exactly as the infants incorporate only the *successful* movements into their repertory, one-year-olds, too, incorporate into their behavior only those results of their attempts that have proven themselves *successful* in the children's relationship to their caregiver. However, in contrast, children in the eighth month also relinquish all those ways of behavior that proved to be useless and in this sense react exactly as young infants, who give up all movements of no use to them. Among the incidental movements, they choose those that lead them to their goal; they keep those various sequences of behavior and emotional reactions that bring children success in the sense of desire and gratification.

Near the end of the first year, then, children no longer move exclusively toward the satisfaction of immediate desires, but also already toward those of the future. While the motor behavior patterns in the first months of life had a clearly defined *reason*, they now, on the other hand, have an unmistakable *goal*. Margaret Mahler, who calls this age the *subphase of exercise*, distinguishes between the *early phase of exercise*, the age of the children who are crawling or are on all fours, and the *actual phase of exercise*, the period of learning to walk, the transition from quadruped to biped. Phyllis Greenacre designates the second phase as the *children's love relationship with their environment*, because simultaneous with upright locomotion numerous other sensory functions and perceptual possibilities develop.

With that, not only does the children's "perspective" change, their "horizon," but also their self-confidence. Greenacre says learning to walk is connected "with a transport of physical exhilaration in general." Mahler says children "appear to be intoxicated by their own abilities and the size of their world." At no other period of early childhood does the process of individuation make so much progress as in the month after learning to walk. However, we have to distinguish between two phases of learning to walk—first, the phase of separation from the mother or caregiver, in which children attempt their first tentative steps *away from the mother* or even in her absence, and then the phase of perfecting the walking, which is mostly carried out with the help of the mother or caregiver and *toward her*. In 1846 Kierkegaard had already given a very convincing description of this second phase.

A loving mother teaches her child to walk alone. She is far enough away from him to be able to offer little real support, but she extends her arms to him. She imitates his movements, and when he totters, she bends down quickly as if she wanted to seize him, so that the child could believe he is not walking alone—and still the mother is doing more. The glance with which she beckons her child onward is like a reward, an encouragement. So, the child walks alone, while his eyes are turned toward his mother's face and not at the difficulties lying in his path. He helps himself with the arms that do not hold him—

he steadily struggles to reach the refuge in his mother's arms. In so doing he has hardly any idea that, in exactly that moment that he shows his need of her, that he can get along without his mother, because he can walk alone.

With a brilliant power of observation, Kierkegaard described how the same process appears when a frightened or less self-confident, perhaps even a less loving, mother tries to teach her child to walk.

There is no smiling encouragement, no praise, when the walk is ended. The wish to teach the child to walk is here, too, but not, surely, as a loving mother embodies it. Because, fear reigns now, which holds the child captive. It encumbers him, and he cannot move himself forward. Even the wish to lead him to his goal is the same, but suddenly the goal calls forth terror.

If, thanks to the teachers' lack of skill, children fall behind their average age-specific standard for motility, they often can—if the caregiver is only unskilled, but not unloving—compensate for their relative immobility with perceptive and cognitive advances. In the opposite direction, children with especially high perceptive and cognitive intelligence often develop more slowly physically than their contemporaries. However, for the most part the rule is that the parents' or caregivers' loving, yet not spoiling or possessive, attitude stimulates both self-confidence as well as physical and emotional progress in children.

The more freely children can move, the less they need the mothers' or caregivers' help, the more independent they become. The more independent they become, the greater their pride in their abilities. And the greater their pride, the more quickly the process of separation.

With the age of separation, however, we come across sex-specific problems that we have already encountered in chapter 2, namely, the different forms of separation from the mother or caregiver in girls and boys. Just as the separation of boys from the mother's body at the moment of birth demands not only an adaptation from the mother's circulatory system to their own, but also a complete conversion from the mother's female tissue and from the placenta to autonomous male tissue, the phase of the psychical separation from the mother or caregiver between the third and thirty-sixth months makes higher demands on boys than on girls. For, with the exception of that very limited number of infants who have been bottle fed by their fathers or other male attendants, all children in our social order from birth on are imprinted with the feminine.

The more time mothers and the less time fathers spend with their children, the greater the probability that the psychosexuality will be feminine, no matter if they are daughters or sons. Just as in the prenatal phase the somatic maleness differentiates from the somatic female tendency, so now too, in the separation phase the psychical maleness differentiates from the psychical feminine imprint that the children receive from their mother or caregiver (in our social order almost always female). Since fathers work mostly outside the home, their influence is at best passing, even if they often take interest in the children.

On the other hand, girls, can identify with their mother sexually from their birth on, and now in the process of separation can disconnect from a sexually equal being without any sexual alternation of poles. No matter how hard the girls' process of separation may be in every other respect (jealousy between mother and daughter, for example), it at least demands no new sexual identity. If, however, boys separate from the psychical identity of their mother at this age, they have to assign themselves their own identity, a new, totally foreign, unexplained one that they do not as yet understand. How do they do that? How should they succeed in this?

They can succeed in this only if their mother or caregiver

promotes their masculinity. However, that is difficult in the age of the women's movement. Because if the mother or female attendant is aware of women's oppression, the domination over women, and the disadvantages of women in a patriarchal society, even with the best intentions she will find it difficult to raise her son to assist in the perpetuation of a misogynistic social order. The male infant's separation from the pseudofemale role becomes all the more difficult, therefore, the farther along the socially important and morally justified process of women's liberation advances.

If boys are not to become the images of their mother—thus, to become transsexuals—at this age (from the fourth month on), she has to encourage them to disengage themselves from her; otherwise they will be able to realize themselves neither as individuals nor as sexual beings. If she does not encourage them, she retards the process of individuation and reinforces their primary femininity. However, if she forces the process of separation by sending them away from her, she then possibly reinforces their need to stay with her and to merge with her. That would be the end of their hopes for autonomous masculinity.

But what is masculinity? Is it the stereotypical roles our society has developed in the course of thousands of years of male domination? Is there no other concept of masculinity except that of lords and masters? Of lords and masters over women and children? The answers lie outside the scope of a textbook in developmental psychology. Here we can only point to the difficulties of this phase and suggest that parents together think over these questions and decide how the "masculine" behavior of their son should appear, which now has to be stimulated by both parents.

This is not as difficult as it sounds, because children have an innate desire to learn to master their own functions. But these functions also enable sons to part from their mother. So, in spite of their yearning to blend with her, they nevertheless insist upon a new identification, separation, and individuation. Both parents are now obligated to promote these efforts. The more the father takes part in them, the easier the son has it. If the son is accepted as a man by both parents, he begins to affirm his sexual identity joyfully. That is important, because he now must immediately establish a barrier against the temptation of a relapse into blissful symbiosis with his mother. The barrier is necessary to enable the entry into the next developmental phase. Because if he again fuses with the maternal body, he will not be able to experience her body in the next stage as an independent and desirable object and so will fail to break through to sexual maturity.

Many men lament the painful necessity of establishing a barrier against the mother's body at this stage up to the ends of their lives, and their complaint appears then as either *male protest* (Alfred Adler) or as a lifelong fear of a woman's body. The task of penetrating the substitute mother's body is either perceived by such men as too dangerous or rejected as repugnant. They develop hostility toward the body, fear of sex, asceticism, or transsexuality—and in a few cases, homosexuality, which, however, generally has other origins. Robert J. Stoller believes that the main condition for children's successful establishment of a new identifty other than with their mother rests not in the relationship between her and them, but rather in that between her and the father. If separation is to work out all right, according to Stoller, the mother must be so fond of her husband that she can offer him to her son as a worthy object of identification. Only then can the four additional conditions of a successful separation by the son from his mother follow. She will have to carry on:

1. with great intensity, persistence, and vigilance;
2. at the right time;
3. without fear of failure;
4. mitigated by the correct measure of love, care and sympathy.

However, mothers have to promote not only separation but also the independence of their children. This happens only if mothers are proud of their femininity, like their children as much as their husbands, and treat both as autonomous people.

The American women's movement justifiably reproached Stoller that this interpretation pushes onto the wife and mother all of the responsibility for her son's sexual fate and largely relieves the father from mutual responsibility. Yet, as long as women and men by mutual consent accept different working conditions—the husband an occupation primarily outside of the home, the wife primarily inside the home—the children can never orient themselves sufficiently to their father, no matter how prepared he might be to devote his free time exclusively to his children. If Stoller should be right, then there is only one way out: half-day work for both sexes, and certainly the same pay for husband and wife, so that the mother has an equal opportunity to earn money and to gather experience outside the home, and the father, the same opportunity to engage in a meaningful way in the fate of their mutual children.

However, according to Stoller, as long as boys spend most of their time with their mother or a female caregiver, masculinity can generally be explained only as a product of differentiation and the setting aside of femininity—as a product of the fear of symbiosis that forces boys to mobilize powerful defenses against fusing with femininity. According to this definition, the awareness of being a man therefore would be neither the psychic result of somatic masculinity, as biologists believe, nor the individual outcome of that which the social order establishes as masculinity, as sociologists believe, but rather the sum of the defenses against the sex of the mother or caregiver.

This not uninteresting thesis naturally provokes the question whether the same phenomenon would not appear among daughters raised by fathers, or whether bottle feeding does not reduce the fear of symbiosis from the start since in the first place it does not at all create so intensive a symbiosis as breastfeeding.

Those who have learned the body language of children and their caregivers can recognize the children's process of separation from their first love object just as clearly as that of individuation. Both certainly occur more or less simultaneously, but they are not identical. In many cases they contend with each other or mutually impede each other. The caregiver's attitude can accelerate, slow down, or even block both processes for life.

It is of great significance to the children that, during the phase of physical distancing from the attendant—thus while creeping, crawling, and walking—they can reach the attendant with their eyes. For, no matter how terribly clever the little people are in carrying out their expeditions into the adult world, for example, into another room, they nevertheless remain dependent on the attendant with a part of their psyche and from time to time need assurance that the attendant is still there.

During this period we can observe that those children who have the best relationship with their attendants are also those who dare to go farthest from them. So, it is in no way true that children who are treated tenderly turn out "spoiled" and do not develop any enterprising spirit, but exactly the opposite: The more stable the relationship between caregivers and children, the earlier they find their independence; the more inconsistent the relationship, the greater the children's fear of the unfamiliar world of adults.

One can recognize by the body language of the caregivers as well as that of the children whether they in the separation phase maintain contact with each other from a distance. Many caregivers and children lose contact as soon as one or both withdraws only a few steps from the other. Others remain in unmistakable communication with each other even when they find themselves in another part of the room, apartment, or house. If caregivers are emotionally available at all times, healthy children crawl away from them as soon as possible. But if children feel they do not have the caregivers' full attention, they continue to cling to them.

Children who gain independence early certainly do also return to their attendants from time to time to "refuel" by having physical contact with them, but when caregivers support the children's interest in practicing independence, these periods of emotional refueling become shorter and shorter, and the space between them longer and longer. In contrast, in the case of children who do not feel totally secure in their caregiver's loyalty and availability, one often sees a pleading facial expression directed toward the eyes of the attendant while the children hesitantly extend an arm or a leg away from the caregiver to make an initial attempt at crawling alone. If caregivers do not return this glance with a smile or an encouraging gesture, children continue to hold on to them and will need weeks or months before they finally find the courage to part.

Caregivers can sustain the process of separation only through emotional availability, but not through the active driving away of children. If caregivers believe children must gain their independence as early as possible, or if mothers think that each attempt to hold the children back emotionally can damage their germinating independence, children feel lost. They certainly do follow the instructions to try to crawl away, but they look back fearfully and often fall down and injure themselves. The fear of the mother or caregiver that the children could hurt themselves, combined with the caregivers' wish that the children be independent, often gives the mothers' bodies an expression of petrified ambivalence—as if in the middle of the attempt to push the children forward, the mothers were struck by lightning and were paralyzed. Alternating periods of trust in the children's independence and fear of just this independence have an extremely negative effect on the children, because they never know what attendants want from them, what the attendants encourage and what they deny. Here, as everywhere in education, changing between two alternative styles of education has a more negative effect than an incorrect but more consistent style.

To the body language theme we have addressed here must be added that during the past three decades, pedologists in greater numbers have focused their attention on the significance of the preverbal developmental stages of children, and in doing so, pedologists had to refer back to observation methods that had been developed by zoologists and ethologists in the observation of infants. During these attempts at learning the "silent" body language of animals and small children, we came to recognize that not only can adults learn children's body language but children must also learn that of adults. But in this one area children either learn a lot more quickly than adults, or their knowledge of adult body language is inborn. Most pedologists today lean toward the second thesis and also believe that this innate knowledge first begins to fade when children learn to talk; however, even up to adolescence, children know very much more about their parents and other adults than they can express in words. Because, without being aware of it, children are still fully conversant with a certain part of the vocabulary of body language and recognize adult lies mostly from the contradiction between words and gestures, between the language of the mouth and that of the body.

The most important difference between human body language and that of other mammals, then, is that human children from birth on can certainly interpret the body language of their mother or caregiver, but most mothers and caregivers cannot understand that of children. In all other mammals the mother interprets her young's desires and needs without being taught by anyone. In contrast, in humans that does not work, even if mothers are taught infants' body language with the help of films and videotapes.

A few pedologists in the forties of this century, among

them M. Mahler, W. Daltroff, and I. H. Gross, already began to draw verifying conclusions from the intrapsychical events from the motor, emotionally dynamic, mental, and kinesthetic behavior of infants. In the sixties, J. M. Kestenberg drew groundbreaking conclusions from infants' physical movements. "The complex, expression-filled, and emotional motor gestures of the entire body of small children as well as the backward and forward motions of the approach and inspection behavior on the one hand, and distancing behavior between mothers and children on the other—their frequency, regularity, and intensity—serve as important guidelines that offer many indications of phenomena we meet with in later stages through verbal communication" (Margaret Mahler, Fred Pine, and Anni Bergman, "Human Psychical Birth" [Die psychische Geburt des Menschen], [1975, German trans., 1978]).

Among the questions Mahler and her associates have asked themselves to investigate regarding body-language communication between children and their caregivers belong the following: How do mothers or caregivers carry their children? Do they carry them like a sack of potatoes or as if they were part of their self? How do the children react when mothers dress or undress them? With joy, with anger, with protest, with devotion, with rejection? Do the mothers separate themselves emotionally from the children whenever they give them over to the research team, or do they continue their invisible contact with them? Is the final eye contact reciprocal? Do their bodies show a repetition of the children's physical signals? Do they give them farewell consolation by gesture or facial expression? How quickly, how willingly, and how skillfully do they react to the children's physical signals? Does their tenderness serve the children or their own self-validation? Do they nourish the children's emotional hunger with their physical devotion, or do they feed themselves on the children's emotional states like parasites?

Also, the fact that mothers breast-feed their children

instead of giving them the bottle does not necessarily indicate that they are physically and mentally mature for motherhood; rather it can mean that they submit themselves to socially determined attitudes without understanding them, that they believe in certain health principles ("mother's milk is better than bottled milk") without feeling an emotional bond with the children. Finally, it can also mean that it gives them too much trouble to boil the formula and to sterilize bottles. When such mothers are observed while nursing, you often notice from the mothers' and children's physical behavior that they do not understand each other. The mothers do not maintain eye contact with the children, do not smile at them, do not rock them (for example, because they want to keep a hand free to read at the same time), and do not caress them. The children react with apathy or protest. They do not drink or they spit up the milk. They do not reach for the mother's breast or the mother's arm, but rather lie there indifferently or even push against the mother's body.

On the other hand, mothers who do not breast-feed their children can also explain to them that they are loved through body language. If mothers maintain eye or physical contact with the children while feeding, smile at them, and talk to them, mothers give the children their complete attention instead of doing several other things at the same time; then, children notice that and express their satisfaction in their own body language. They drink their milk and digest it well, they smile at their mother, they touch her, they fall asleep with a smile on their face.

We have already pointed out again and again the frequently neglected observation that in approximately the sixth month children begin to distinguish their own body from the mother's or caregiver's and express this knowledge unmistakably in their body language. They explore the mother's or caregiver's body as a newly discovered continent. They inspect the mouth, nose, ears, hair. If the mother or caregiver allows them to discover their bodies, too, the children's joy in this new pleasure is obvious. They investigate the land-scape of the other body tirelessly like a lover the body of the beloved.

If by exploring the body of their love object children gain a certain amount of security and knowledge of the other person, they at least diminish the children's *eighth-month fear*, first mentioned by Spitz—their fear of strangers. This fear, however, is also proof that children can now clearly distinguish themselves from other people (and others from each other). This fear indicates progress, and so it always is accompanied by curiosity. Children's body language allows one to compare their behavior toward strangers with that of domestic cats. In their case, too, we find the bodily ambivalence between curiosity and fear in which all the muscles of the body communicate and prepare for the alternative between fight or flight.

If children lose their initial surprise at an unfamiliar body by being initiated into the mysteries of the bodies of other people by their mother or caregiver, their curiosity triumphs over their fear. They begin that process of investigation that Sylvia Brody has termed "customs inspection": They inspect the other persons dutifully and methodically from head to toe, thoroughly searching their pockets, rummaging in their baggage, and becoming more secure and satisfied by the minute. The eighth-month fear disappears and gives way to a game accented by pleasure. So, René Spitz calls this childhood developmental phase the *stage of the libidinous object*.

The progression from the newborn age across the different stages of infancy up to the toddler age, therefore, ensues on several paths: first from the experience of nearby things to perception at a distance; second, from the prenatal and perinatal fantasies to the awareness of reality; third, from the objectless condition to the awareness of objects; fourth, through separation from the symbiosis with the mother or caregiver; fifth, by the shift of the libido from their own body to that of the caregiver.

From the children's point of view this process appears as if the progress occurred centrifugally (from inner feelings to grasping the environment). On the other hand, objectively we find that the opposite process occurs: The environment acts centripetally (from the outside inward toward the center) on the children's psyche and by means of gratification of their needs brings about a gradual clarification of their illusion of omnipotence and a gradual metamorphosis of their self-love into object love.

Up to the end of the first half of the first year of life children possess no personal image of the world, because they still do not recognize as signals the stimuli streaming in from the outside and could not process them as memories. Only in the second half of the first year are the effects of the external world now recognized as meaningful experiences and become thereby those signals out of which children construct a coherent image of their world.

Spitz distinguished the infants' perceptual system from that of toddlers and named the first *kinesthetic*, the second *diacritical.* By that he meant, in the case of the first system, that perception is supposed to be extensive and visceral. It has its center in the autonomic nervous system and manifests itself in the form of emotion. It is receptive and unconscious. In contrast, the second system is active and conscious. It has its center in the cortex of the brain and manifests itself in the form of perceptions that are both intensive as well as cognitive.

Since people in general can learn what their contemporaries think only from the spoken or written word, they naturally can hardly understand that small children, who can neither speak nor write, can produce cognitive feedback—thus, can *think.* In humans, however, thought develops even before birth, although at first it is a precognitive, fantasizing, prelogical thinking. But in contradiction to what many linguists postulate—that thinking is more likely a result of speech than speech a result of thinking—pedologists in general, and sex pedologists in particular, believe that children can think before they learn to speak. Already in 1920, psychiatrist Paul Schilder had carried out a series of experiments that has never been disproved, and the results of which are that every single thought first passes through a speechless state, before it is formulated.

Thinking in late infancy age is not yet logical, but rather still graphic. Freud's thesis that, while dreaming, people transform an "archaic" *vocabulary* common to all languages into images, is topsy-turvy. It is more probable that dreamers have at their disposal an archaic, common-to-all-people store of images—a reservoir of primal images that has taken on different verbal forms in different languages. The image is primary, the word secondary. As yet there has been little research on the process of translating archaic symbols into dreamlike, precognizant, and prelogical forms of thought. It probably develops according to the principle of emotional discharge, but nevertheless it constitutes a rudimentary form of thought, because it "consists of ideas according to which later deeds will be performed" (Otto Fenichel). As soon as children learn to talk (near the end of the first year, the beginning of the second year), their thinking changes and takes on more organized, more thoroughly realistic forms. So, speech is an instrument for separating the conscious from the unconscious, a guide to the conquest of reality.

Children's first object ideas develop from privation. If a gratfication still living in memory is not attainable in current reality (because the mother is absent or the children's caregiver does not change, does not embrace, rock, or caress them), children imagine the gratification and with that create the first independent images of a love object: "They are both a substitute for the missing concrete object as well as an attempt magically to control the concrete object" (Fenichel). For childish magical thinking wants control over its object magically and at the same time considers magic as something real. When children's later thinking that strives to control their objects fails and does not gain control over the objects, children in the second or third year often regress to the stage of magical thinking. Children's ability to distinguish objects from each other first develops a couple of months after they have learned to perceive their mother or caregiver as an individual. So it is the love for the attendant that delivers the thrust of energy to think. However, during this phase, since the love for the attendant develops from the love for the oral object, the ability to distinguish people from each other in this phase of life is also a side product of the development of oral sensuality. For orality is not only the acquisition of food and drink, but also the incorporation of knowledge. The Latin word for understanding, wisdom, science, and philosophy, *sapientia,* is derived from *sapiere* (to taste) and with that unmasks the oral roots of the process of human perception. Since children learn to distinguish the taste of one object from that of another before they ask themselves how their own bodies would taste to another person, they learn to distinguish objects from one another earlier than to distinguish themselves from other objects (for example, in the mirror).

All sensory imprinting in the seventh to twelfth month is *oral* and still determined by taking nourishment and the sensual primacy of the oral zone. Therefore, the worst fate of this age is weaning. Now, it is certainly true that in our social order each phase of the development of the libido in childhood is divided into two stages by some action: the oral phase by weaning from the breast or the bottle, the anal phase by toilet training, the genital phase by the prohibition of sexual intercourse. However, no normal mother expects children in the oral phase to take solid food before they can halfway chew. So the hardening of the parodontium, of the bed of the teeth, marks the biological entrance into the second oral stage.

The first dentition, the development of the milk teeth,

currently occurs in Western Europe between the fifth and sixth months. Up until a short time ago people spoke of early teething (*dentitio praecox*) whenever the milk teeth penetrated the gums before the sixth month. Thanks to the general workings of acceleration (see the Introduction), today we can more likely speak of late teething (*dentitio tarda*) when the teeth first break through even near the end of the sixth month. Many pedologists believe children seek to speed up this process by gnawing on every available object and by biting everything, even the mother's breast. In any case this is the latest time at which breast-feeding mothers in Europe wean their children and change to bottle feeding or to a cup. It is the time between the first and second periods of infant development called the *first and second stage of the oral phase.*

In German-speaking areas weaning is usually completed between the second and third months. That is relatively early according to international standards and may explain certain lifelong problems of withdrawal that emerge in Germany, Austria, and in the German-speaking cantons of Switzerland. Upon the symbiotic dream of union with the world in love and desire now follows the discovery that the pleasure— that is, the mother's breast—disappears, is taken away. Children at first hesitate to take this perception as really "true": They reject knowledge of the external world; they suppress it. With this act of primal repression begins the chain of suppressions in which each link is connected with the one preceding. The narcissistic desired object of loving union with the world is now paired off with the unrealistic goal of becoming the whole world oneself: secondary narcissism flourishes.

With unmistakable clarity breast-fed children make known their annoyance at every change (no matter how justified) to the bottle or cup. They tear at the mother's clothing, try to get at the breast with force you can hardly imagine, and allow no diversion to console them for the lost happiness of oral contact with the skin. If one forces children to re-linquish the gratification of the desire of sucking, which of course was the most important sign of the first oral phase, they now try to get as much pleasure from biting, the sign of the second oral stage: They take every available object into their mouth and try with all their might to destroy it, and taking sheer delight in the activity.

So, here again the ambivalence of desire comes to light: Satisfaction through destruction. In children who felt disappointed in the first oral phase (but also in those whose suckling period was extended so long by pampering that it was dragged into the next phase), the desire to bite will be especially emphasized. The beginning of *character development* takes place then in the indication of an abnormally accentuated ambivalence.

In a developmental phase of the motor system in which the hands are at best used for grasping and holding, the teeth, then, represent the first organ with which children can wield destruction on objects of the external world. In this way they experience the external world as an autonomous, independent-from-themselves, existing something that one can incorporate, but also at the same time as something that is destroyed by the fusion. Here our designation of the oral phase as a cannibalistic phase gains genuine plasticity.

Children's cannibalism becomes evident not only in that they, as we observed in the previous chapter, want to eat up the mother, but also that they, as we have just noted, want to bore into the mother's body. From the numerous dreams, myths, and medical case histories we now know that the tooth is often a symbol of the penis. (In mythology if heroes knock out an opponent's tooth, they then also castrate them.) In this way the infants' eagerness to penetrate the mother's body already paves the way for the man's desire for penetration into the body of the substitute mother. But since at this early developmental stage there is still no heterosexuality, the desire for penetration into the womb is still not sex-specific: It is found in small girls of this age with exactly the same intensity as in small boys.

Questioning under hypnosis of adults fixated in or regressed to this stage has revealed that they have all too often imagined a biting into or eating into the womb in their dreams and masturbatory fantasies of the second oral phase. Perhaps the children's attempts at separation, which begin shortly before teething begins and end only in the third year, play a role in conquering these dreams and fantasies.

Sexual Pathology of Late Infancy Age

The etiology of psychosexual disorders that have their origins in the seventh to twelfth months can be summed up in six categories:

1. Effects of unresolved ambivalence problems.
2. Weaning syndrome.
3. Oral and oral-sadistic regressions.
4. Problems of the transition from the oral to the anal phase.
5. Effects of the frustration of the discovery of infantile sex.
6. Separation trauma.

From an etiological standpoint, the two most important symptoms are fixation in and regression to the period of weaning and the transition to solid food:

1. Withdrawal symptoms linked to the loss of the mother's breast.
2. Destructive, "crunching" fantasies that develop during the teething period.
3. Problems of ambivalence—results of the ambiguous, childish passions of this phase.

The specific form of ambivalence of the seventh to twelfth months reveals itself in the tendency to *bite* the beloved individual (for example, the mother) and beloved things (toys, for example). Therefore, many pedologists have called this period of childhood sex development the *stage of early childhood love-hate;* others have designated it as the *oral-sadistic phase.* While the first oral stage, the early infancy period, can be designated as *preambivalent,* the second oral stage, the time of teething, represents the beginning of the *ambivalence conflict,* which governs the entire sex life in our social order, when it is not in the second genital stage, puberty, and adolescence, subordinated by object love and demolished by it.

However, only very few people in the present phase of the Western social order succeed in this dismantling. Its failure can lead to a wide range of disorders, from simple, relatively harmless forms of the instability of the love life, to compulsive neuroses, to serious psychoses. Healthy, mature, stable people who have liberated themselves from the wastefulness of infantile sexuality and have also thereby overcome their oral ambivalence, are more likely exceptions than the rule in the later middle-class culture of our day. People who have attained a postambivalent stage of their sexual development, and with that have found the ability to master the object world, are rare today.

Another symptom of oral ambivalence in the second half of the first year is the back-and-forth move between voracious hunger and refusal to eat. On the one hand it is expressed in eagerness for possession, on the other hand in depression at every denial; on the one hand in unrest and excitement, on the other hand in discouragement, withdrawal, passivity, and apathy. Since both impulses are usually directed toward the same attendant, they combine libidinous and aggressive inclinations in the relationship between the children and their attendants. If these caretakers are not willing to be at the disposal of the children in *both* relationships—as beloved *and* as hated objects—the children direct their aggression toward themselves: oral-sadistic tendencies change into oral-masochistic behavior.

Clinically, that means these infants no longer digest food and sleep only a little. When they become older they beat their heads with their fists; hammer their heads against walls, against the edge of the bed or railings; or pull the hair out of their heads in bunches. If no sexual-pediatric help is ordered, deterioration advances to infirmity, wasting, and death.

So, such children behave like adults who say to their sex partner, "If you are not available to me in every respect I will kill myself!" If the caregiver refuses, children lose not only their high spirits but also their aggression. And that is dangerous, because aggression is an age-specific form of love. Except that at this age love and hate appear *combined*. The danger lies in that the adults, who do not understand that, try to *separate* the tendencies and thereby create exactly what the adults want to avoid: the children's deterioration.

As a result, children at first become pretentious and domineering, then lachrymose, and finally despondent. For a time they cling to every person who comes close to them. Spitz believes that this is always a kind of aggression with the help of which children want to conquer their love-hate object. If they are also not successful in this last attempt, self-destruction begins: aggression breaks down and with it the will to live. The children lose weight and die. If they survive they usually remain disturbed for life.

Those who cannot develop a successful love relationship with the mother or caregiver in the first year of life often remain incapable of building one in later years. Such children are not equipped for more progressive, more complex forms of personal and social exchange without which we would not be able to continue to exist as spouses, Spitz believes. The children become handicapped sexually *and* socially. If they are not helped in infancy age, they become lifelong burdens to their fellow citizens not only sexually, but also in every other respect. In such cases we realize to what great extent timely sexual-pedological or sexual-pediatric advice can help to spare society grief and expense. In no other area of today's science than in that of preventive sexual pedology can we save so much future expense with so little outlay here and now.

The behavior of other oral-regressive adults points to the wishes to fuse that were already mentioned in the previous chapter. Such people now in adult age try to make up for the failed symbiosis with the mother or caregiver with the help of the sex partner. Externally, that sometimes looks as if they themselves took over the role of the nurturing mother, because they overload their sex partner with gifts and acts of kindness. But in reality their gifts are only expressions of how much love they wish to receive from the other, with whom they, of course, symbiotically identify. This behavior is often very painful for sex partners, because in the other's need to overwhelm with love, they recognize all too clearly the ambivalence of the infant in whom love and hate are always so closely related that one can no longer distinguish the border between them. At infancy age that is normal; in adulthood unbearable.

The most profound trauma of infancy age is weaning, the loss of the mother's breast. It can lead to acute depression or a state of mourning that lasts the whole life through. When mothers react to the children's first teeth by immediate weaning, children feel that as a vengeful act and react with lifelong bitterness against all things motherly and womanly. Many of these orally damaged persons in adulthood can no longer find the courage to strive for satisfaction. Since they had already been discouraged in their earliest childhood, they no longer find the courage to court a sex partner.

When mothers wean their sons too early, they often in adulthood develop the obsessive conviction: "All women must make up for my mother's denial, must furnish me with oral satisfaction that my mother has denied me. If not, I will take it by force." Such men allow themselves to be nurtured by their wives, live off of their money, and in spite of that still always feel wronged by them. The inclination to react to disappointments with force, and the simultaneous inclination toward groveling submission is characteristic for the oral fixations of this phase. They also frequently appear in orally damaged women, whose vindictiveness toward the mother can be expressed in a lifelong hostility toward women.

A woman the author knows has for her entire life held her father responsible for divorcing her mother when she—his daughter—was four months old. Although the mother was the guilty party and child custody rights were awarded to the father the child developed the conviction that her father had robbed her of her portion of oral pleasure. The father's later, second wife very lovingly brought the child up on the bottle, but that was not sufficient to give her a minimum of oral stability. Her entire sex life as an adult woman stood under the shadow of the accusation against her father. She considered all men as substitute fathers and felt herself duty bound to suck each of these men dry, both emotionally as well as financially. So, her sexual relationships did not serve her genitals, but her oral satisfaction.

Other children, frustrated by premature weaning, behave toward their sex partners as adults in a frustrating manner that can only be explained as a symbolic identification with the frustrating mother. These adults take revenge on their sex partner for the frustration they had suffered during weaning. This unconscious and repressed motivation is the basis of many cases of erection and ejaculation disorders in men (for example, *ejaculatio retardata*); but also in many cases of "vaginismus" and "frigidity" among daughters. The unconscious motive is the mortification of the sex partner. They make allowances for their own loss of desire only to allow the other person no prize of carnal pleasure.

From the fact that food decreases when people eat it, that it therefore disappears in the process of the gratification of hunger, many children just weaned from the breast to the cup conclude that the satisfying object must disappear in the course of gratification. As adults, such people often cannot bear the presence of their sex partner as soon as they have received satisfaction. They expect that the other person will then voluntarily disappear and do not hesitate to throw out the sex partner who does not take the initiative to leave.

Every form of addictive oral pleasure—drinking, smoking, excessive eating—is a form of oral regression and originates in insufficient nursing in infancy. Addictions of another type—for example, dependency on sniffing or injecting drugs into the bloodstream—are also dangerous effects of incorrect nursing in infancy. In any case, orally damaged people are much more at risk for addictive drugs of all kinds than orally satisfied and balanced persons. So, "therapy" for alcoholics is usually just as unsuccessful as the criminal prosecution of addicts. What the parents have botched cannot be repaired in later years by the doctor or the judge. The only therapy for drug addiction is the prophylactic advising of parents on the oral stage of their children.

All adult sexual practices that have to do with the lips or tongue develop out of the desires, fears, and activities of infancy. The preference for certain practices in adulthood (kissing, biting, fellatio, cunnilingus, analingus) results from later regressions out of the anal or genital phase to the first or second oral stage. Kissing goes to the first oral stage, biting to the second. *Analingus* is a regression from the anal to the first oral stage; *cunnilingus* and *fellatio* are regressions from the genital phase to the first oral stage. However, the first oral stage is also the origin of a notable number of sexual deviations, especially all of those fetishes that use the pleasure of nurture as a substitute for coitus—for example, not only all forms of *picacism,* in which the man or the (lesbian) woman licks food out of the sex partner's vagina, but also those forms of regression where the person in question only wants to suck on the partner's breast instead of having coitus with her.

Autopedophilia, the hallucination of seeing oneself as a child, belongs to the sexual infantilisms of this phase (the so-called perversions). Pedophiles search for gratification by means of a child's body. In opposition to "normal" pedophiles, who feel object love in the face of children, autopedophiles, on the other hand, search for gratification with their own body, which they perceive as that of a child. They need partners who represent the mother or caregiver, and they allow themselves to be served by those partners, as they were once served, or would like to have been served, by their caregivers. There are prostitutes who specialize in the gratification of the desires of such infancy-regressed clients. Such women have at their disposal diapers, baby powder, milk bottles, end other aids. Clients are undressed, diapered, powdered, and fed. Orgasm sometimes occurs without any other aid; in other cases, clients are masturbated while being bottle fed.

In cultures where children are nursed longer, none of the disorders mentioned here have ever been observed. However, nursing, just as any other mode of nurturing and rearing, follows the rules of the cultural-specific norms. Mothers who try to avoid some of those disadvantages of our relatively early weaning by nursing her children up until their third or fourth year (for example, as in the case of many Bantu tribes, who know no endogenous depressions) in our culture would probably prepare her children for more disadvantages than advantages. Culture-specific forms of behavior can be changed and corrected only socially and not individually.

That is also true for the regressive aspects of the parents' reaction to teething. Since biting is children's initial aggressive reaction to their mother or caregiver, parents' reaction to their biting is one of the turning points of all of childhood sexual development. If parents' allow children their age-specific behavior, the prognosis of the progression to the next developmental stage is a good one for the time being. If parents react with horror, fear, or protest, the children's first reaction is to bite their nails. Later biting of pens and pencils are regressions to this first fixation. Likewise, passive desires of aggression can also develop from this developmental phase, fantasies of being destroyed accompanied by carnal pleasure. Many later fantasies of raping small girls and boys and also many of the adolescents' masochistic masturbational ideas originate in unsurmounted stages of this developmental phase.

Spitz views the hazards of the first year as chiefly conflicts between physical and psychical development. Only when children have reached and mastered a certain phase of their psychosexual development can their development continue in the direction of the next phase. If, however, overcoming the phase fails, psychosexual development stands still while somatic development continues undisturbed. The psychosexual systems, which should have become integrated by the interaction with the environment, remain at the previous less-differentiated stage.

A disorder is created by that, because now the psychosexual and the physiosexual forces are no longer in balance: "This kind of developmental balance disorder is limited largely to the first years of life, where it also occurs most frequently. With the increase in age it appears less frequently, only to disappear totally after puberty" (Spitz). In contrast to classical sex psychology, for which sexual conflicts in general become acute only in and after puberty, developmental psychologists of our day, instructed in sex science, for that reason see their most important field of work in early childhood, which the majority of parents and schoolteachers believe to be free of sexual problems.

If children in the final stages of the symbolic phase have

not gotten accustomed to the mothers' or caregivers' bodies, if, for example, on "moral" grounds, caregivers have avoided exposing themselves to the exploratory drives of their children, the first meeting with a stranger in the following phase can have serious effects. Children are then not only confronted by a new person, but are also forced additionally to come to terms with a strange body. If children have not had the opportunity to inspect a human body up until then, for all of their future life they connect the negative experiences of fear and strangeness with the experience of another body. This is one of the main reasons for later fear and hostility toward the body.

In no phase of sexual development do children search so urgently for new love objects as in this one. If children now lose the love object they have just won, instead of gaining a new one they are thrown back from secondary to primary narcissism, i.e., to the autoerotic phase of infancy. If the mother becomes ill, dies, or leaves them, many children and adolescents reach adulthood never having come out of this phase.

This enormously increased dependence on the caregiver begins in the second month and gradually diminishes thereafter, but it is still prevalent up to the end of the first year of life. To a limited degree children in the second to fifth years are still endangered by the loss of the caregiver. After that children can better cope with the parting or even the death of the caregiver. However, if they lose the caregiver before the fifth year, they all too often can become infirm. That is, they develop retardation of development, fear of contact, disorders of the primal trust, and loss of the sense of security.

These dangers are highest in early infancy because at this time children have no strong object relations but only have such relations to object precursors. If children are traumatized in this phase, they remain at the stage of object forerunners in their human relations, i.e., they are forever unable to enter into sexual relations with another person.

If children lose their attendant between the sixth and eighth months, they fall into depression and possibly die. If all relations with their caregiver are withheld from children in the first year for longer than five months, the decline resulting from it is irreversible. Abandoned children begin the stereotypical shaking while standing after a few weeks. At no other time than at this one is it so difficult for children to cope with the effects of a parental separation or divorce.

5

Second Year
Toddler Age

In spite of many difficulties of toilet training and individuation, the second year of life—toddler age—is above all a time of relaxation and consolidation of what has been accomplished. It is the time of the broadening of the childhood vocabulary and the completion of the transition from quadruped to biped. But it is also the beginning of childhood sex investigation and the beginning of the first clearly genital impulses.

At the beginning of the year the boy is approximately 77 cm (2.52 ft) tall, at the end 89 cm (2.91 ft). At the beginning he weighs approximately 10.3 kg (22.7 lb), at the end 12.8 kg (28.2 lb). On her first birthday the girl weighs approximately 9.3 kg (20.5 lb), on her second about 12.2 kg (26.8 lb). On her first birthday she was 75 cm (2.48 ft) tall, on her second she is 12 cm (4.72 in) taller. Numbers for mid-year: boys 82 cm (2.68 ft), 11.4 kg (25.1 lb); girls 81 cm (2.65 ft), 10.8 kg (23.8 lb). So, although the weight gain comes to approximately 2-3 kg (4.4-6.6 lb), this is a year for linear growth especially. Many children even reach half of their size as adults near the end of the year. The legs, especially, grow during the year and at year's end amount to more than a third of the total size of the body.

In Western cultures one can also designate the second year as the age at which many children can see what is on the table for the first time, and for the first time are able to open doors with their own hands and to flush the toilet. While until nearly the end of the first year children had seen only the pipes and cobwebs under the wash basin, they now see the faucets, the overflow, the water, and the soap. From their new point of view they discover not only hitherto unimagined and constantly changing perspectives but also continual new joys and new frustrations. This sharpens their perception and their reasoning power.

The weight of their brain now reaches 70 percent of its later weight in adulthood—1.4 kg (3.08 lb) in men, 1.3 kg (2.86 lb) in women. If its size is converted into percentage of body weight, women have a larger brain than men. The increase and differentiation of the brain cells are correlated with the increase in weight (which reaches its high point in the nineteenth to twentieth years). In the first two years especially, the number of dendrites and synapses increases, that is, the number of processes of the nerve cells and the association between them increase, so that a tightly woven net of these structures develops in the cortex. This process is completed toward the end of the second year. So the brain of the two-year-old is structurally almost finished.

With the maturation of the brain, the reasoning power, and the upright posture, toddlers develop into children and into individuals. During the first half of their second year children captivate the adult world. While the ego formation makes dramatic progress, however, childhood narcissism also grows. That means children fall in love not only with their expanding world, but also with their own ability to master this environment. In the jargon: They fill their own body with narcissistic libido. However, they also simultaneously begin to experience their body as personal property.

They no longer want to be handled. They resist being dressed or undressed—they want to do everything themselves. They sometimes even avoid being embraced, held, kissed, or coddled. In our social order, this claim to physical autonomy is expressed earlier in boys than in girls. In both of them, especially in boys, the sadness of the late infancy phase simultaneously disappears. Children now become relatively less sensitive to bumps, physical wounds, and aches. When the children fall or when other children take away their toys, indeed, even when their mother or caregiver leaves them alone for short periods, two-year-olds are willing to give in to that without protest, because they are so preoccupied with what is new that what is old loses significance.

Margaret Mahler says,

> We can take into consideration the possibility that the high spirits of this subphase are connected not only with testing the ego apparatus, but also with the playful escape from fusion with the mother, from being swallowed up by her. From this viewpoint we would suppose that just as the infants' hide-and-seek games appear to turn from passive to active, from the loss to the regaining of the gratifying object and later of the love object, so the toddlers' constant running away until they are caught by their mother, the fear of again being swallowed up by the mother turns from the passive to the active. This behavior also assures the children that their mother wants to catch them and take them in her arms.

So toddler age is also an age of transition in which children seek safe harbor yet simultaneously want to flee again and again. This indicates the lasting condition of *ambivalence,* along with the great dangers it brings for the children's psychical stability. More about this at the end of the chapter in the section "Pathology."

An important change begins to establish itself in children's behavior toward their parents or caregivers. Children now harbor less fear of being left alone, thus of the temporary loss of attendants as well as of the loss of their love. Near the end of the year—in many children, of course, only in the third year—this fear will be overcome when children surrender their total claim to their parents' love and recognize their importance in their caregivers' affection—for example, the children's relative significance compared with their older and younger siblings, but also their relative status as love objects compared with the parents' status in their mutual devotion.

In small European families, at this time, the father (unfortunately, in many families also for the first time) begins to become increasingly significant to the sons and daughters. Sons and daughters often flee from the mother's hitherto prevailing love-and-power sphere into the father's world, which is less emotional and less structured by past obligations and violent emotions, while the newly won independence is defended with stubbornness in the face of the mother. On the one hand the stubbornness is supported by the faculty of *negation* described in the previous chapter, on the other hand, however, by the stubborn avoidance of *toilet training*, to which we will turn in detail in the next chapter, because it plays a significant role in childhood sexual development.

Both sexes in toddler age turn not only to the father but also to other male individuals. We believe that this has no sex-specific meaning, but rather has only to do with the higher (in the children's mind: the more "adult") status of men in the patriarchy of our day.

Out of all of these experiences, children begin to develop self-awareness and the first fundamentals of their conscience. The conscience (psychoanalysts speak of *superego*) develops from objects internalized in the first year. So, the *biting stage,* the *second oral stage* (the seventh to twelfth months) that was just overcome, can also be defined as the *period of the first formation of conscience*. In the thirteenth month, children now learn to defer many of their needs. From the sixteenth to eighteenth months on, they learn to tolerate frustrations, and near the middle of the year they learn to influence the social surroundings by their own behavior. By also learning to endure parental prohibitions, they establish their identity and their self-understanding.

On the other hand, near the middle of their second year, children also begin to recognize the *limitations* of their autonomy and of their abilities. With deep depression they discover that the world does not belong to them, that they are small and powerless, that their parents are not there to help fulfill their every wish, but rather are independent individuals with their own interests, and that these interests only rarely coincide with their own. Almost all children react to this awareness with blind rage, feeble beating of the parents or caregivers, and desperate destruction of those things with which the parents are preoccupied (books, newspapers, cutlery, bottles, glasses, etc.).

In the final quarter of the second year children's resistance often wears down and results in total resignation. It is as if they now wanted to yield to the authorities for better or worse. So, Mahler calls this the *re-approach phase*. In many children it occurs in the last month of the second year. On the other hand, after a difficult *crisis of re-approach* in mid-year, others retreat into a condition of relative self-satisfaction—a condition that begins with the perception of separation and ends with the ability to come to terms with the separateness and to accept the parents as independent individuals. Mahler calls this condition, which in most children takes up all of the third year, the *subphase of the consolidation of individuality*.

An indispensable aid on the path to the consolidation of individuality is the parents' or caregivers' encouragement of progress toward emancipation. Before the end of the year they have to give the children a gentle nudge to push them out of the nest. This is "an essential condition of normal, healthy individuation" (Mahler). The gentle nudge also leads to the consolidation of sex-specific behavior and to the awareness of sexual identity. Both precipitate into the children's behavior toward their attendants, but afterward also into their behavior toward other children and to their own body.

In the euphoric phases of this year filled with changes, children seek parental tenderness (especially when tired, anxious, or wet), show joy in gentle words, and kiss their parents or caregivers before going to bed.

Small girls like to nestle and are especially loving toward their father. Little boys intentionally snuggle up in their mother's lap, as if they knew exactly where her genitals were to be found. The opinion of many mothers that this is "by coincidence" is false. The explanation that the head of the two-year-old happens to be the same height as the mother's lap is also not right, because the same behavior of young boys can be observed in short children with tall mothers and tall children with short mothers.

Without a doubt, for many two-year-old children the genitals already mean the center of the body, indeed, perhaps, the body absolutely. L. J. Stone and J. Church, two American pediatricians, report that when investigating the question whether two-year-olds could already name the parts of the body, they found a little girl who was by all means in the position to identify the eyes, ears, arms, and legs correctly, but at the question of where her "body" was, she spread her legs and pointed to her genitals.

Adults who ask themselves if "masculinity" and "femininity" already has behavior-specific forms of expression in late toddler age can conduct an important experiment with their two-year-olds. It consists of hanging a bell under a rocking chair and setting the chair in motion. Girls delight in the tinkling of the bell, sit on the chair, and spread the enjoyment and the peal of the bell. Boys of the same age crawl under the chair to find out from where the noise comes. In a series of experiments in Germany, Austria, and in Switzerland, which now has lasted more than twenty years, up to this time I have met with no two-year-old girl from any social class who was the first to attempt to discover how the chair rang, and no boy who *did not* immediately attempt to do it. Other experiments have yielded results that girls are moved more by aesthetics, boys more by mechanics. Or that girls are more inclined toward passivity, boys toward activity. To the author, the experiment appears to express more about our culture and our methods of rearing than about congenital sex differences.

In their relationship to toys and animals also boys and girls in the second year display new dimensions of sex-specific behavior. Small girls treat domestic animals gently, ones that they had up till now been afraid of or had not yet noticed at all. For the first time in their life, they develop a kind of sympathy, especially toward small animals. Boys, too, kiss and caress their teddy bears or their sister's dolls when they feel they are not being watched by her and adults. Many parents are horrified when their "big" boy of two years suddenly takes up his sister's dolls and takes them to bed. But boys not only feed and discipline the dolls, not only clean their bottoms and noses, but also dress and undress them, hug and kiss them, say loving words to them, rub two dolls together and say, "Mommy and Daddy."

At this age boys consolidate the discovery of their penis and their sexuality. Between the sixteenth and twentieth months, girls, too, begin to explore their own sex parts. In boys, this exploration is promoted by the fact that while in the standing position, they now for the first time become consciously aware of the involuntary erection of their penis and now attempt to influence the process voluntarily: "In any case, during the exercise subphase, the boy's exploration of his penis appears first to be an experience of sheer joy; several mothers report that their small boys often masturbate peacefully at home. That stood in opposition to our later observation in the separation and individuation phases (near the end of the second year and the beginning of the third year), that boys seized their penis to make sure it was there" (Mahler).

Sigmund Freud probably erred when at the beginning of our century he for the first time postulated the idea of a dominant inborn *penis envy* in women in all cultures and in every age. But there can be no doubt about the unpleasant fact that in our patriarchal social order, it has been suggested that from birth on, girls are less valuable and less desirable than boys. So sex educators cannot conceal the fact that in our culture, to almost all girls from the second year on, no matter how much enlightened parents and educators try to prevent it, the discovery of the sex difference is the discovery of a *missing* limb. In small girls at this age this creates anxiety, vexation, and defiance, especially when the daughter is the first born and the boy the second born. Mahler, who has observed many girls at this age, writes, "They want to destroy the sex difference. Consequently, it appears to us that masturbation occurs more often and earlier in girls than in boys, and characteristically is more desperate and aggressive. . . . In many of our small girls penis envy could explain why envy remained their predominant characteristic."

Mahler wrote that about North American girls and women. The extremely competitive character of the American social order no doubt has something to do with the formation of lifelong envy. In any case, there are no biological reasons why women should be envious of men. To the contrary, as we have stressed from the first chapter on, in every biological respect, women are favored by nature, so that it would be very much more justified for men to be envious of women as biologically privileged individuals, who over and above all also still possess a monopoly on childbearing.

In practice, however, toward the middle or the end of

the second year, penis envy appears in almost every girl in our social order, and almost without exception the girls blame their *mother*, not their father, for the "loss" of the penis or complain that their mother has not equipped them with such a nice toy. This attributing the responsibility to the mother is very noteworthy, because it also appears in those girls who still do not know that they come from the mother's body (and not out of their father's). It also appears in those girls who hold to the strange fantasy that parents, through mutual activity in the bedroom, formed the children out of blood, feces, and food.

Toward the end of the second year, the first daddy-and-mommy games occur between boys and girls. The children make a "bed" for themselves, embrace and kiss each other, in many cases even intentionally reach out for each other's genitals—but obviously less for conscious stimulation or gratification than in simple imitation of parents or other adults. It is worthy of note that in all countries of the Western and industrialized world in which we could exchange experiences with other sex pedologists, there is the opinion that in the second year, boys take the initiative in these sex games, in the third year, on the other hand, girls.

The actual age-specific, erogenous zone of the second and third years, however, is not the genital (which only in the fourth or fifth year becomes significant as the most important erogenous zone), but the *anal*. This has a good reason. In the child's transition from liquid to solid food, the colon, rectum, and anus become exposed to totally new burdens, which would cause enormous pain if nature had not provided for the libidinization of this pain. The difference between painful and pleasurable stimuli of the human body lies, as is well known, not in the irritation of the epidermis and of the nerve endings bordering on the stimulated spot, but in the ways and means in which the brain interprets this stimulation. The details of this process, which English-speaking brain researchers call *scanning*, are not yet satisfactorily established, but one thing is certain: If an adult had eaten nothing but liquid food for a lifetime and then converted to solid food, the pain of digestion and excretion would be unbearable. In the case of a two-year-old child, on the other hand, the process is obviously not only free of pain, but also pleasurable.

This libidinization of the anal region in the second year has a number of effects. First, pleasurable stimuli that attach themselves to other erogenous zones, for example, to the genitals, can be gratified directly only to a limited degree—thus, at the place of stimulation—and instead must be discharged over the anal zone. That holds great danger for those persons who remain in this phase or later regress to it, because they will never be in the position to attain full satisfaction from their genitals during sexual intercourse and will have to yield to anal stimulation (anal intercourse, anal masturbation, analingus, etc.).

Second, not only is the anal region invested with libido, but also its product, feces. It thereby assumes a disproportionate and highly significant place in the life of the two-year-old. As long as the parents do not intervene, the childish smearing and kneading of feces is one of the most gratifying activities of the second year. Those who prevent children from this gratification rob them of a great measure of their growing self-confidence and of their emerging creativity, because children proudly present their parents or caregivers their first independent, "made" themselves product. If the parents or attendants reject it with disgust, the child is confused and frightened. This rejection can traumatize the child for life.

On the other hand, people who are fixated on the pleasure of feces of the second year in adulthood also tend toward a quasi-magical worship, as it were, of their feces. They are the symbol of possession and are hoarded as if they were a part of the children's own body. And indeed, they once were, and they thereby assume the status of something irretrievably lost and become the central object of melancholy. So, in many schools of psychiatry, nostalgia is considered an anal emotion.

Third, children discover very soon, namely, in the *second anal stage* (the third year), that they can heighten the pleasurable stimulation of the anal mucus membrane even more by retaining the feces as long as possible and then joyfully forcing it out.

Fourth, the close relationship between pleasure and pain causes many persons fixated in this phase to prefer active or passive forms of the pleasure of pain during coitus in their later sex life, thus, to search for sadistic or masochistic gratification. So, many pedologists call the entire anal phase the *anal sadistic phase.*

To the anal erotic activities of this developmental stage belong the strange practice of two-year-olds to stick into their anus or into that of other children all kinds of objects (modeling clay from the children's room, beans and peas from the kitchen, the little sister's pacifier, the big brother's marbles, the last bit of Daddy's eraser, the last piece of Mommy's lipstick), but also the joyful watching of adults and children defecating. More than half a century ago, Alice Balint established that the initial expressions of tenderness between two-year-olds emerges when they go to the toilet together: "It has been my experience that children who are indifferent or even hostile toward each other came closer under the stamp of such experiences and for the first time embraced and kissed each other of their own initiative and without the urging of their parents."

Sexual Pathology of the Second Year

A great part of the fixations on a certain childhood developmental phase reverts to the fact that children either cling with all their might to the habit of a phase familiar to them or resist the next phase with a panicky fear of the new and unknown. One can say in general that the transition from one developmental stage to the next on the whole only succeeds when two forces work simultaneously: a decreasing interest in one particular erogenous zone and an increasing interest in another. Children's libido, as it were, is pulled from one side and pushed to the other. So, children can only overcome the *oral phase* of the first year when their joy in eating and biting decreases and their joy in defecating increases. If this process does not occur from both sides, the age-specific joys turn into regressive fears. The oral desire for fusion becomes oral fear of fusion. The anal desire for separation from the love objects becomes the fear of being abandoned by, rejected by, and separated from them.

Another symptom of insurmountable difficulties in the transition from the oral to the anal phase is some children's compulsive eating of feces. During the first year almost all children certainly do place into their mouth almost everything within their reach that is small enough to fit into it. Sometimes this also includes small bits of feces they roll up into small balls with their fingers. But most children do not like the taste of feces. They spit it out again. If children do not do this, but rather take obvious pleasure in it, then it is a warning sign that the transition from the oral to the anal phase has miscarried, because the objects of the anal phase have obviously been regressively retained in that of the oral.

Spitz, who carefully studied the phenomenon of *coprophagy* in two-year-old children, concluded that the parents or caregivers of coprophageous children are almost without exception unstable and ambivalent. They swing back and forth between oversolicitousness and indifference, between constant pampering and sudden neglect, between dependence on the child bordering on bondage and annoyance bordering on rage whenever the child does not return their love. A surprisingly great number of coprophageous children suffer "accidental" injuries or even death through the careless behavior of their parents or attendants. The children burn or scald themselves, swallow medications left freely lying around, fall out of their beds or are allowed to fall, drown in the bathtub or die of electric shock by badly insulated wiring. Spitz attributes it to the attendants' unkindness, hostility, or even suppressed death wish toward their children. In any case, the inability to accomplish the transition from the oral to the anal phase appears to have something to do with the negative behavior of the parents or attendant toward the children.

If an inadequacy in the establishment of the children's ego occurs in the first anal stage because of too lenient or too strict an upbringing, then in later years the children also often fail to shift libidinous emotions onto cultural activities. That can result in emotional and cultural infantilism in adulthood. Adults such as these, then, exert an especially negative influence on their own children and thereby perpetuate the process of infantilism. An unmistakable indication of such conduct are certain words of endearment. If a mother uses words such as "little stinker," "my old troublemaker," "my little shit bag," "my little piggy," "my little dirt bag," "my little pain-in-the-ass" toward her children or teases the child with unconsciously anal-sadistic words such as "little pest," "nasty boy," "nasty girl," "dirty beast," then all experienced pedologists know that they are dealing with a woman who has run aground in her own anal phase, and the aggressive feelings that she had felt toward the person who raised her are now turned toward her children in a squabbling manner. That sounds more harmless than it is because behind such a vocabulary hide disorders that make clinicians fear for the well-being of the child.

When raising their children, regressive persons tend to raise their own regressions to the level of educational maxims. This becomes especially clear in the weaning, toilet training, and false or withheld "enlightenment" of their children. In all three tasks such adults treat their children either too harshly or too leniently. Oral neurotics wean their children too early or too late; anal neurotics begin to teach toilet training too early or too late; genital neurotics give their children sex education too early or too late, or give them incorrect or no sex education at all. All neurotics unconsciously tend to perpetuate their own anomalies (which often were also those of their parents) when raising their children. According to the rule that parents try to continue their life in their children, this also occurs in anal fixations and regressions.

Anal-erotic persons are mostly tolerant and permissive in the face of dirt, disorder, and other weaknesses of children. Only dysfunctional, childish anal-erotic persons, who through repression to an *anal character* or through regression and reaction formation to *anal neurotics,* later also behave repressively toward their children and thereby continue the tragic escalation of anal neurosis from generation to generation. While anal-erotic persons anally wean their children without especial strictness and speed and thereby support and extend the stage of pleasurable feces elimination, anal characters and anal neurotics train their children for "cleanliness" especially early and drastically, and thereby drive them too early into the second anal phase, the period of stubbornly withholding feces. So, each of the three variations of fixated, anal parental types produces children who exhibit their own anomalies. But parents do not produce these children through heredity, as people believed for a long time, but through unconscious aspects of their behavior.

One of the most frequent reasons of later misconduct at school age is the parents' or caregivers' unkind or irritable conduct, obviously motivated by their disgust for the feces of their children. When the mother or attendant disgustedly removes the potty immediately after the children have produced something, the children feel cheated and robbed. The fear of such children, that the parents will never return to them the products they have produced, appears years later, as Tobias Brocher observed a long time ago, in the fear that teachers could keep or lose the handed-in homework. Certain determined children ask about the whereabouts of these products with astounding frequency. A question such as this should always be a warning signal to schooled educators that the children have not conquered a part of their anal phase.

Since children consider their feces as their first independent creation, they also tend to see it as their first "possession": as that which they have earned through patient sitting. People who are fixated on or regressed to this phase tend to regard their later sex partner as a possession and react with immeasurable jealousy at any sign of independence of the other person. If children's age-specific inclination to squeeze out their feces joyfully is through fixation strengthened beyond the anal phase, in adulthood it can lead to taking great joy in squeezing out other people, especially their own sex partner.

As we said in the Introduction, children's regressive behavior can lead to many different disorders in later life. If adults act out their regressions, they develop deviances or perversions. If they suppress them, they develop neuroses or psychoses. Many variations of anal eroticism—for example, *pedicatio* (active or passive anal intercourse), *analingus* (licking the anus of another person or having one's own anus licked), *anal masturbation* (passive or active), *fecal fetishism* (for example, the desire to defecate on others or be defecated on by them), *coprophagy* (taking joy in eating feces in adulthood), *coprolalia* (compulsive use of obscene language), *coprography* (writing scatological words or texts), and many others—belong to the deviances originating out of the first anal phase.

Anal conversion neuroses and *paranoia* belong to the neuroses and psychoses of this stage. Under conversion neuroses we understand to be those disorders in which childish desires or fears that focus on a certain organ or a certain region of the body lead to an apparent somatic disorder of this zone or this organ in adulthood. Almost all non-somatically based digestive disorders in adulthood (for example, "nervous" constipation or "hysterical" diarrhea) are symptoms of anal conversion neuroses with first causes in the second or third year.

Paranoia, the appearance of hallucinations in otherwise intact personalities, can arise from the infantile translation of the functions of separation. Paranoiacs project their hallucinations onto their social surroundings, as fecal fetishists defecate on their beloved. One of the most frequent paranoiac hallucinations is that the world is peeled off of their own body or that their enemies cut open their stomach and pull out their entrails. Fantasies such as these reach their high point in paranoic persecution mania, in which the persecutor represents the fears that anal paranoiacs connect with their intestines.

So-called *borderline symptoms* in adulthood belong to the effects of wrongful parental conduct during the child's second year, especially during the *subphase of re-approach* (months eighteen to twenty-four). These are psychical disorders that lie on the border between neuroses and psychoses and are not categorized as one or the other. Simply stated, it is a matter of fixations on or regressions to childish *conditions of ambivalence,* as they appear with great frequency during the second year. One can often recognize the danger of later borderline symptoms when children at this age express violent and volatile emotions with regard to their parents or caregivers, for example, desperately clinging to them followed by furiously pushing them away, or even simultaneously clinging and pushing away ("split body language"). That means the children cling to their father with one arm and hit him with the other. Or they clasp their mother's neck with their arms and at the same time kick her in the stomach with their knees. In cases such as these, Melanie Klein speaks of *division of the object world* and believes children separate the entire world of objects, including their preferred love objects, their parents or caregivers, into "good" and "bad" objects. With the aid of this division the "good" part of the parents can, at least for a time, be loved and maintained in the presence of the "bad," the denying, the prohibiting, or absent part. On the one hand, the more tenderly the parents treat their children, the more they deny them, on the other hand; however and especially, the more harshly and quickly they push toilet training at the same time, the greater is the danger that the children's endogenous ambivalence will shatter because of this exogenous severity.

According to Mahler, the conclusive clinical result, however, is determined not only by the events of the second year, but is codetermined in the following years by five other factors:

1. by the question whether in the third year (the stage of the second anal phase) the children succeeded in reaching libidinous object constancy;
2. by the amount and type of sexual frustrations in the fourth year (phallic phase);
3. by possible stress and shock trauma in the fifth year (oedipal phase);
4. by the degree of fear of castration during the transition from the oedipal phase to the latent period; and
5. by the developmental crises of puberty.

The wrongful conduct of the parents or caregivers need not only consist in prohibitions or excessive insistence on toilet training, but can also be expressed in simple indecision, in the inability to decide, or in emotional immaturity. As we already said, children recognize expressions such as indecision and contradiction much more clearly than many adults. They more lovingly and more reliably perceive the body language of parents or caregivers, given from their love and safety, just as clearly and positively as they react negatively to the constrained body language of the insecure, indecisive, immature, or frustrated ones—especially when such adults drain their children emotionally instead of offering them consolation and strength.

From the end of the first to the middle of the second year of life the apparently insignificant events in the children's life and that of their parents or attendant can have traumatic effects. For in this period of life the children's somatic development ensues so resolutely and unstoppably that even the slightest psychical setback can lead to schizophrenia-like disorders—disorders that Mahler has called *differentiation* and *fragmentation*. They express themselves above all in the inability to bear even the slightest separation from the mother or caregiver.

So this is also a very inopportune time for children or their caregivers to be separated because of hospitalization. A separate vacation at this time can also have a traumatic effect, not to speak of the parents' separation or divorce. During the last war it became evident that the psychical effects of the separation of evacuated children from their parents were more persistent than those fears created by bomb attacks.

At no stage of childhood must parents so urgently be dissuaded from any kind of punishment, especially of physical punishment, as in the second year. Because of the predominant libidinization of the gluteal region at this time, children should not be spanked on the rear under any circumstance because this can lead to lifelong masochistic tendencies. Sadism and masochism are effects of an ambivalent and painful love that is created when a beloved individual (for example, a father or mother) inflicts pain on the child. If this infliction of pain occurs in the highly ambivalent stage of the anal phase, the effects can hardly ever be remedied.

Instead, children in this phase of life need special tenderness. If in their second year they receive neither cutane gratification nor fulfillment of their anal needs, they develop a psychical insatiability that in adulthood can lead to serious neuroses. The premature attempt to discipline small children and to harden their character by refusing their wishes does not lead to the ability to master their environment, but rather turns the children into lifelong slaves to their contemporaries by the premature breaking of their still-fragile ego. Children such as these develop neither the ability to succeed nor the capability to love because both abilities are products of parental love or the love given by other adults. Independence cannot be created either by prohibitions nor through privation or denial.

It is absolutely wrong to forbid children at this age to masturbate or to let them know by word, gesture, or facial expression that you disapprove of their autoerotic behavior, because most of the masturbatory dream desires in the second year relate to their own parents or caregivers, and children release their emotions not over their genitals, but rather over the anal zone. Paradoxically, the anal pleasure intensifies when the parents or caregivers deprive the children emotionally. For then the masturbatory activities become attempts at consolation and combine with a pleasurable defiance toward the parents or attendants. So the anal zone is libidinized even more intensively, but also invested with highly aggressive emotions, which later precipitate into aggressive, defiant behavior toward their own sex partner.

However, on the other hand, it can also happen that, if she encourages an all-too-narrow identification with her body in this developmental phase of her son, a mother provokes a transsexual choice of partner. That means: She rears a son who feels as a woman and needs a male partner. The risk of the identification of a daughter with her father and the risk of a transsexual condition of the girl arising from that are much less, thanks to our social order, which encourages fathers to work outside the home.

In almost all boys and girls, the late toddler age brings

with it the initial curiosity about sexual intercourse and procreation. The children want to know what the parents do when they close the bedroom door at night. They want to know where small children come from, especially when they have just received a small brother or a small sister. We call this learning process *childish sexual investigation*, because it represents the most important impetus to thinking and investigating in later years. That which appears as sexual curiosity in late toddler age becomes the thirst for knowledge in adulthood. Those who have developed no burning interest in this question in their second year will also show no burning interest in questions of understanding, research, and science in adulthood.

On the other hand, late toddler age is also a time of great narcissistic vulnerability. If parents do not answer their questions and do not take their sexuality seriously enough, children feel offended. If the little girl's pleasure in displaying herself was still tolerated in early toddler age, but is now no longer honored with smiles of admiration, but rather with serious warnings, the child feels not only confused but also begins to doubt the consistency of the parents or caregivers. Likewise if parents or caregivers say "That won't do!" to a small boy who proudly presents his genitals. For then the small man, whose first erection in early toddler age perhaps created pleasant surprise, begins to question the honesty of the parents or caregivers. His whole image of the world wavers. The security he had just won disappears. This is honestly dangerous. It should not be taken lightly.

Children naturally perceive the social sex differences earlier than the morphological ones. Yet, before the end of their first year, average children undertake to categorize themselves as belonging to one or the other sex. However, this categorization is nothing but a reaction to the parents' or caregivers' signals. Those who are treated like boys feel as boys do. Those who are treated like girls feel as girls do. This is true for all social orders, no matter how differently they may establish the sex-specific behavior of their children.

Now, in the second year, children perceive the morphological sex differences for the first time and now, in many social orders—for example, in our own—feel confronted by an inexplicable tabu: the prohibition against inspecting the genitals of the other sex. The threat of punishment by the adults and the abhorrence readable in their facial expression increase the children's curiosity, yet also create fear of the difference and of the great secret. From the age-specific and thoroughly justified desire to orient oneself in the world of the sexes, and the adults' highly charged emotional denial of this wish, there develops from this phase a *nevermore unbridgeable* conflict between desire and fear, between fascination and fear of punishment. A conflict that can never more be bridged over.

Therefore, even by the second year, a bad conscience already becomes the dynamic of sexuality in many persons. They can find satisfaction only as long as the activity is forbidden; or at least only when they feel the activity is forbidden. If they meet other people who have a healthy childhood behind them, and therefore do not require an itch for the forbidden as well, they react with impotence and frigidity.

6

Third Year
Beginning of the Toddler's Puberty

The third year—for many called the *kindergarten age*, for others the *play age*—has for many years been called the *age of defiance* by developmental psychologists. Although this terminology expresses more about certain educational methods than about the children's biomorphosis, it makes sense, because it describes the area of tension to which many children of our social order are exposed at this age. Since the area of tension varies in extent and duration from country to country and from social class to social class, we should not be surprised when we find that the data of different developmental psychologists on the beginning and end of the so-called age of defiance diverge from one another not only by a matter of months but also of years—from the middle of the second to the end of the fifth year. That would mean— if we were to take it seriously—that the age of defiance would be about identical to the *preschool age* or at least run simultaneously with it.

But that is not correct. It would be more correct to say that the "age of defiance" depends on the behavior of the parents or the persons in charge of raising the children and, in children treated differently, can appear very early (the third year), or very late (the fifth year), or in the middle of this developmental phase (the fourth year), or not at all. On the other hand, it is true that between the third and fifth years, a *pseudopuberty* is ascertainable in many children. So, we have labeled these three years as the toddler's puberty [*kleine Pubertät*] and divided it into the *beginning* (the third year), the *middle* (the fourth year), and the *end* (the fifth year).

It is without a doubt a phase of tension that is interrupted for only a short period (in the fourth year) by a period of relaxation or a number of short periods of relaxation. The growth in height becomes slower; the growth in breadth increases. The difference in height between boys and girls is reduced. Toward the beginning of the third year the little girl is approximately 87 cm (2.85 ft) tall; the small boy, approximately 89 cm (2.91 ft). She weighs 12.2 kg (26.89 lb); he, 12.8 kg (28.21 lb). Toward the middle of the year she has grown about 4 cm (1.57 in), he only about 3 cm (1.18 in). He now weighs 13.1 kg (28.88 lb), she 12.8 kg (28.21 lb). Both have twenty milk teeth. Toward the end of the third year, she is 96 cm (3.14 ft) tall and weighs 14.5 kg (31.96 lb); he is 97 cm (3.18 ft) tall and weighs 14.9 kg (32.84 lb).

In the girl, now, the *reproductive phase of the ovaries,* which began even before birth, has ended. That means that a part of the fate of the children who the girl will one day bear as an adult woman is already preprogrammed in the third year of childhood. The production of her lifetime supply of fertilizable oocytes is completed. After *menarche,* the first monthly period, each month one or several of these oocytes are made ripe for fertilization by mitotic cell division. This foresight of nature, too, shows the falsity of the general public's opinion, that sexuality and procreation begin only with puberty.

In the third year, the children's physical and psychical independence grows. They recognize themselves in the mirror and no longer call themselves by their first name, but on the contrary use the personal pronoun "I." While still in the second year they largely conformed to adults' observations; now they begin to orient themselves by their own perceptions. Their emotions develop quickly, especially the ego feelings. The ability for self-criticism increases, but especially the power for making decisions and exerting their will. Now the children decide whether they want to play with others or not, whether they want to be good or ill-behaved, whether they want to be "nice" to their parents or defy them. However, the defiance is directed not only toward the parents or caregivers, but also toward things, toward animals, and toward other children. Toys, domestic animals, and children, which they loved up until now, are now rejected. Other toys, other children, and other animals take their place.

It is diagnostically significant that the distancing and reorienting, the increasing contradiction, and the intensified aggressiveness of this phase of life possess no endocrinal basis—thus no genuine appearance of puberty in the sense of a physically analyzable somatic maturity—but are more like adolescent-type phenomena, thus products of a psychical maturity, by which new ideas especially of desire are developed. In "primitive" cultures in which children are encouraged to participate in the process of production as early as possible, the children's will to act independently and to integrate into the adult world with some useful work is eagerly snapped up to the advantage of the community. Under these circumstances, a "phase of defiance" never appears, because children may do whatever they wish, namely, bring their own life playfully, yet also independently, into the adult community.

Our labels of this phase in life, for example, "play age" and "kindergarten age" show, in contrast, what we inflict on our children when we reject their desire for independence and thereby provoke defiance, or when we try to bend the defiance back into a game and thereby force the children into an infantilism that they in part have already outgrown.

An often-cited signal of this phase, the slackening of affection toward the parents or caregivers, must, therefore, be regarded on the one hand as the children's growing independence; but also, however, on the other hand, it must be seen as a reaction to the prevention of their struggle for independence by parents or persons who are rearing them. A part of this reaction is a characteristic back-and-forth between attack and defense, between pride and embarrassment—a compulsive unrest that is dismissed by most parents with the word "impoliteness." But this unrest is a characteristic of the childhood phase of tension. It grows with each phase up into late puberty and is at least partly the child's justified reaction to incorrect upbringing.

Now, the harder the parents or caregivers try to bond the children to themselves, the greater will be the children's "defiance," i.e., their lack of independence. Part of this syndrome is that at this age children for the first time turn to other adults, for example, to the parents of other children or the female kindergarten schoolteacher. One recognizes this behavior in the children's body language, when they passionately embrace and kiss strangers but ignore or push away their parents or caregivers. In the sense of our thesis of a cutaneous phase, children behave as if they wanted systematically to reduce skin contact with their parents or caregivers and just as systematically to broaden that with strangers.

Another aspect of the growing independence of this phase and of the growing pride in new accomplishments is a sudden talkativeness. Not only have the words "I" and "you" practically simultaneously entered into the children's vocabulary, but also prepositions and adverbs. A simultaneously appearing and sexually very significant factor, to which we will return again, is the urge to relive their own toddler age in words. That means three-year-old children plague their parents or caregivers with repeated questions about their own past. They now also want to anchor their personality historically, but they can do that only with the aid of their newly acquired linguistic accomplishments. The result is the talkativeness mentioned above.

In the third year the nonsensical words and nonsensical verses of the second year favored up until now are replaced by qualitative children's rhymes of descriptive content. Here, too, something sexually significant comes to light: the children become interested in "forbidden" verses. They acquire from older children verses, rhymes, and songs in which "forbidden" words appear.

In the twenty years of research by the author and his team, the question whether the children "understand" the "forbidden" words has been discussed by all associates even to total exhaustion. Up to now, these three of the existing five volumes of our research reports in process have been published: *Studien zur Befreiung des Kindes* (Studies on children's liberation) (Olten and Freiburg i. Br., 1973–76; Berlin, 1980–81) gives a detailed account of our findings. Here it should be repeated that according to our opinion children have no rational understanding of the colloquial synonyms for genital organs and processes, but infer from the contradictory body language of adults (laughter, horror, fascination, disgust) and of older children (giggling, red faces, fidgety gestures) that here something significant, but forbidden, is addressed. With the defiance caused by the parents and educators, the more children quote such verses, the more violently the adults react. On the other hand, the children's interest in such verses wanes the more quickly, the less emotionally the adults react.

But, too, the viewpoint of the psychoanalysts and psychologists of the Jungian school that deviates from our opinion should also not be kept secret here, that there is an "archaic reservoir" of genital words that is common among all humans and on certain occasions (dreams, semiconsciousness, hypnosis) can already be recalled and translated by children into the current language of the people to whom they belong. This thesis, developed toward the beginning of our century by linguist Hans Sperber, is supposed to explain why the "forbidden" words of every language immediately and directly call forth before the eyes of everyone— even the most protected child and the most puritanical adults—the image of the organs or processes the words describe. We should also mention here that the thesis appears to have recently found confirmation through the work of the Austrian neuropediatrician Andreas Rett. Rett has repeatedly verified that among brain-damaged children who could not repress, the emotional receptiveness to these words is too intense to be explained as the result of a postnatal acquisition of the knowledge of the meaning of these words.

Although Rett's findings are biased, in our culture the interest of healthy three-year-olds not only in these words but also in "childish sexual investigation" explains the unusually heightened interest of children of our social order in the genital processes. An interest as intense as this derives neither from the children's "nature" nor from the children's "natural" processes of maturation, but is the product of a social order that, from birth on, withholds from children any sensual knowledge of the processes of the pairing and procreation of their own species perceived through the five senses. In cultures that are less restrictive and less secretive about the reproductive organs and activities, such a profusion of childhood sexual curiosity is ascertainable just as infrequently as those harmful hothouse atmospheres in which sexual incidents among us still take place in adulthood.

Sigmund Freud has coined the strange thesis that not only the sight of parental sexual intercourse, but even the idea of such an act in the child's brain can cause lifelong disorders. If that were so, up until the invention of separate children's rooms, almost all people would have been traumatized. For only in a tiny part of the world—and even there only for people with a relatively high income—has it been possible within the last century and a half to keep children from the vital knowledge of mating and procreation. The results have been indicated in such a drastic increase of neuroses, psychoses, and psychosomatic illnesses as in no other culture in the entire history of the race.

Today, sexual pedologists know for certain that children who by their second year have not perceived with their five senses what occurs in mating and procreative behavior, try in a thoroughly desperate way from the third year on to make up for the omission by observation and/or interrogation of their elders. They want to know where they themselves come from. They want to know where their brothers and sisters come from. They want to know where the other children come from. They want to know where the parents and the other adults have come from.

All of that is legitimate. But provoked by the adults' secretiveness, they also want to know what the adults do in their bedrooms after the door is locked, the curtains drawn, and the lights turned off. If the parents have not expressly forbidden the children to disturb them in their bedroom during the night, the curiosity would have been less. The closing of the bathroom and toilet doors, too, stimulates the children's curiosity until it is unbearable. The result of this adult's hide-and-seek game is a fear of nakedness that becomes evident for the first time in three-year-olds. They lock all the doors when they go to the toilet and banish the parents from the bathroom when they are washing or bathing. It is absurd to see in this a "natural" form of human modesty, because it is a part of the children's general defiance, of the protest against parental behavior, and never appears when parents act freely or spontaneously.

The first indications of childhood sexual investigation in the second or third years are the already mentioned children's questions about their origin: "Daddy, where was I before I came to you?" But they soon also develop characteristic questions about their own sexuality: "Mommy, what was I when I was small? A boy or a girl?" Newborn siblings are viewed with envy not only because they demand the parents' time, affection, and energy, but also because they have a sex: because from the moment of birth on, they are introduced as either the same ("your little sister") or different ("your little brother").

This difference plays a large role in the development of the image of the specific sexual membership of the three-year-olds. So, they ask a constantly growing number of questions about sex differences, develop a great interest in sex life and the sex organs of the parents or caregivers, try to observe them dressing or undressing in the toilet or bathroom, ask questions about Mommy's breast when the small sibling is being fed ("What's in there?" "Is the baby drinking your blood?"), or ask strangers quite frankly: "Can I open your trousers?" "Can I look up your dress?"

Already very important in this year is the following question, one that reaches its greatest urgency two years later: "Mommy, can I marry you when Daddy is dead?" "Daddy, we'll get married if Mommy has to go to the hospital, okay?" Then, parental attempts to teach the children that relatives may not marry often give way to awkward questions: "But Mommy, you married Daddy! Aren't you related?" Or (the angry reply of a three-year-old to the explanation of the incest tabu by the female kindergarten teacher): "That's a lot of nonsense; my father married my mother, and he would never do anything wrong. He's a policeman!"

We already mentioned in the previous chapter that in our Western industrialized nations the little girl currently discovers in her second year that boys "have something she does not have." If she has a small brother, she ultimately wants to see the thing and play with it again and again. That means the little woman wants to have it. And, to be sure, have it immediately and irrevocably. For three-quarters of a century psychoanalysts have asserted that with this begins the tragedy of the woman in a patriarchal society. For in the beginning she still may hope it may confer such a thing as equal rights, thus the thing still might grow; you just have to have a little patience, which is proper for women to do. However, when that does not help, she begins to despair and blames her misfortune on her mother, whom she reproaches for having brought her into the world mutilated.

In contrast to boys, who, at the discovery that they have something that girls do not have, also at first believe it will still certainly grow on the girls, but then conclude that it must have been cut off, perhaps as punishment for something, and now begin to fear their parents would do the same to them if they do not "behave." Therefore, according to psychoanalysts' opinion, the phallic castration for girls is not a threat, but rather a reality.

We do not believe that this psychoanalytic assertion is totally correct, but from 1960 to 1980 we have observed a certain solidarity between mothers and daughters, a partnership in destiny for mutual defense against the domination by men. At the same time, we noticed in the course of the two decades of our examinations an ever-growing envy of breasts and child-bearing in the boys. It is today (1981), at least in the case of boys of enlightened, liberated mothers, about as widespread as penis envy in the case of daughters of authoritative fathers in the early twentieth century.

In both sexes a growing interest in the individual's body forms as a result of parental disapproval of genital relationships of children with each other. Therefore, children are made aware of their genitals not because of a biological drive, but rather because of parents' rejection of their unsatisfied curiosity about their genitals, and so children handle them when they are undressed. Masturbation gains an enormously excessive significance, thanks to parental prohibition, and feeds on images of parental genitals and sexuality. These notions are dangerous because they just do not project a correct image of loving, tender, adult relationships, but rather become stamped by age-specific obsessions with feces and anal stimulation.

Next, for the understanding of these processes it must be shown that all of these substituted activities of children do not occur in sexually healthy cultures. Even as a transitory activity, masturbation itself is not customary in childhood where children have free entry into age-specific sexual play with children of the same age. With the exception of infant masturbation, which is the norm in all regions of the world, masturbation from the third year on is always and everywhere a necessary release, a substitute for the childhood homo- and heterosexual exercise phases customary in the case of other primates. On the other hand, in our case the age-specific sexual relationships of three-year-olds reduce themselves to the suspicious staring at others, to hesitant sharing, touches of the face and of the body, to sharing of favorite play areas, to swapping of toys, to consoling offers of a child's own playthings, to consoling embraces and kisses. In our case, too, when parents have no objections, at this age the age-specific necessary examination of the genitals occurs, mostly initiated by the girls. The boys are often a little surprised and caught unawares by these games.

The girls' ambivalent behavior toward the boys in this phase has been very nicely described by Françoise Dolto, who observed a two-and-a-half-year-old girl as she watched a brawl between two not-too-much-older boys, and, with folded arms and an admiring look of wonder, said, "Boys, they are all crazy!"

To prevent parental misunderstanding of the motives and results of childhood sexual activities in this age phase, it should be pointed out that sexual disorders in childhood almost never originate in children's excessive sexual behavior, but are caused by insufficient sexual contact with other children and in difficulties in making contacts. What serves as a warning sign to alert observers of childhood interpersonal relations is not the fact that children try to have sexual relations with each other, but the absence of such an attempt.

In the sense of the processes of *negation* already mentioned again and again, children learn to define their own sexual identity through defiance: "No, I am *not* a girl, isn't that right, Mommy?" "No, Daddy, I am *not* a boy, right?" The sexual identity acquired in this manner is to be shaken once again during puberty (and in the case of transsexuals in adolescence). For all others the principle holds true, that the sexual identity imprinted up until the third year can no longer be changed by anything—regardless whether it is identical to the genetic or morphological sexual membership or not.

As we have stated at another place, the majority of all boys raised as girls (a highly obscure figure!) remain feminine in their understanding of their own sexuality for their entire life, while the majority of girls raised as boys (a somewhat less obscure figure) remain masculine in their subjective sexuality up to their death. That has nothing to do with the conduct toward the other sex, thus with heterosexuality or homosexuality, because these are behaviors toward *other* persons; sexual identity, on the other hand, is behavior toward one's *own* person.

Perhaps I should also take the opportunity to state the obvious: Homosexuality is no "perversion," but rather encompasses a great number of very different causes of non-heterosexual behavior. The idea of a single homosexuality with one single, monolinear cause is just as unscientific as the thought of one single form of heterosexuality with one single biological or social cause. There is, no doubt, a very narrow association between the current social order and the number of deviations from sexual norms postulated by it. But the precise causes of this association have as yet been insufficiently researched.

However, one thing is certain: Just as the genital region is stimulated rather than relieved by prohibitive and secretive behavior by parents or educators, the anal region, the actual erogenous zone of three-year-olds, is also libidinized to its highest degree by prohibitive behavior (toilet training). Parents' enormous interest in the earliest possible "cleanliness" of children creates that highly libidinized defiance we have described as characteristic of this phase, without as yet explaining its precise occurrence. The cause is the great pleasure children get from *holding back* the feces and from the later orgasmic-like squeezing out of the stool. In the second and third years this delight is much greater than that of masturbation. On the other hand, even at this age, the crucial points of later genital desire develop: the more children desire to retain their feces between the second and third years the more they as adults will desire to prolong foreplay and delay orgasm during coitus. Finally, by the retention of feces in this phase, children also learn that retention is valued in our largely anal culture. The far-too-frank person is, as you know, considered by us as a little naive, as infantile. In contrast, to be adult means: Think first, then act. Or: Think first, then speak. One should first hold back the information that one wishes to give or not to give to another. This "I know more than what I am telling you" gives the anal character the same feeling of superiority that three-year-olds feel toward their mother or caregiver when the children retain their stool, instead of giving it to her when she wants it. Therefore, the secret of the second anal phase lies in that the children now learn to enrage that big person who up until now had dominated them by retaining their feces when they are placed on the potty, and then go in their diaper, or on the carpet, or in the bed, as soon as the adult is gone. In this way children experience for the first time the extent of their power. On the other hand, they thereby also learn to identify power with defiance and resistance. From this spring forth certain dangers, with which we will concern ourselves in the "Pathology" section at the end of this chapter.

Although most parents have recognized that children

cannot control their bowels before they have learned to walk and so strive to toilet train between the eighteenth and twenty-fourth months, half of all children up until the thirtieth month have an occasional "accident," mostly during the night. So, even a half-century ago, the founder of empirical pedology, Arnold Gesell, said toilet training "is founded on the naive theory that practice makes perfect and that through an early start the longed-for cleanliness can be attained early. In this area parents often give way to excesses. They have recourse to punishment, promises, shaming, scoffing, and to unremitting corrections, and nevertheless the children do not understand. Is that the children's fault?"

No, certainly not. Bowel control truly is an extremely difficult function. The involuntary act of evacuation consists in peristaltic contractions of the rectum, called forth by the vegetative nervous system. However, so that evacuation can be delayed voluntarily under changing circumstances and then released, the higher functions of the brain have to be checked. This suppression cannot be attained by way of linear progression, i.e., not through mere habit training, because bowel control is not only a matter of the sphincter muscles, but also of the total organism. So, voluntary stool evacuation is also an ability that has to do with the children's total intellectual development: The more the parents lead the children by the hand and order them about, the more slowly their total development progresses.

If for the entire second and third year the parents persist in demanding that the children be "obedient" and be "clean" out of obedience, they can most certainly force a certain measure of obedience. At the same time, however, the children's will is also broken by it, and indeed often until the end of their life. On the other hand, if children succeed in the breakthrough to sphincter control, succeed as a result of the children's love toward the parents or caregiver, they gain control over their ego as a token of their love and then are mostly also in the position to make sacrifices to their sex partner in later life, without feeling this as a loss of their own self-respect.

Even when children are themselves clean for the sake of the love for their attendant, there is still the danger that the whole process will collapse if the attendant is absent for even a short time. Not only does the stool then become irregular, not only do the children begin anew to evacuate in their bed and clothing, but it also often leads back to a relapse to a much earlier stage than the one just attained. It is as if the children were protesting with defiance and rage against the absence of the attendant, an absence they felt as aggression. This is also true when children have already developed a sufficiently strong conscience and have already themselves laid claim to cleanliness themselves, on their own. For children can maintain the demand of their own cleanliness only so long as the attendant, on whose account the children have even addressed the challenge to themselves, remains available in the environment. If the persons disappear (because of illness, divorce, or death), their representation in the young, unstable conscience of the three-year-old also disappears.

On the one hand, the three-year-olds' refusal to comply with the parents' wishes for toilet training has the positive function of forming the children's own ego; on the other hand, however, strong sadistic tendencies also develop here, ones that are honored as positive by our social order ("perseverance," "will power," "diligence," "energy") and therefore cause great dangers for the stability of the ego. Those who feel they have the moral duty always to be the *first* develop their "moral" power from the desire to make others persons *second*, to *degrade* them, to cause them *displeasure*. The less they are aware of the sadistic motives of their conduct, the greater the danger that they will drive them through suppression into neuroses or through acting them out into perversion.

Something active is also always connected with the

squeezing out, an ejaculatory act that our social order falsely associates with the masculine. On the other hand, something receptive, passive, is connected with holding back, which our social order falsely associates with the feminine: something held back in the inner body, as a castrated penis by the vaginal muscles. In any case the contrast of activity and passivity exhibits the actual dialectic of the anal phase, while that of the oral phase had been overcome in the polarity of subject and object. Children's narcissism, which had denied the dependency on the mother or caregiver in a hallucination during the oral phase, now translates the hallucination into active protest: into defiance and the favored game of this stage of life: "I am the mother and you are my child!"

So, three-year-old children categorize the entire social surroundings according to active/passive standards. They try to divide all objects into active and passive by comparative environmental investigation. If they walk into a chair, they hit it and say, "Naughty chair!" They hit into the fire to punish the flames that burned them. Living individuals, too, are categorized according to the same standard. Yet, the "good" dog over which children trip defends itself, bites, and becomes a "bad" dog. The "nice" cat turns into a "bad" cat when children do not pet it just right and it hurts them. "Mommy, dearest," too, turns into "naughty Mommy" when she does something the children do not like. If parents and caregivers conduct themselves badly in this phase of children's development, children learn to identify "good" or "nice" with "passive"; "bad," or "angry" with "active": They become passive, lethargic, apathetic, or even begin to garnish their passivity with pleasure—they become masochistic.

So, the entire relationship between parents or caregivers and the children is highly ambivalent in this developmental phase, for example, in the sense that the feces can represent the mother and therefore can become a love object with a doubly libidinous trimming. In this case the relationship between the children and their body product would be *alloerotic* (from Greek *alloios*: "other"), a relationship to *other* people. However, as long as the body product still remains in the body, it is a part of one's own body. So the children's relationship to their bowel content in this case would be an *autoerotic,* a narcissistic one. If children themselves explain how this happens through successful potty training, to offer their feces as a sacrifice to their mother or caregiver out of love and to "bequeath" them to her as a gift whenever and wherever she wants it, for the first time in the children's history we see genuine object love: selfless and ready to sacrifice for the love of another person. Becoming an adult begins with that.

If we investigate this process of breaking through from the narcissistic self-love to altruistic object love, we find that the continuing development from the first anal stage, at which the love object, the feces, is joyfully rejected and thereby sacrificed, to the second anal stage, at which it should be retained, thus saved, is also an advance from indifference to care about the survival of the object—thus also a form of object love as it underlies the mature love of adults. The status of the second anal phase, in which the first signs of an object love show themselves thereby becomes stronger.

The psychical progression from the oral to the anal phase ultimately lies also in that the orality bases itself upon the taking, the anality in contrast, to the giving. That appears in the children's tendency toward giving the mother or caregiver their feces as a first personal achievement, as a first creation made by themselves, as a first present, as if in preparation to present the feces where she wants to have it, considering the mother's or caregiver's successful potty training—in the pot and not in the diaper.

If the mother or caregiver does not succeed in moving the children to this voluntary gift of their body product, the children—even if they appear to obey and do their duty when and where they should—turn to a number of alternative behaviors and substitute objects. These "transitional objects" are dented, have already been given up some time before, and have now regained a place in the heart—mostly worn-out dolls, stuffed animals, or other playthings, but sometimes even scraps of material, pillows, or corners of beloved blankets that now must serve as substitutes for the parents whom they actually want to love.

Picking the nose and ears, poking at the navel and between the teeth, smearing tables and walls with dirt and other material that stinks or makes marks are part of the substitute activities that serve as surrogates for pleasurable defecation. Girls grope about their nipples for hours and scratch their behinds. Small boys play with their hand in their trouser pockets and there jingle keys, change, marbles, and buttons. Also characteristic is the symbolic masochism of many of these behaviors of this play phase: chewing on the lips, biting on the tongue, nibbling their nails, scratching themselves until sore, tearing out hair. Every mother and many fathers are thoroughly familiar with these activities of their three-year-old. Except that they refuse to think about why their children do it.

Almost simultaneously with the problems of anal toilet training, but already beginning just a little bit earlier and ending a little later, appears the no-less-complex problem of urethral hygiene. Many of the somatic, psychical, and psychosexual implications of urethral development are similar to those of the anal. In spite of this there are differences that, because of the chronological overlap with that of the anal phase, have not yet been sufficiently distinguished from the latter, and have not been sufficiently analyzed as an independent phase. Since bladder evacuation is more often successful than bowel evacuation, the opportunities to learn bladder control as well as the possibilities of losing this control are greater. Totally independent of the children's gradually growing control over their bladder activity, however, a later mastery of it in sleep as in wakefulness occurs within every stage. That means even when children have long since been "dry" during the day, they can almost always suffer "accidents" at night.

Children do not like to take the time to go to the toilet and often wet themselves because they just do not want to stop playing. So, bladder toilet training should not begin before the end of the first year. When there are unexpected setbacks toward the middle or the end of the second year, punishment should not be given, because at this age the number of times the bladder is emptied increases in all children:

> Wetting occurs more frequently, and besides, children call their mother many times after they are put to bed. To the head of the family all of this appears a sheer setback. That is the time the father intervenes and inflicts strict punishment. And this is the worst measure of all, because the children find themselves in the midst of a constructive, growth-limited transitional stage in which they bring the opposing functions of bladder closing and bladder opening into well-weighted balance. (Arnold Gesell)

In the case of bladder control, the same rules of teaching apply as for bowel control and all other measures of training: The less parents exert their own will, the more quickly and easily children learn. Girls usually acquire bladder control somewhat earlier than boys. Children who have attained control of their bladder for a long time do, however, revert to their incontinence whenever they leave their usual surroundings or lose their regular attendant. During the evacuation of London in the Second World War, so many of the schoolchildren who were separated from their parents exhibited a relapse into bedwetting that "half of London stood under water" (Anna Freud).

Up until adulthood there is a close relationship between

bladder control and the triad ambition-pride-shame: ambition as striving toward bladder control; pride as the result of successful bladder control; shame as the result of frustrated bladder control. Freud speaks about the "burning ambition of the onetime enuretic" and by that certainly means the ambition to solve the problems of adult life better than those of childhood bladder control. The American pediatrician Joseph Church reports that his daughter, Ruth, when praised because she went on the potty by herself, had replied, "I sometimes wet my diaper, and then you are not proud of me. Now you are proud of me." Pause. "And *I* am proud of myself."

From newborn age on there is a close relationship between urethral eroticism and genital eroticism. They can certainly be diagnostically distinguished, but since the organs of evacuation of the urogenital system overlap, many common factors and many libidinous associations can be found. Since the penis ontogenetically develops from the lower intestine, it is hardly surprising that it is not only beset with genital but also with urethral and anal libido. Even at newborn age the penis of most boys becomes erect just before urinating and approximately one half hour after going to sleep.

With sitting up, urinating begins to assume a new meaning for both sexes, but especially for the boy. For the first time he perceives his penis as a special organ. At age two-and-one-half, both sexes then begin to understand their bladder activity and become interested in the difference between boys and girls while urinating. As often as they can, they try to see their parents, their brothers and sisters, their playmates, and also domestic animals urinating. When they are not allowed to watch, they begin to distinguish the sexes by the noise they make while urinating, especially into the potty, where that is very easily possible. At this age they also begin to talk about the different positions when urinating: "Right, Mommy, when the child is standing, it's a boy. When it sits, it's a girl." Girls react to this discovery mostly by trying to do it while standing; boys also try it sitting down.

Between the third and fourth years, boys who are raised restrictively and have never seen their mother or their sisters, or any other girls or women, naked develop two interesting theories of reproduction: that children are made by the father piddling into the mother's stomach, and that women piddle from their anus.

In their third and fourth years, boys like to piddle publicly so they can display their genitals. Many even begin in preschool age to make snakes and arabesques while urinating in the snow, sand, on tree trunks, and on house walls. At the same age, many girls try to obtain urethral gratification by pressing their legs together upon the urgent need to urinate and retaining the urine for as long as possible. In children's language: "I have to go."

If we divide the typology of urethral erotic children into two groups, namely, according to those who find greater satisfaction in urinating and those others who seek their satisfaction in retaining their urine, we find more boys in the first group and more girls in the second. However, it is characteristic for the complementary behavior from urethral to genital libido that urination for the purpose of elimination of libidinous impulses satisfies most children up until the mastering of bladder control. Urethral erotic children rarely masturbate in this phase, but turn to masturbation as soon as they are "clean." It is as if the renunciation of the pleasure of urinating unhindered at any time is only possible thanks to the gift for genital release of the age-specific libido. According to whether parents allow or prohibit the children to masturbate will they later on remain dry or (at least temporarily) return to bedwetting.

Sexual Pathology of the Third Year

From the third year of life on we begin to demonstrate only the psychosexual regressions up to the actual age of life, but also some of the somatic and psychosomatic sexual disorders of the actual developmental phase. So, for example, it must be pointed out that from the third year on, specific cells in undescended testicles degenerate if no operation is performed within the first two years. In 4 to 5 percent of newborn boys the testicles have not fully descended into the scrotum. In most cases such as these the scrotum is so shriveled that newborns—especially one whose penis is underdeveloped—are considered to be and raised as girls. Then, if one or the other testicles descends by itself, the parents are ashamed to have the mistake corrected by operation and to report the change of sex to the authorities. From the second year on the condition no longer normalizes itself spontaneously and can no longer be corrected by surgical intervention.

During the last decade pediatricians have begun to confirm psychosomatic diseases such as asthma and eczema on a large scale, even in three-year-olds. Almost without exception these disorders refer back to unresolved sexual problems in the family—not necessarily to the children's sexual disorders, but also to ones of the parents or caregivers, ones that precipitate in the children as psychosomatic effects of "family neuroses" (Spitz). To these effects also belong skin diseases, especially urticaria (hives), psychogenic body disorders, nervous breathing syndrome (mostly in girls), colic, gastric ulcers, and colitis ulcerosa, a serious compound disease of the colon—a part of the large intestine—with slimy-bloody evacuation. The last two disorders are often interpreted as psychosexual effects of unsuccessful toilet training in the second and third years.

One clearly psychosexual phenomenon of the family is pavor nocturnus, the nightly startling of the child. Three-year-olds wake up bathed in sweat, cling to the bed or to the parents, and exhibit all the signs of fear of death. In the morning there is no memory of the nocturnal scene. The cause almost always lies in the parents, often in unresolved marital crises that the children perceive with their sensitive antennae and, without being aware of the rational content of their fears, interpret as life threatening.

Other children's reactions to parental marital problems are eating disorders that are unconsciously used as weapons by the children against the parents or caregivers. Psychogenic obesity, exactly as psychogenic emaciation, which up until just a short time ago were still considered illnesses of puberty, often appear today even in the third year. They have an unmistakably imploring character: They point to a yearning for affection and satisfaction of pleasure.

Behavioral disorders that a short time ago appeared at the earliest in youth are likewise found today in three-year-olds—motor unrest; jactitations; tics such as sniffing, blinking, raising the eyebrows, grimaces, turning of the head, shoulder jerking, uttering certain sounds. Here, too, the causes often are the lack of the parents' ability to find love for each other as well as for their children.

Neuropaths with headaches, dizziness, and fainting spells today are frequently observed in the third year. They are often connected with an abnormally intensified sensitivity to odors during toilet training and likewise have their origin in the disturbed sexual relationships of the parents and a lack of tender affection for the children.

Children with different constitutions react to psychical stress with different bodily zones—in many the mucous membranes of the throat become swollen; in others the skin becomes red or pale, forms allergies or eczema; in still others their blood pressure rises or falls; others get muscle cramps; yet others have digestive problems: they vomit or cannot eat, they get diarrhea or constipation (J. I. Lacey). But by and large symptoms develop in the age-specific libidinized zones and can be explained as regressions to the corresponding developmental phases: skin diseases to the cutaneous phase, diseases of the mouth and throat to the oral, disorders of the digestive system to the anal, psychosexual disorders to the genital phase. Since the third year stands in indication of anal and urethral weaning, we will concern ourselves here especially with anal and urethral psychosomatic.

While the persons rearing the children also demand strict regularity besides cleanliness, they expose the narcissism of the oral phase to a hard test of endurance. The majority of children sooner or later meet these challenges. In the most favorable cases the children succeed in identifying with the parents' or caregivers' demands and are proud of the measure of continence they have reached (on this subject see the remark by Joseph Church's daughter, Ruth, cited above). If the children stay clean out of the love for their attendants, the children compensate for the injury to their primary narcissism by taking satisfaction in the successful accomplishment and in the attendants' praise.

But it often happens that attendants try to force continence from children who are not yet mature enough for it. They become mature only when they have succeeded in transferring the feelings originally bound to narcissism to their attendants. Only then can they become punctual and clean for the love of these persons. But if cleanliness and punctuality of urinating and defecating are required too early, as, unfortunately, it almost always is in our case, the children train themselves alone out of fear. The inner resistance remains and the libido persists with tenacity in narcissistic fixation. Result: A lasting disorder of the ability to love.

The full impact of premature toilet training becomes clear only when one pursues the transitional stages of the narcissistic desire in particular. If we recognize a justifiable feeling of power in the children's pride of evacuation, the characteristic feeling of fainting that we meet with in neurotic, severely constipated victims of premature toilet training becomes understandable. Their libido has shifted from the genital zone to the anal zone—with the result that they feel their constipation as a kind of impotence. One can sometimes relieve characteristically habitual constipation through therapy in which one exposes and brings to awareness the potency complex of such anal neurotics.

One of the most well-known results of toilet training carried out with threats and punishment is *encopresis*, involuntary defecation, which with the usual time delay of such disorders appears from the fourth year on, thus about one year after the children have been "clean." In the etiology of encopresis (and also of feces smearing) in the preschool and school years, an unsuccessful relationship to the parents or caregivers appears in most cases, particularly in children of "cleanliness freaks," especially of mothers who demand cleanliness, order, and morality or especially frigid, disciplinarian, and domineering fathers. If such parents succeed in moving their children at least for a time to anal or urethral continence by punishment or threats of punishment, the continence often, and certainly up into adulthood, has a forced, automatic character.

As a schoolteacher, one often meets with that type of "fine," "good," "shining" child who never participates in "dirty" games, but also not in clean ones. Such children obviously never give teachers as much trouble as the dirty fellows and mischief-makers, but for educators schooled in psychology the fear of dirt is a warning sign to be taken seriously just as is the pleasure in dirt. Both expose an unsuccessful stage of age-specific development in the home. So both behaviors can also be a plea of the children to the teachers: "Help me! My parents did not help me." If teachers misunderstand the pupils' desire for contact or refuse it, then both types of conduct—the pleasure in dirt in some children, the fear of dirt in others—are made much worse.

Forced and therefore compulsive cleanliness in childhood can become compulsive washing in adolescence and com-

pulsive neurosis in adulthood. With it a tormenting washing
ritual connected with great sexual fears plays a leading role.
Certain body parts have to be washed with a certain soap
for a certain amount of time in a certain series of steps and
be dried off with a certain towel. For example, if, on vacation
or on a visit, there is no possibility of celebrating the ritual
in the "prescribed" manner, the obsessive compulsive falls
into panic. The attempt to become rid of the imaginary dirt
often leads to severe skin injuries, especially in the anal
region. In practicing Catholics the confessing of minor sins
appears as a frequent accompanying phenomenon of the
symptom.

At no time in life is the self identified with the body
to such a high degree as during the anal phase. This is one
of the reasons why children feel that toilet training is an
attempt by the parents or caregivers to deprive them of the
power of decision over their body. On the other hand,
however, under the stress of the training children also
attempt to gain a kind of power of decision over the product
of their own body—over the words that come from their
mouth, over the tears that stream from their eyes, but especially over the feces that come from their insides. If they
succeed in doing that under the adults' pressure, the danger
arises that later the children will one day treat their contemporaries, especially their sex partner, as feces. In adulthood, such children then try to manipulate their sex partners,
to cling to them or to throw them out of their living space,
just as feces can be retained, evacuated, and manipulated.

On the other hand, fear of the failure of sphincter and
bladder control in later life can result in the fear of the failure of genital control: as the fear of frigidity or impotence.
In the fantasies of anally or urethrally disordered persons
frequently emerges the hallucinatory fear that, if during
sexual intercourse they allowed themselves to let go they
would lose control of their sphincter muscles and go in bed.

Girls' toilet training contains certain dangers that boys

are largely, if not totally, spared. For, the more the mother suggests to the girl that anal products are dirty the greater the probability that the daughter will relate this disparagement of the anal zone to the bordering vaginal zone and thereby perceive her own sexuality as "dirty." If one year later the mother discovers the daughter masturbating and prohibits it without being able to state clearly why it is "bad," she confirms the suspicion that everything that has to do with sexuality is bad and dirty. Result: lifelong frigidity and anorgasmy.

If the children finally obtain full control of their sphincter muscles, in many cases that gives the already described feeling of power pleasurably exercised. Persons who are fixated at this stage, or later regress to it, for that reason also tend to feel every exercise of power as pleasurable. As we know from medical history, Caesar, Napoleon, and Hitler were anal hypochondriacs whose manic striving for power was closely connected with their anal character. Since sphincter control is often strived for even at the age of the primary fantasies of omnipotence, in such cases these fantasies combine with the pride at achieving a measure of control and then not only lead the individual to the later wish to control other people in this manner, as they learned to control the products of their own body, but also lead to symptoms of megalomania, to delusions of grandeur.

To summarize: While the first anal stage (the second year) was marked by pleasure at the evacuation of feces, the second anal stage (the third year) is now characterized by the control of the evacuation functions, and certainly in two contradictory forms that actually require a subdivision of this stage into two subphases: first, through toilet training, small persons are delivered from the illusion of power they had gained in the first anal stage. Second, however, the illusion of this omnipotence in a certain sense reappears when they now discover that they can control their caregivers. Children learn that they can elicit compliments and rewards from their attendants when they evacuate where and when the children should or can bring these caregivers to despair whenever they either go in bed or defiantly retain their feces. The stimulation in evacuation is intensified by the rewards, and the anal zone is more highly libidinized by the retention of feces and the powerful evacuation following it.

So, during the anal phase, children take four important steps forward:

1. The discovery that evacuation is a kind of self-satisfaction. This perception still belongs in the first anal phase.

2. The discovery that rewards can be earned by evacuating promptly. This experience leads us from the first to the second anal stage.

3. The discovery that greater pleasure is attained by retaining the feces than by an immediate evacuation. The second anal phase begins with this perception.

4. The discovery that retaining the feces (thus self-will, obstinacy, and defiance) can elicit negative emotions (rage, annoyance, anger) out of other people. This concurrence of anal pleasure and satisfaction of aggression led Sigmund Freud to call the whole phase "anal sadistic." But the terminology applies only to this, the children's fourth discovery, which is in general first made in the second anal stage.

When they are not sufficiently assimilated, each of these discoveries can in later life lead to regressions clearly resting on this phase. A few examples:

1. *The discovery that evacuation can be pleasurable* leads to a narcissistic libidinization of the anal zone, to anal masturbation, and to the desire to have the anus masturbated, licked, or used in sexual intercourse. Forms of regression to this discovery are acted upon in anal fetishism, enema mania, and anal exhibitionism.

On the other hand, the discovery that evacuation of bodily products can be pleasurable can even forestall later processes of the satisfaction of genital pleasure, such as ejaculation in men and orgasmic reactions in women. Finally, the fixation on the anus as a pleasurable source contains highly ambivalent elements. As a bodily orifice the rectum is a kind of vagina and so makes the passive anal erotics into receivers, into false female sex partners. They simultaneously also identify themselves with the feces as love object, equate it with the penis, and in this sense tend toward active anal eroticism. So most adult anal erotics possess a heavy bisexual component.

Since uninhibited anal erotics who do not suppress or sublimate the fact have no place in our social order, extraordinarily severe social pressure works on them to move them to suppress their inclination nevertheless. It is often too late for sublimation. So, by every means of social pressure, our society tends to turn anal erotics even in adulthood into compulsive neurotics. Other anal erotics are driven to hypochondria and conversion neurosis by shifting their non-sublimated coprophilic libido onto other parts of the body.

2. *The discovery that prompt evacuation can earn rewards* is typified by "ass kissers," those types of characters who on the one hand seek to fit in perfectly into the current social order because they want the maximum amount of personal advantages promised by it, but who, on the other hand, deliver their work all too promptly. So, regressions from the genital phase of puberty and adolescence to this aspect of the anal phase often lead to premature ejaculation and to excessive submissiveness in later life.

3. *The discovery that greater pleasure can be attained by retaining feces than by immediate evacuation* is probably the cause of the pleasure of collecting, hoarding, and avarice— also the pleasure of collecting as many sex partners as possible, who are then promptly "screwed up the ass." In contrast, other retention fetishists tend to hold back their feelings. They suffer not only from bottling up their emotions, but often also from ejaculation disorders. In their sex life, still others tend to withhold their orgasm so long that foreplay becomes the actual sex act.

The discovery of the pleasure of retention contains a high degree of ambivalence. On the one hand, the object beset with desire, feces, must be *evacuated*. On the other hand, however, it should also be *retained*. Adult anal erotics remain loyal to this ambivalent conduct toward their love object mostly their whole life long.

The desire to keep the love object back in the body all too easily transforms itself into the fear of being retained by it. In several anal psychoses the notion emerges that the sufferer will be sucked into the bowels of the other person and held there. On the other hand, the wish to retain the feces can, by resistance and regression, also turn into the fear they could be torn out of you. The fear of the loss of the bowels is a central phobia of anal neurotics.

4. *The pleasurable discovery that retaining feces can enrage other people* is one of the main reasons for human sadism. This discovery, as do all of the others of the anal phase, certainly does also contain positive components, especially the recognition of reality and the understanding processes of interaction, but regressions to this discovery are especially insidious. Men and women who feel this discovery as too pleasurable to be able to separate themselves from it ever in life provoke their sex partner by a constant mixture of seduction and denial. They save their orgasm not for the sake of gratification, but to frustrate their partner. They become all the more excited the more their partner suffers. This type, once very prominent among men, has been appearing more and more among women for about the past twenty years.

Inevitably, anal sadists such as these also develop great fears of reprisal. They are therefore exposed to the fear that what they did to or wished to do to others will happen to them. They show an especially great susceptibility to conversion neuroses, such as, for example, to the idea that their pleasurably retained feces will be forcefully torn out of their body by their sex partner.

In this syndrome even a sudden change from anal sadism into anal masochism stands out. It is not rare and assumes many forms. When children retain feces, they not only enrage the mother, but also bind her to them, themselves. They "extort" her presence by not squeezing out their feces. That means they bribe her presence with the sacrifice of being scolded or even beaten. So, the regression from the genital to this aspect of the anal phase appears such that the adults accept the insults by the sex partner only to bind the sex partner to them. More exactly stated: They seek for themselves a sadistic partner whose presence they ensure for themselves because they already propose to be abused by the partner.

The pleasure-tinged defiance against toilet training not only arises out of the anal source, but is also supported mostly by a regression to the second oral stage, in which the sadistic desire to bite arose. In this sense the aggressiveness of the second anal stage is a recapitulation of the cannibalistic tendencies of the second oral stage, a shifting from above to below, from the entrance gate of nourishment to the exit gate, from the teeth to the anus. Psychoanalysts speak of the "toothed anus" in analogy to the mythical concept of the "toothed vagina" (vagina dentata).

Those regressions in which elements of the second anal stage pair with those of the first oral stage reach even further back into past early childhood. This oral stage, as you know, is characterized by the children's sucking. If it combines with the wish for retention, which is characteristic for the second anal phase, compulsive neuroses of an especially obstinate kind often develop. Such persons show traces of an unsatisfied infancy all their life.

Even worse are the cases in which sadistic partial wishes combine in the sucking of the first oral stage and the retention of the second anal stage. "In the social behavior of these persons, something constantly longing stands out, that is expressed now more in the form of begging, later in that of demanding . . . they allow themselves to be rejected as infrequently by the discussion of facts as by pertinent objections, but continue to urge and to insist" (Karl Abraham). As sex partners they make it very difficult for their lovers to build any kind of loving, reciprocal relationship.

All these regressions have their common denominator in that the derailments of anal eroticism revert to signals that had already been falsely regulated during the oral phase. Wrong switch signals of this type, which are almost always the result of incorrect training, can bring the children's psychical life to derailment even in the third year. These occur especially frequently whenever the illusion of childhood omnipotence is not conquered at the end of the second year and then unites with the defiance and willfulness of the third year.

Anal erotics are almost always children of anally burdened parents. Parents such as these reenact their own anal complex by premature and too drastic anal training. Under the pretext of wanting only the best for the children and helping them to become accustomed to the precepts of the world at the earliest possible moment, they use "discipline" and "strictness." They are only doing their "duty." But where strictness serves as a substitute for love, one has to fear that the children, when grown up, can also give only a substitute for love, also only strictness.

Therapy for the various anal neuroses promises only limited success if they have already developed fully. As in almost all childhood neuroses the only effective therapy is the prophylactic one. And the preventive measures must be used by the parents.

The symptomatics and susceptibility to therapy of urethral disorders of the third year minimally distinguish themselves from those of the anal. Among chronic *bedwetters* there are two different types with different etiology of the enuresis. Some are prematurely trained for "cleanliness" and take unconscious revenge up into their youth by urinating in bed. Others are trained for "cleanliness" too late, mostly only in the third year or later, and so have passed the critical period in which bladder muscles can be most easily controlled.

According to Sandor Ferenczi, bedwetting is an attempt to enjoy the pleasure of masturbating without the guilt, thus, an unconscious masturbation surrogate. But this logic is wrong, because urethral eroticism is an earlier impulse than the genital. So, it is more justified to postulate that masturbation in the fourth year is a surrogate form of the lost urethral delights of the second and third years. It appears to us that nocturnal bedwetting is an attempt to get during the night what parents and caregivers forbid during the day. In this sense it is indeed unconscious, to be sure, but for that reason no less the desired intention of the children to take revenge on the prohibiting parents.

Passive as well as active efforts combine with urethral eroticism exactly as with anal eroticism, both of them often in an ambivalent mixture. Many urethral erotics feel the desire for urination as the pleasure of letting flow, of letting go of oneself, of the joyful surrender of control over one's own body, as a giving in to the "oceanic" feeling. Others consider urination as an active deed, a kind of ejaculation. Still others connect sadistic associations with the thought of urinating on other people, to dirty them against their will. And yet still others experience the same syndrome in the opposite direction: in the wish that someone else might urinate on them. The last two practices are truly frequent in clients of prostitutes specialized in intercourse with urethral erotics.

Sexual pedologists have never contested that one of the unmistakable regressions to certain aspects of the third year, especially to the pleasure of urinating, is premature ejaculation. There are also seemingly convincing notions that totally determined ejaculatory disorders reveal close relationships to stuttering and that both have a common origin in incorrect urethral toilet training.

Like anal erotics, urethral erotics, too, tend toward sadomasochism. The diagnosis of premature ejaculation almost always also uncovers, beside accentuated pleasure of urinating, psychical resistance against heterosexual sexual intercourse, fear of women, misogyny, desire for revenge against women, and also the wish for a "strong," "strict" female sex partner. Both tendencies are results of the regressive wish to use the present sexual relationship as compensation for the unsuccessful childhood relationship to the urethral mother. If the mother was weak, the female partner should be strong. If the mother was strong, the female partner should be weak. If during urethral training one felt unjustly punished, one now assumes the right to "punish" your female partner. If at that time we felt neglected by our mother, we now would like our female partner to treat us "severely."

In the third year, many children already develop practices of urethral masturbation, ones that unmistakably distinguish themselves from those of the genital. They are thereby characterized by the fact that not the external epidermis of the penis or the clitoris is stimulated, but rather the urethral passage. But since it is not easily accessible by hand and finger, objects are mostly used as aids. The practice of urethral passage manipulation in children and adults is thus in general first made known by the fact that surgeons have had to intervene for removal of objects from the urethral passage and bladder. Magnus Hirschfeld already in 1926 wrote, "We have repeatedly observed that children as well as adults introduce all kinds of objects into their urethral passages, such as peas, beans, flower stalks, pieces of straw, ears of corn, toothpicks, knitting needles, pins, pencils, pen-holders, probes, matches, and similar things. Male as well as female persons have been found doing such things as this, and in 1862 masturbation with hairpins was so widespread that one surgeon invented a special instrument to remove hairpins from the female bladder."

In 1942, L. Kielleutner, in a question-and-answer column in the *München medizinischen Wochenschrift* (Munich medical weekly) again pointed out the injuries "to the urethra and bladder entrance caused by masturbation. . . . The frequent finding of foreign bodies used for stimulation in the bladder proves how often frictions are carried out." A correspondent writes to us in a personal message: "When I was about two years of age I had two masturbation buddies from the same family. We used to dig out a hole in the haystacks of one of our neighboring farmers and study our genitals. These two boys showed signs of great pleasure in introducing dry pieces of straw between about 2–5 cm (.78–1.9 in) long into their urethra until the stems completely disappeared. By pressing the shaft of the penis the piece of straw came a few millimeters out of the glans and could be grasped and be pulled out again, and the game began anew. The thrill of the thing consisted in the danger that it could stay in; that was the essential thing of doing it."

The same correspondent wrote to us explaining this syndrome. "As an essential point I could imagine for myself an unconscious feminine level of identification that is first suppressed in puberty to the advantage of the patriarchal standard of identification and only later can still be proven to become transformed into characteristic behavior."

My associates and I have observed very similar manners of behavior in the third year of our informants. They obviously serve to aid children with a rudimentary sexual identity. That parents and educational authorities are afraid of such practices, and do everything in their power to prevent them, may be understandable in the light of the risks to health. But that most parents dismiss with refusal, annoyance, disgust, or uncertain laughter even the most harmless attempts by their children to form a sexual identity, is less understandable. For the results of such parental conduct often are hostile. Many later "perversions" are results of parental offenses against the children's striving for sexual autonomy. The hatred resulting from it can be overcome in later life only by a compensatory behavior—behavior we call "perverse": behavior with the help of which children who have reached mature adulthood take revenge on their parents by carrying out joyfully and defiantly what was then forbidden or not acknowledged.

So we have to complete our explanation of "perversions" or also past psychosexual infantilism, that it is a question not only of acted-out regressions to a certain childhood phase, but also of such that are unconsciously felt as revenge on parents or caregivers. If the "perversion" is a behavior prohibited by law, then it has an especially stimulating effect because it creates a tension between the hope that prohibitions in those days can be successfully acted out today, and the risk of failure and getting caught.

The later sex partners of these parentally damaged adults for the most part do not know that they are mere actors of a scenario that the other person has constructed since the third year. In the imposture that is now being performed with the unknowing help of the sex partner, there is no place for love, but only one for the hatred caused by the parents. So the sexual intercourse of such persons has only one goal: overcoming the hurt suffered in the third year.

The metamorphosis that transforms the childhood trauma of such parentally harmed persons into pleasure is always at the cost of the sex partner. For in this complex scenario it is the partner's function to embody either the injurious mother or the punitive father. What now in adulthood is said to be an act of "love" is in reality an act of revenge against the parents: This form of revenge changes me, the one-time victim, into today's victor, and my present sex partner, in contrast, into the victim of yesteryear. This etiology of "love," unfortunately, affects the majority, rather than the minority, in our present Western society.

Since persons wronged by their parents manipulate their

sex partner like a marionette, they place their partner into the past and themselves into the present. One-time children imagine themselves taking the part of the parents and thus give the parents the children's role. The resulting orgasm is intense, because it is not only an explosive release of lifelong hatred, but also a triumph over time and space, but especially over punishment.

We already said at the outset that in the childhood development of this syndrome it is unimportant whether the parents consciously or unconsciously hurt the children. The tragic thing about the syndrome is indeed the fact that parents mostly have absolutely no idea that they have highly damaged the children for life by a prohibition appearing legitimate to the parents, or by a doubt seeming justified to them, in respect to the—immature—sexuality of the children. So, it is in no way the ill will of the parents or educational authorities that calls forth the misfortune, but mostly parental ignorance, their ignorance about childhood sexuality.

This is exactly what is wrong with our social order. Parents do not at all suspect that their children do not understand the motive of parental behavior. They do not know that the children, because of the immaturity of their sexual ego, are driven to despair by the smiling doubt of the parents. They have no idea that one day the later sex partner of their child will have to pay the costs of their misbehavior and then also step forth promptly and often as a critic of the partner. This is a hopelessly botched situation that has become one of the central sexual problems of our social order.

Toward the end of the third year, children discover death. If they find a dead bird, if the dog gets run over, if a relative lies in a casket, from the children's standpoint that means: They do not move; they make no sounds. From this children then learn: Motionlessness equals death. If parents now say to them, "Stop running about so much; sit down and behave yourself; don't talk so much; shut your trap, for crying out loud!" from now on that means, "My parents want to kill me!" Children then either control themselves and try to survive or accept the imaginary parental death wish and begin to become aware of it. Characteristic intermediary stages of such a development are insomnia, refusal to eat, immobility, and catatonia. The obscure rate of such unexplainable, premature child mortality is much greater than the general public realizes.

7

Fourth Year
Middle of the Toddler's Puberty

The fourth year of life is a relaxational phase. Sexuality certainly does begin to make itself known to a greater measure than in the third year, but the most difficult battles with individual sexuality are reserved for the fifth year.

Growth in height slows down; growth in breadth increases. Toward the beginning of the fourth year boys are approximately 97 cm (3.18 ft) tall; toward the end, approximately 104 cm (3.41 ft). Girls grow from 96 cm (3.14 ft) to 103 cm (3.37 ft) tall. So, difference in height of the sexes is only 1 cm (.39 in) at the beginning as well as at the end of the year. The same goes for weight. At the beginning of the year girls weigh 14.5 kg (31.9 lb); at year's end 16.6 kg (36.5 lb). At the beginning of the year boys weigh only .4 kg (14.1 oz) more and at the end, only .2 kg (7.1 oz) more.

Motility increases. Children run, hop, jump, skip, and climb. They learn to ride the bicycle and to balance themselves. They can cut out precise patterns with scissors, can go around with the fretsaw and—what is more difficult—can tie their shoelaces. They eat cleanly and adeptly. While eating and changing clothes they can speak and listen. In the third year most could do these only separately.

The ability to learn and the interest in the environment increase. The narcissism of the anal phase decreases. Adults, who still believe children at this stage of life are at best halfpersons and cannot think "right," should be reminded that 50 percent of the growth of human intelligence occurs before the fifth year, 30 percent between years five and eight, and the remaining 20 percent between the eighth and seventeenth years. Thereafter, only growth of experience still occurs, but not of intelligence (Benjamin Bloom).

Children's fantasy increases. During the fourth year many children make up imaginary friends with whom they hold long conversations. They can be very comical, because the children play the role of these invisible friends with pretended voices. In such dialogues, four-year-olds give a hint of very much more of their sexual desires and fears than in the questions directed to their parents about the origin of little children and the secret acts in the parents' bedroom.

But that in no way reduces the quantity of questions, because childhood sexual investigation now assumes the character of an almost endless series of questions. At the same time, the actual object of curiosity often is no longer mentioned. Nevertheless, the experienced pedologist knows that the seemingly senseless and in many cases long since answered questions are only paraphrases of the suppressed main question about the origin of life. However, the main question doubtless is not only the one about the origin of children, but also that about individual sexual identity. It is characteristic that the "age of questions" does not appear in cultures that make no secret of the processes of sex and procreation. Also unknown there is the ascertainable attempt among us in the fifth year to spy on parents and others at washing, bathing, showering, urinating, and defecating. In contrast, in our case, four-year-olds are intensely interested in strange toilets and bathrooms. While visiting the residences of other children, they insist on going to the toilet or bathroom and inspecting all of the objects and pieces of clothing found there.

The age-specific sex games ("Mommy and Daddy," "Doctor," "I see something you don't see") are not childhood surrogate forms of coitus, but rather learning games, part of childhood sexual investigation. In the fourth year, boys take over the initiative that girls had taken in the third year. Only when the parents are especially hostile toward the body and forbid children to play these games does something like the fear of retaliation appear in many, which then is expressed as excessive shyness. It is a sure indication that parents have acted incorrectly. If defiance is the price of the forbidden anal desires of years one and two, shame the price of the forbidden urethral desires of years two and three, then bashfulness is the price of the forbidden genital desires of years three and four.

The father now gains more significance for both sexes, while the mother loses another piece of the monopoly she had had up until now as attendant. To the father are now directed those questions that in previous years had still been addressed to the mother, "But Daddy, how does the child get *out* of the stomach?" Before the end of the fourth year most children know that their parents engage in sexual intercourse with each other, but they do not know *how* they do it. They know that the father sticks his member into the mother's "stomach," but they do not know that while so doing he *moves about*. They know that children grow "under the heart" of the mother, but they do not know how and where they *come out*.

Certain parts of the body that possess no sexual character, for example, the navel, now become embued with libido. It could be that this happens because children believe it is the opening through which the fetus slips out. Until only recently this was a traditional theory among pedologists. Among the four thousand children and youths we questioned in the last twenty years, we found not even one child who expressed this hypothesis of birth. In contrast, since four-year-olds tend to expose their navel and display it proudly to other children (or also to adults), the reason for the existing libido, according to our opinion, must be a substitute for the anus and a precursor of the genital phase. Perhaps there is such a thing as a "navel phase."

During the fourth year "immoral" children's verses become very popular, but the content turns from scatological to genital themes.

Toilet training now lies in the distant past. Only very rarely, especially after a day filled with stress, can an accident again occur during sleep. But that can upset the child only if the parents become upset. Certainly, toilet training succeeds perfectly only when the children can replace the fascination of feces and urine by another fascination. This is the allurement of the genitals, and with that begins that developmental phase that Sigmund Freud called the *phallic phase* and sex pedologists have designated as the *first genital stage*. Among other things, it expresses itself in play with knives, toy guns, and similar objects. Toddlers envy their older brothers and secretly try to get to their airguns. In the course of this phase, sexual stimulation, no matter in what body part it might have formed, is discharged across the genitals: "There is no specific oral, anal, or genital, but rather only one libido that can be shifted from one erogenous zone to another" (Fenichel).

Erections, which already begin in many boys with the elimination of the first solid food and thereafter more or less link themselves with bowel action, now begin to come on by themselves and to assume their own regularity. So, many boys now begin to boast, "Mine is bigger than yours!" The girls boast about their conquests, "That is *my* friend, and that is *also* my friend! I have *many* friends!" With the exception of twosomes, mostly between neighboring children, play groups now divide according to sex. But that does not mean, as was believed up to only a few years ago, that this is an expression of dwindling interest in the other sex, but, on the contrary, it expresses the growing tension between the sexes. At the same time, totally in contrast to the superficial impression of a turning toward the group, a sexual turning to the single person begins. While toward the end of the third year everything was a matter of *the* girls or *the* boys, now it is a matter of one certain girl and of a certain favorite boy. That is also symbolically expressed in the play with dolls, because in the fourth year many girls begin to lay aside their old dolls and to turn to one single doll.

Both sexes begin to become intensely interested in the formulation of sex relationships and bombard their parents with questions about engagement and marriage, about weddings and nuptials, about brides and bridegrooms, about husbands and wives. But that in no way means that children have taken a sudden interest in the institution of monogamy, but that they begin to identify with their parents. So there are many questions about the parents' childhoods and the question of when and how you can have your own children also often occurs.

So four-year-olds do not think about only sexuality, but also about procreation, and they do both totally harmlessly with regard to the parent of the opposite sex as the spouse nearest at hand. Small girls try to court their father, little boys their mother. Both repeatedly offer marriage to the chosen parent. Also, they do not hesitate to say to the parent, without any fear of sentimentality, "I love you!"

In the techniques of seduction, girls are certainly at least a half-year ahead of the boys. They are coquettish, raise their little skirts, and try to attract their father's attention. On the other hand, you may often experience that, while changing their clothes, boys will grab their penis by the hand, point it at the mother like a weapon, and smile at her slyly and cunningly.

A favorite game is role reversal, by which the children make unmistakably clear that they want to take the role of the same-sex parent in the presence of the opposite-sex parent, "Daddy, I am now the father and you are my son. You must now wash yourself and I will go to bed with Mommy." Jealousy is clearly and unmistakably present. Every time the father or mother says, "Go play; leave us alone now," or, "Go to bed; we still have things to do," the children ask with a jealous voice, "Why do I have to go? Why not *Daddy*? Why not *Mommy*?" Or, "What do you *two* still have to do every night? Why can't *I* stay?"

Our team of researchers observed that four-year-old girls turned photographs of their mother with the face to the wall, that four-year-old boys have smashed framed photographs of their father and torn the photographs. A colleague reported that his four-year-old daughter sliced a portrait of her mother with one of his straight-edge razors. We have often observed that boys, while playing, have stepped with their feet on, knocked down, stabbed, knifed, and scalped their father. A mother told us that her daughter first became aware of her mother's bosom in her fourth year and said, "How nice! How big! How fat!" And then, with a suddenly changed facial expression, "I'll cut them off of you and make chopped meat of them!" A father described the following scene: "I'm in the head taking a pee. Maxi comes in, stands as if petrified and says, 'What, you've got one of those too?' And then in a tone of jealous defense, said, 'But yours is no good. It's much too long!' " The lifelong illusion of many men that their penis is too small is no doubt based on the comparison of their penis at age four or five with that of their father.

Many parents are horrified when they notice that their children have sexual impulses and that the impulses are directed right at their own parents. But at whom else should they be directed? The human infant is biologically more helpless than the young of other mammals. Infants need not only nourishment, warmth, and protection, but also a high degree of affection. So they cannot help demanding love from their parents. Since children are certainly born as sexual beings but learn to distinguish love and sexuality only later, there is the innate tendency for the son to direct his first wishes for love toward his mother and the daughter her first ones toward her father. The other parent is thereby inevitably felt to be the rival for the affections of the favored parent.

This stressful parent-child relationship, which develops between the third and fifth years, sex pedologists call the *Oedipus complex*. The concept originates with Sigmund Freud and is borrowed from Greek mythology. The king's son, Oedipus, raised by strangers, thought his foster parents were his biological parents; in manhood he meets his mother, then unknown to him, and marries her after he in a street brawl has killed his father, who likewise was unknown to him.

So, the name "Oedipus complex" is badly chosen, because Oedipus in no way fell in love with his mother because she had brought him up, although on the contrary she had *not* raised him. Also, he in no way killed his father because he considered him the rival for the affection of his mother, *before* he really got to know his mother and *before* he knew that the man killed by him was his sire.

According to the present understanding of sex pedology, what Freud called the "Oedipus complex" should actually be called "small family complex," because it develops only when no attendants other than the biological parents are at the disposal of the children. In prehistoric cultures in which the part of the father in procreation was still unknown (and where the fathers also did not live with the mothers), no Oedipus complex could therefore develop between father and daughter. In communes and in Israeli kibbutz settlements it appears that children raised there rarely exhibit any Oedipus-type complexes. So, the Oedipus complex most probably is not a biological, but rather a social phenomenon. It is the product of the small family and only in this small family does it appear as Freud and his students described it. But it can hardly be argued, even by opponents of psychoanalysis, that it determines the fate of all people who are raised in small families of our kind up to the end of their lives.

The reason why social and class-specific aspects result in the Oedipus complex very much less than sociologists expected and supposed has especially to do with the fact that different forms of sexual morals link less to career and income than to parents' style of childrearing. In no other area is there so little affinity between economy and world view as in that of parental sex education. That also operates in the Oedipus complex.

The *castration complex,* too, is very closely related to the Oedipus complex. It is based on the observation that in the fourth year children recognize only *one* sex part, the *male* one. When girls discover they will never have a penis, they choose the father as love object because he has a penis and can give her a substitute for a penis, namely, a child. Adult women and mothers also, according to this logic, regard their children especially as penis substitutes.

Empirical sex pedologists have registered different doubts with regard to these psychoanalytical concepts. Some of the phenomena described surely do occur in a relatively high number of children and adults. But our empirical observations during the last two decades allow us to suppose that these days we should rather establish that the man perceives his penis to be a substitute for the child he cannot bear. Certainly in our social order, more men suffer from birth envy than women from penis envy. We have established besides a pronounced envy of the bosom in small boys in the fourth year. The fact that the mother can nourish her children with her breast gives her, in the son's opinion, a higher "potency" than the father's penis possesses according to the daughter's standards. For during the last decade we have also discovered in four-year-old girls growing bosom envy—envy of something that the mother already has, but the daughter does not have as yet.

We asked ourselves: Why does the female breast have

a sexually stimulating effect not only on most men, but also on many women? Obviously, because it serves in breast-feeding. Those who were bottle-fed feel an unexplainable, deeply repressed yearning for what they had missed as infants, while those who were breast-fed feel a lifelong homesickness for this happiest time of their childhood. But how does an experience felt as happy in childhood change into a sexually stimulating one in later years? Because human sexuality no longer serves just procreation exclusively, but rather derives its thrusting power from the pregenital desires of childhood. However, whenever the memory of childhood happiness as well as the yearning for past childhood happiness possesses a sexual character, then the parent-child relationship is a sexual one from the start. Then neither the myth of a sexless parental love nor an asexual child can be maintained. If people fail to recognize this, they reject sexuality. They remain sexually frustrated for life and express their frustration by seeking on "moral" grounds to forbid sexually healthy persons all that they lack themselves.

The discovery that four-year-olds suffer more from bosom envy than from penis envy should not mislead us to the overreaction that in general there is nothing to penis envy. The opposite stares us in the face. Such as, for example, the experience that four-year-old girls in our society especially like to tell tales about the boys to their parents. That is without a doubt a kind of revenge for the discovery that nature gave boys something that it withheld from girls. The experience that girls learn to speak much, much earlier and in the fourth year can express themselves incomparably better than most boys their age can be understood as a compensation. Finally, girls' preference for clothing, jewelry, decoration, finery, ribbons, and flowers in their hair can be explained as compensation for the withheld penis—at least in our patriarchal social order. In many others it is the man who decorates himself. Perhaps such a love of decoration in men can then be explained as compensation for the inability to bear children and to breast-feed.

From our research practice we know many cases that, at least in our linguistic region, furnish clear indications of penis envy and castration complex. Thus a famous sculptor reported to us that one day his four-year-old daughter smashed or tried to smash with a hammer the sex parts of several male statues. A painter told us a comparable case of his four-year-old daughter, who crossed out the genitals of male nude-drawings with a black felt-tip pen.

In the individual sketches by children (we have collected about one thousand examples from kindergartens in the Federal Republic of Germany, Austria, and Switzerland), breasts and male genitals appear. Human and animal figures made with molding clay appear with oversized male sex parts. In contrast, female genitals never appear, even in the figures molded by girls, but on the other hand, there are often women with enormously large breasts.

It also came to our attention that during the fourth year, children discover a sudden interest in games such as blindman's buff, in which they pretend to be blind or physically disabled, and we suppose that these are attempts at overcoming the fear of castration. As so many children's games, they obviously function according to the model of preventive magic: "If I do something to myself, no one else can do it to me." That means the children prefer to "castrate" themselves instead of running the risk of being "castrated" by their parents. "Becoming blind," in the myths of almost all peoples, means becoming impotent. When Oedipus discovered he had married his own mother, he "castrated" himself: He gouged out his eyes with his mother's belt buckle.

We already mentioned in the previous chapter that in the third year many girls discover a peculiar form of mammary masturbation, a compulsive plucking around their nipples. Now, in the fourth year, a characteristic further development begins: The little girl develops an inexplicable fear of losing her nipples. Psychoanalysts have explained this as a regression to the infant's fear of the loss of the mother's nourishing, consoling breast. However, it still remains unclear why in the fourth year so many girls and almost no boys at this age regress to this aspect of the infancy phase. Psychoanalysts answer the question by seeing in the girls' fear of the loss of her nipples the female counterpart to that fear that is the trauma of boys of the same age: fear of castration.

There, too, one understands the fear that the father could actualize the mother's articulated threats: "Listen you! If you don't stop playing with your little thing there, Daddy is going to come with the scissors and cut it off!" Sex pedologists certainly believe that this threat must never be spoken, because children, with their inborn understanding of body language, can read the adults' horror in the presence of childhood masturbation in their facial expressions and in the gestures of their parents, even if they make the effort to hide it. The fact that in social orders in which no masturbation prohibition exists there also appears to be no existence of the fear of castration confirms this presumption.

On the other hand, there is obviously a sequence of separation fears, in which each new process reinforces the older ones—birth trauma (separation from the womb), weaning trauma (separation from the mother's breast), trauma of disassociation (separation from the mother), trauma of toilet training (separation from the products of one's own body), youth trauma (separation from childhood), independence trauma (separation from the parents' home), death trauma (separation from life). In this sequence of the fears of separation the fear of losing one's own erogenous zones is placed absolutely in the series as a link of the long chain, because with them one has undertaken something forbidden by the parents.

Human desire is based in great part on the conquest of aversion and the fear of separation. The greater the fear, the greater the desire. The sex act is filled with desire because it is a conquest of the fear of separation, an ending of separation by the pairing of two bodies. The primary human fear as such, then, is that of banishment from the paradise of the womb. Heterosexual men conquer the fear by returning to the womb of a substitute mother during sexual intercourse. Heterosexual women conquer the fear by receiving the man back in the womb of the substitute mother in each sexual intercourse. The fetuses' fear at birth is conquered step by step when the children seek to liberate themselves from it by active reenactment of the passively suffered situation of fear.

This attempt at overcoming fear by recapitulation or reenactment occurs in children's dreams as well as in their earliest games. They later dramatize in play not only the fear-inspiring experiences of the past but also those anticipated in the future. Only in this way do they succeed in overcoming the new dangers awaiting them without fear. Then, as soon as they discover that they develop the confidence to be able to master life, they feel a great sense of joy—the joy of conquering reality. From the fourth or fifth year on, the joy flows into genital desire and subordinates itself to it step by step from puberty on.

Although the psychoanalytical thesis that children in the fourth to fifth years assume there is only one sex, namely, the male, cannot be maintained for certain, many pedologists and sex scientists retain the concept of the "phallic phase," because in fact boys at this age develop a strong, quasi-phallic tendency to penetrate things, to bore through them, to take them apart to learn about the inside, while in girls at this age are frequently found dreams and fantasies about being bored through and penetrated, being taken apart and explored from the inside.

Freud brings these fantasies into connection with an age-specific misunderstanding of coitus: with the idea that behind the parents' locked bedroom door something powerful is occurring. The children hear moaning and panting, find bloody tampons in the toilet, have notions of the vulva as a wound, assume that at some time the father once cut off the mother's penis. So, thanks to the parents' dangerous secretiveness, it happens that the fears and aggressions of the anal-sadistic phase, which still have not been totally conquered, combine in the soul of the child with a false notion of the adults' sex life and allow the act of love to appear as an act of hatred. This wrong interpretation remains for life in many children, who have not been enlightened at the right time, and changes the hope of a happy love and married life into a lifelong fear of sex.

Sexual Pathology of the Fourth Year

The fourth year of life shows an increased incidence of skin irritations, nose and throat diseases, digestive disorders, stomach cramps, colic, constipation, diarrhea, encopresis, bedwetting, urethral, bladder, and kidney disorders. Besides this, we find loss of appetite, nausea, sickness, vomiting, speech disorders, and chronic, seemingly baseless lying (pseudology). With the exception of purely somatic illnesses, we have to distinguish among regressions of the fourth year to earlier developmental stages; actual neurotic disorders caused by incorrect parental conduct, disorders that were already acute during the fourth year; fixations in the fourth year that appear in year five or six; and later regressions from adolescence or adulthood to the oedipal aspects of the fourth year.

The regressions of the fourth year often reveal themselves as repressed fears of the responsibilities of the now maturing genitality. The skin irritations, allergic eruptions, and the variations of neuralgic skin hyperesthesia often appear as regressions to the cutane phase. Throat diseases, but also speech disorders, chronic lying, loss of appetite, nausea, sickness, vomiting, and stomach cramps—thus phenomena that have absolutely nothing to do with each other according to somatic diagnosis—find a peculiar common denominator in unresolved crises of the oral phase. Digestive disorders, colic, constipation, diarrhea, and encopresis stools often point to unresolved problems of the anal phase. "Nervous" disorders of the bladder, urethra, and of the kidneys (bladder neuralgia, urethral colic, urethral blockage, bedwetting) can often be treated by helping the children to become aware of the repressed urethral problems of the second and third years.

The diagnosis of regressions into bedwetting and uncontrolled stools make clear that children evacuate their urine and feces as a jealous protest against the parents' sexual behavior. The actual motive is certainly just as unknown to the children as it is understood by the parents, but the connection is clearly in evidence in thousands of cases. Children lose control of their stool exactly when the parents are having sexual intercourse. They wet their bed when parents refuse the love offerings of the children or make fun of them. In contrast, they stay clean as long as the parents devote themselves more to the children than to sexual intercourse. Even more than a half-century ago, Alice Balint reported about a small girl who wet herself every time her parents slept together, but when her mother was menstruating, when the parents were abstinent, always stayed clean. That means the girl rewarded parental sexual abstinence with her own abstinence and parental desire with her own desire.

At this example it bears repeating that parental behavior can lead to childhood behavioral disorders. But from that it cannot be inferred that the Oedipus complex arises only when parents behave wrongfully. Totally the opposite: In patriarchal social orders with small family structures, the Oedipus complex is an indispensable catalyst of childhood processes of maturity. So children who grow up in this society without parents or with only one parent have to muster incomparably much more energy for the stabilization of their egos than sons and daughters of stable small families.

But it should also not be said that the small family is the best of all constellations in which to raise children. Neither should it be asserted that patriarchy is the best of all social orders. Finally, it should in no way be maintained that adaptation is better than resistance. But it should be stated that resistance requires much more energy than adaptation. So among the mothers of democracy and the fathers of humanism who organized the resistance against the feudal order, we find strong people who have a stabilizing childhood behind them, rather than weak or already-damaged-in-childhood individuals. The damaged ones, too, are certainly capable of resistance, but their opposition expresses itself in neuroses, psychoses, or delinquency, while children of stable marriages raised with love find the courage for protest and political resistance earlier.

The choice of the way into adult society is in practice determined less by consciousness and will power than by the ability to love and the disposition of the available parent or the available attendant. If children receive tender affection they will try to compensate for the absent parent by devoting themselves as adults to the creation of a better social order. If they receive rejection, emotional coldness, hostility toward the body, and punishment, we should not complain if they devote their life to destroying the society represented by their parents.

If during the oedipal phase the boy's father or another male attendant is absent, that can lead to psychosexual feminization, just as the absence of the mother or another female attendant can contribute to the psychical masculinization of the daughter. Since children at this age not only desire and need the parent of the opposite sex but also persecute the same-sex parent with jealous hatred, the death of the same-sex parent during the oedipal phase often produces strong guilt feelings. If the opposite-sex parent dies, the opposite occurs: children will idealize that parent in the hereafter just as excessively as one feels excessively responsible for the death of the same-sex parent.

> The details of such an idealization depend on when and how children discovered the death of the parent. Three effects appear especially significant. First, an increased attachment to the remaining parent; the type of attachment is determined by the affection of the respective parent for the child and is usually ambivalent. Second, a frequent and intensive association between the notions of sexuality and death, whereby both are for them connected as a matter of "adults' secrets." An intense fear of sex can result from it, one that traces back to the idea that sexual gratification can cause death. Or children can develop from it a masochistic inclination, as a result of which death (the union with the dead parent) becomes a sexual goal. Third, those who grieve regress to the oral stage; if this occurs in early childhood it brings with it a lasting effect on the structure of the oedipal complex and on the character; the oedipal love as well as all later object relationships then become mixed with identifications. What is mentioned in the second and third effects is also true in connection with the early experience of the death of a sibling. (Fenichel)

Since children are condemned to lose the battle with the same-sex parent for the favors of the opposite-sex parent, they can, if they regress to this situation in adulthood, react in two different ways: Either they accept defeat and from the beginning forego any competition for the favors of the chosen sex partner, or they elevate jealousy to an actually stimulating practice of sexuality. Adults fixated in oedipal rivalry are motivated neither by love nor by the desire for reciprocal love, but rather require only that the sex partner make them jealous. If no rivals make the effort to win the favors of the partner, they are totally disinterested in the entire matter. Their interest in the sex partner blossoms again only when someone becomes interested in "their" partner or partners. In such cases, therefore, jealousy is no product of love, but rather love a product of jealousy.

Conflicts between parents are especially dangerous in the oedipal age of the children, whenever (such as in divorce) the children themselves are the object of the altercation or are asked to take the side of one parent against the other. In such cases the oedipal situation is heated up and the narcissistic illusion is given to the children that their later sex partner might at least strive for their favor with the same intensity as their parents once did.

Much more dangerous at this age is a climate of tender spoiling of the boy by the mother or of the girl by the father that all too easily suddenly changes into scolding or punishment whenever the parents do not encounter sufficient reciprocal love from their children. In such families it is not the children who are acting out their oedipal tendencies, but rather the parents who strive for the favors of the children and become jealous of each other when the children show too much favoritism to the other parent (or the other parent to the children). Such parents tend to punish especially quickly, often by bodily thrashing, because they unconsciously expect that the children behave like an adult love partner—faithfully, loyally, and especially tenderly.

However, since children at this age are not at all capable of such behavior, they disappoint their parents again and again, no matter how well the relationship between the adults and the children might be in every other respect. As soon as the children do anything at all that contradicts the father's image of a miniature beloved or the mother's of a miniature lover, such parents exhibit fully irrational attacks of rage, overwhelming the children with reproaches or even striking them—often on their naked behind. The result is the unconscious breeding of a masochistic tendency in the children.

The law of the conversion of passive behavior into active brings about the humiliations borne by the battered children being promptly passed on from generation to generation. As adults, such children not only defend the humiliating behavior of their parents, but also do this with especial emotion: "A sound thrashing never hurt anybody. I was beaten and nevertheless I am a decent person!" This all-too-often heard statement reveals that such people consider only physically punished people as "respectable" and therefore encounter those not physically punished with fear, mistrust, and aggression.

The less parents sexually gratify each other, the greater the danger they will sexually seduce their children. Since this seduction is mostly not openly genital, and since the parents are mostly not aware of their own role as seducer, they deny the claim of incestuous tendencies with especial vehemence. And since in such families no coitus actually takes place between parents and children, in such a situation the parents always feel wrongfully accused by pedologists and sex scientists. But the children, who still cannot at all think in terms of genital intercourse but who nevertheless are already in possession of intense genital stimuli, feel the parental devotion otherwise than the parents "meant"— namely, as solicitation. Then, when the parents for their part notice what is happening in the children, and, filled with horror, react with sudden aversion and intentionally hurtful behavior, children become totally uncertain and no longer at all understand what the parents really want of them.

Since at this age we find a remarkable fusion of childish parental love and genital self-gratification, each regression out of adulthood into the first genital stage of the fourth to fifth years creates a peculiar ambivalent conduct toward the adult sex partner. The sexuality of the adult regressed to the oedipal situation divides into object love and self-love. But, since the object love of such people has remained infantile, the relationship to the sex partner also remains infantile: The partner is not treated as an adult sex partner, but rather as a substitute for the father or the mother—perhaps with respect or attention, but perhaps also with fear—at any rate without mature genital love. The sexual gift remains reserved for their own body, which is now regarded and treated as if it were the body of the other person.

So, the problem of masturbation during the oedipal phase does not lie in the masturbation as such, but rather in the danger of later regressions to secondary narcissism. This danger is all the greater the more closely the parental prohibition of masturbation is linked to the fear of castration. During the oedipal period, many boys begin to fear their penis is at the wrong angle to the abdomen. They believe it should be exactly at a right angle to the abdominal wall and think they are ill when it points upward. This especially affects those boys who imagine they have damaged their penis by forbidden masturbation.

We have already indicated again and again how dangerously parental threat of punishment can affect the highly emotionally and highly ambivalent masturbation fantasies of this phase. We should also point out something here that normally remains unmentioned in the discussion of our theme, namely, the tendency of many adults to threaten each other in jest with castration: "If you don't stop harassing me, I'll kick you in your balls!" Or: "If you keep that up, I'll cut your cock off!" In spite of their "humorous" masks, such threats are always expressions of one's own fears of castration. To put fear into others or to make fun of the fears of others is a long-established method of warding off one's own fears. By projecting them onto others one liberates oneself from them. But children hear such remarks, relate them to themselves, and have a panic attack, for their fear of castration is the predominant fear at this age and influences everything heard, seen, and experienced.

Fear of castration in four-year-olds often causes serious sleeping disorders, because they are afraid of being castrated in sleep, when they are helpless; indeed, many children feel that sleep itself is castration and therefore fear it. Sometimes the fear of castration also displaces itself in the notion of being ill. One can understand accompanying symptoms such as fever in such cases as an expression of sexual excitement. Such children are not "displacing" themselves, also, they are not "playing" sick; they *are* ill, although it is not viruses or bacteria but inner conflicts that have made them ill.

Children who experience a conflict between oedipal desires and fear of castration regress mostly to the anal-sadistic phase. This is the constellation out of which compulsive neurosis can develop in later life.

If parents feel their son is not "masculine" enough or their daughter insufficiently "feminine," children always notice that, no matter if parents put it into words or not, and perceive it as a kind of castration. Also if parents make it clear to their children at this age that they consider them less clever, less honest, or less loyal than other children, this symbolic castration often results in automatic behavior of the children: They take refuge in compulsive masturbation, bedwetting, uncontrolled stool, excessive gluttony, or total refusal of food.

Different children react to other forms of parental castrative behavior with different means. Introverted children develop excessive distrust and withdraw from adults as well as from children. Extroverted children begin to lie, boast, or steal. Others suddenly develop a deterioration of their motility, an awkwardness unknown until then. Everything they hold falls apart. They fall down, hurt themselves, burn themselves, cut their fingers. All these are forms of self-castration by which the children will anticipate parental castration or loyally carry it out.

The later effects are serious. If a mother cuts off her daughter's self-confidence in this developmental phase by forbidding her to dress and to act as other girls do, a vaginal castration complex can develop in the daughter. If the mother intentionally seeks to frustrate her daughter, which occurs to frustrated mothers all too often, by representing all of woman's life as a series of torments—marriage as a fall-and-tumble and love as inevitable disappointment—then fear-instilled fantasies often arise in the four-year-old daughter based on the age-specific guilt feelings toward the mother: An animal wants to swallow her up, a knife is going to be stuck into her body, her stomach is going to explode. In the dreams of such girls there appear punched-out teeth, gaps between the teeth, fallen-out hair, a bald head, and similar dream symbols of castration.

It makes no difference whether the mother has good reasons (for example, justifiable criticism of the patriarchy) or bad ones (for example, unjustifiable criticism of her husband). In using her daughter as the garbage can for her anger the psychosexual effects are always the same: The fear of castration is carried over from the subject to the object. The mother's passive fear of castration changes into the active castration behavior of the daughter. Penis envy becomes penis hatred.

An American investigation into the sex life of female striptease dancers and peep show girls convincingly reveals that for all of those who did not practice their occupation for economical reasons, but rather out of interest, a strong fixation in the castrating aspects of the oedipal phase existed. All suffered under the delusion of having been "castrated" in the fourth year. Yet in contrast to men, who have foundered on the castration complex and, by means of that psychical form of exhibitionism we call Don Juanism, must again and again give proof of their perfect masculinity, in these women the need to prove to themselves that they are perfect women took on the form of a legitimized physical exhibitionism.

The social phenomenon of penis envy that Freud tried to base on biology is, therefore, no characteristic of the human species, but rather only one of the patriarchal social order. Since such societies always consider women inferior and furnish fewer rights to daughters than to sons, both receive a patriarchal image of their own body. Boys, to whom it is suggested by both fathers and mothers that they belong to the dominant, "strong" sex, reduce it unquestioningly to physical power. Girls, who from earliest childhood have learned to consider themselves members of the weak, dominated sex, also promptly feel their body as inferior and envy the genitals of the other sex as symbols of its power. One of the catastrophic effects of the limited patriarchal interpretation of human sexuality is the difficulty many women of our social order have in reaching genital gratification ever in life. Those who have already in childhood learned to categorize their own genitals as inferior will later also categorize as inferior their own ability to have orgasm.

Many women rescue themselves from frigidity in motherhood. This works especially well when the child is male. Because she then compensates her penis envy by assigning herself a penis in the form of her son. That is not at all good for the son, because sooner or later he will discover that he is loved not for himself but only as a penis substitute.

A later result of parental castrating behavior in the children's oedipal phase is a castrating behavior of the boy or girl who has matured to adulthood. The unresolved castration conflict in this case causes a kind of time-bomb effect and transfers the whole unresolved problem from the father to the beloved man and from the mother to the beloved woman. In order not to be castrated by the father, the daughter castrates her husband. In order not to be castrated by the mother, the son castrates his wife. Such marital relationships only appear to be based on personal affection, but in truth are parental relationships transferred to the spouse.

In the Western industrialized society of our days this

kind of syndrome appears so frequently that we have to ask ourselves if we should still understand it at all as a result of an abnormal castrating behavior of the parents or whether it is not a phenomenon specific to society. In the second case a collective failure of the castration complex would be present, and not the individual parent but rather the structure of the patriarchy would be responsible.

8

Fifth Year
End of the Toddler's Puberty

The fifth year is one of great stress. So it is also called the *third stress phase of childhood* by adherents of the stress theory, and *toddler's puberty crisis* by those theoreticians of crisis. In a somatic sense it is the *year of the first change of shape, of the first bodily stretching*, of the accelerated growth in height. The arms and legs grow more quickly than the torso. Toward the end of the fifth year, leg length represents 44 percent of total height. Children are "nicer," according to the aesthetic standards of our society. The soft and roundly shaped contours of the toddlers change in the direction of a simple, muscular profile. Their posture improves, the shoulders broaden, the neck elongates, the head becomes more graceful, the stomach disappears, the waist forms, the cylindrical children's torso loses fat from front and back and begins to narrow from below. The last milk teeth fall out; the first molars break through.

At the beginning of the year the girl is approximately 103 cm (3.37 ft) tall, the boy 104 cm (3.41 ft). A half-year later the girl has become 3 cm (1.18 in) taller, the boy 4 cm (1.57 in). At the end of the year both are 111 cm (3.64 ft) tall. The period of the more accelerated physical growth of the woman has begun. That also precipitates as weight. Toward the beginning of the year the girl weighed 16.6 kg (36.59 lb), the boy 16.8 kg (37.03 lb). Toward mid-year she has gained .6 kg (1.32 lb), he 1.2 kg (2.64 lb). But toward the end of the year the boy weighs just .1 kg (3.52 oz) more than the girl, and in the next year she overtakes him.

The nimbleness of both sexes increases. But motility is also misused. In boys a severe motor unrest develops. His body language becomes hectic. He begins to make faces.

The girl develops an increased need for love, an enormously intensified instability. Inside of minutes, many vacillate back and forth between euphoria and thoughts of suicide, between a mania for cleanliness to a scorn of clothing, between participation and disinterest, between giggling and crying.

In boys, the tendency toward pseudology increases. They lie without gaining anything by it. Many begin to steal in the same irrational way. Many run away from home and develop great shrewdness in evading the police. Happiness and sadness, offenses and feelings of being offended alternate so quickly that most parents can no longer keep up with them. On the one side children demand praise and recognition from their parents, on the other they call the parents incompetent and dictatorial. Inside of a few seconds obstinacy can turn into tears. So, on the one hand, children begin to judge their own behavior. They develop their own standards. On the other hand, their self-confidence fades. They develop doubt and self-doubt. On the one hand, the relationship to the social surroundings matures, on the other, the ability to learn slackens, especially in boys.

On the one hand, children become aware of their feelings, especially of self-confidence, on the other hand, however, the world image also becomes subjective and thereby the unrest and excitability grows. Children oscillate between yearning for independence and the awareness of their dependence on their parents, between pride in newly acquired abilities and disillusion by their own inadequacy, between the discovery of a new maturity and regressions into infantilism. That also shows up in the games of five-year-olds, where aggressive demands of leadership and unconditional submissiveness can be observed inside of a few minutes in the same children.

On the one hand, the awareness of physical identity grows, on the other hand, however, that, too, of physical vulnerability. It appears as if the growing awareness of one's own limbs does not lead to a greater self-assurance, but rather to a desperate battle for maintaining physical integrity. Children begin to recognize dangers everywhere, ones they had known nothing about until now: accidents, operations, wars, crime, hostage taking, murder.

The talkativeness and boasting of boys suddenly stops. They become silent and act uncommunicative, often plainly rejecting. Bombast, showing off, and talebearing are as if wiped away.

The tension between children and adults increases dramatically, especially between daughters and mothers, between sons and fathers. On the other hand, the relationships between sons and mothers and between daughters and fathers sometimes assume something plainly and alarmingly adult, coquettish, and seductive. Children want to be loved—and certainly not as up to now, in a sublimated form, but rather as mature, genital individuals with obvious sexual needs.

If parents are not prepared to acknowledge this progress, children use physical force: This is the first year in which children strike back when they are hit, and often try to hit the parents even without having been hit. The American child psychologists L. J. Stone and J. Church, in the German translation of the book *Childhood and Adolescence* (Kindheit und Jugend), say about the five-year-olds, "If their psychical strength were as strong as their feelings, a preschooler in a fit of anger would think nothing about killing."

Simultaneously the need for skin contact and tenderness grows not only in girls but also in boys. The age-specific sex games now turn from the phase of the exploration of the anatomy and assume the character of genuine sexual behavior. In the fifth year it still happens that boys take the initiative and court the girl, but the page turns: Nowadays you more often notice that girls court the boys, embrace, caress, kiss, hold, and undress them.

When boys are among themselves they behave noticeably differently than in the company of girls. You frequently see competitive pissing: who can go farthest, who can go highest? Sadistic traits are evident in boys' games. Every oblong object becomes a weapon during play. Conversation is bloodthirsty; mutual threats are murderous. Toys are destroyed, animals are tormented; there is a lot of fighting and playing with fire. Sexual play with domestic animals is also not rare. Boys try to masturbate male dogs and cats, stick their member between the female cats' and dogs' legs, try to penetrate and in so doing sometimes get into the animals' anuses. Whenever boys at this age come home with wounds such as bites and scratches, that is often the result of failed attempts at coitus with domestic animals.

The first homoerotic attempts in both sexes occur in the fifth year. Masturbation sometimes assumes a desperate rather than joyful character. Imagined pictures of the parents serve as masturbatory subjects, "giant photographs" of the body parts of parents, often linked with blood, wounds, infliction of pain, and anal representations. The parents' genitals play a role at the same time, but not a main role.

Girls' mental images of the form of male genitals are much more precise than the boys' of the female. In the girls' eyes the penis may be not only desirable but also be dangerous; however, it is not mysterious. The womb, in contrast, is a mystery not only to boys, but also to girls. It even remains hidden when the girl looks at herself naked. This causes a different behavior of the five-year-old boy and girl toward their own sex parts, and also a different one toward the other sex. Both fear the foreignness of the other, but in the case of boys the deeper fear of the unfathomable and hidden joins the fear of the difference of the girl. One of the possible causes of certain forms of homosexuality (there is not only one homosexuality but many, each with its own history of origin) is the flight from the unknown and the turning to the known, to that which one is oneself and has oneself.

So, childhood sexual discovery in the fifth year no longer concerns itself with fundamental questions, but rather with details: "When girls go pee, where does it come out of?" "Why do you have balls down there?" "When the baby comes out of there, does it hurt?" "How often do you do that, every night?" Both sexes now know the father's role in procreation; and both also know that one day they themselves will become mothers and fathers. That brings the parents closer, but also causes increased sexual tension, because the children now consider themselves equal to the parents and therefore can imagine themselves engaging in thoroughly normal sexual intercourse with the parents.

We can quite clearly see that many boys at this age get erections when they see their parents being amorous toward each other. The changing expression on the face of the small girl indicates to any trained eye that at the sight of sexual behavior of adults, but especially when parents are smooching, she becomes greatly excited. On the other hand, the girl's position at this age is more difficult, because both sexes have not yet totally separated from the mother as most important attendant. For boys, the step from childhood, pregenital mother love to investing the mother with libido is relatively easy. For girls, however, the elevation of the father from a secondary figure to a primary one as well as the reduction of the mother from the beloved, nourishing, consoling central figure to female rival for the father's attention is extremely difficult. So, in the fifth year, daughters develop an oscillation, with which parents can hardly sympathize, between mother love and mother hatred. These feelings sometimes even show themselves simultaneously.

A second ambivalence appearing in this year, and certainly in the behavior of both sexes toward the parents, is a homoerotic one. Sons sexually court not only their mother, but also often act like girls toward their father. Girls simultaneously court not only their father, but from time to time act like boys toward their mother. We call this characteristic children's behavior the *negative Oedipus complex.*

All this childhood ambivalence and turbulence cause great difficulties, even for parents filled with good will and understanding. The difficulties of this age mostly get to be too much for those other parents—and unfortunately in our social order that is the majority—who have never in totality come to terms with their own sexuality. They refuse to acknowledge the children's difficulties, because such knowledge would force them to a confrontation with their own carefully repressed childhood sexual problems. For parents who have imagined throughout their entire adult life that they never had any such problems in their own childhood, that would be an unbearable glimpse into the mirror of truth. Such parents candidly carry out foolhardy feats of self-deception when their children enter the oedipal phase and thereby announce unmistakable sexual tendencies toward one of the two parents and obvious feelings of rivalry, jealousy, and murderous desire toward the other.

Every father has heard from his small daughter the statement: "When Mommy dies, I'll marry you, Daddy," and every mother has become aware of her small son's intention: "Mommy, when Daddy is dead, you should be my wife." The fact that parents so systematically attempt to ignore the causes of this exhibition of will of their children and instead assert that they should be laughed at as examples of children's simplicity, says more about the simplicity of the respective parents than about the children.

Even when the boy says to his mother: "I hope Father

finally dies so that I can marry you," she does not believe he means what he says. The daily attacks boys execute against their father, often of the physical kind, and sometimes also those of the girls against their mother, are dismissed as clumsiness, childish defiance, or excusable blunder. At no other time are parents prepared to overlook so much and to forgive so much only in order to shrink away themselves from recognition of the truth staring them in the eyes.

Professional literature of the more than one thousand children's dreams of this age teaches something more important. What is coming together there from the incestuous longings and bloody vengeful desires goes beyond what adult perpetrators of incest and jealous murder actually do. Here, too, is verified the recognition that the son is the father of the man and the daughter the mother of the woman. Everything that we do as adults or let be done to us is either the result of what we did or let be done to us as children or our later counterreaction to it.

Many adults fall into a panic when they can no longer close their eyes and ears to the realization that they are desired as sex partners by their children not only figuratively and symbolically, but rather carnally and concretely. But this desire is indispensable for the children's later sexual development. The later effects of *not* having desires for an adult (or even a contemporary) sex partner in the fifth year are much more serious than those of existing desires. For when boys do not desire the body of the mother or another female at this age then in adulthood, too, they will develop no mature sexuality, but rather will experience their maleness as a burden. Exactly the same thing goes for the femaleness of small girls: If in the oedipal age they find no person whom they can invest with age-specific genital libido, the probability is that in adulthood they will be ashamed of their female body and will never struggle through to a mature sexuality.

On the other hand, toward the end of the fifth year the

Oedipus complex has to be conquered voluntarily and independently by the children, because otherwise here, too, severe disorders appear. The conquest of the male Oedipus complex lies in the boys' not only giving up their battle with their father for the affection of their mother, but also of their being aware that it is unreal, and not only seeing through their fixation on their mother as imaginary, but also drawing back their genital libido bound to their mother and turning it to another object. Both are easy when the boys learn to identify more with their father than to rival him, and that, likewise, occurs only when the rivalry is not suppressed, but rather is openly carried out on the level of the battle between the generations.

The mother has to help with it. She cannot persuade the boys to give up the battle against the father, but rather in this battle she must clearly declare support for the father. If the boys say: "Mommy, if Daddy doesn't come back from the trip, I'll marry you," the mother should reply: "But that won't do, my dear young man, because I'm already married to Daddy. Yes, seek your own wife." Since the age-specific behavior of the son toward his mother is certainly libidinous in content, but playful in form, such an answer is never offensive. To the contrary, the form calls on the independence and initiative of the children, and so flatters them.

But often the problem is still not resolved just like that, because the negative Oedipus complex is often more persistent than the positive: Even if boys free themselves from their mother at the correct time, accept the incest tabu and the reality principle, they sometimes still continue to keep their "men's friendship" for their father. And since our social order not only accepts it in opposition to the incest, but also considers it as something positive, the results are especially tenacious. In the case of these dangers it is in no way a question of homosexuality, but rather of the enormous fears of castration that can cause this postoedipal relationship with the father.

The renunciation of the active strong desire (conquest of the mother) must proceed with the renunciation of the passive strong desire (to be conquered by the father). If the boy succeeds in a stage-by-stage decrease of interest in the parents and a gradual turning to his own contemporaries, he then leaves the parents to their own bedroom and begins to build his own house. That means he designs plans for his future and prepares himself for it in play with his girl- and boyfriends.

Under such conditions, that age-specific period of indifference toward sexual matters that we call the *latent phase* develops totally by itself. It cannot be induced prematurely with any parental persuasion or violent means. To the contrary, the greater the parental pressure, the later the introduction into this period of relative asexuality. If parents do not try to accelerate this process, the boy stops masturbation totally by himself. Childhood sexual investigation abates. When the boy now hears other boys talking about sexual questions, he may join in, but he now does so without guilt feelings.

The girls' Oedipus complex runs its course less dramatically and disappears partly even before the end of the fifth year. They resign from rivalry with the mother, without surrendering the oedipal tendencies toward the father. The authority that helps both sexes to conquer this difficult process is the *conscience*, which forms at the end of the fifth year with unheard-of force.

But what is conscience? It is the internalized authority of the parents. No matter how liberal, how noble, how "anti-authoritarian" the parents might be, conscience always filters those aspects of parental authority out of the total image, from which the simple fact arises that they are the older ones and possess the power. More strongly than the strongest parents themselves ever had done it, conscience now suppresses the sexualization of the opposite-sex parent and the jealousy of the same-sex parent.

However, the love that until now was directed to the opposite-sex parent is not destroyed, but only changed, and certainly into two different forms of libido—one into loving identification with the same-sex parent, into the cementing with the model, the other into tender, no-longer-genital union with the opposite-sex parent.

So, the conscience takes possession of the inheritance of the parents not only as a result of threats and punishments, but also because up until now the parents as protecting force had given a certain measure of security to their children. If this security is lacking, no human conscience can develop. So, children also at first have more difficulties with the internalized voice of their parents than with the parents themselves. Because, the child could shirk the parents' *command*. The child could feign obedience and then do the opposite in secret. But before the voice of one's own conscience there is only a limited possibility of deception. At the same time, the change from obedience to conscience is a prerequisite for the liberation from parental authority. The children's self-reliance is now no longer conditioned by the parents' agreement or refusal, but rather by the children's own conviction to do what is right or wrong. Obeying the demands of conscience provides not only relief but also certain feelings of joy similar to those that the children had experienced in their earlier years through the external supply of love.

On the other hand, the problems mentioned above, can cause themselves. If children refuse to follow the dictates of their new conscience, they crumble into guilt feelings themselves. And these guilt feelings again call to mind the fears of those years in memory in which they were afraid of no longer being loved by their parents. From now on children have to decide according to their own standards which sexual appetites should be gratified and which should be suppressed. The simple decision of earlier years, that one did what was allowed and avoided what was forbidden, is now past. Because now everything has become complicated by guilt feelings. Beside the respect for possibly punishing reality, the ego now has to judge itself according to a contradictory and irrational representative of reality.

So conscience is based on the fact that it has arisen through incorporation with one part of the external world. But the children's ego, too, arose in this way, so you could say conscience actually is a second ego or *superego*. Since the superego forms much later than the ego, it remains more closely bound to the external world and often judges more according to what others may say and think than according to what one thinks oneself.

But in a peculiar way conscience is not only tied to the external world, but also to the unconscious regions of the inner world, because the mental powers with whose help children internalized the parents' commands originate in the deepest layers of the archaic needs of humans, and children are fully unconscious of them. This origin in the gloomiest regions of sentient life explains the urgent, irrational character of many desires of the conscience, which are overcome only in very healthy children by the rational judgment of their intellect. So, on the one side, the sternness of conscience agrees with the parental strictness experienced before. But on the other side, based on the close relationship between conscience and archaic needs, it also depends on the children's sentient constitution. Children who are unaware that they hate their parents also unconsciously fear reprisal and so, without ever being aware of the whole process, experience their conscience as hounding them with fear. The greater the children's fear of their parents, the "stricter"—and therefore more irrational—the conscience is. But also the opposite: The better the children's relationship with their parents, the more trustworthy and more rational their conscience is, too. The more loving the relationship, the easier the success of the conscience in its task to sublimate genital libido.

With the successful resolution of the oedipal conflict

children have legitimated themselves as members of their own sex and their own generation. With that they have acquired clear ego boundaries for themselves and extensively solved their narcissistic problems. So many developmental psychologists designate the fifth year as the *year of character building.*

Why do most adults remember these processes so poorly or even not at all? Because conscience is not only the internalization of parental authority, but also contains the predominant views of the social order to which the children belong. This process of internalization of prevailing opinions, rules, and laws is so subtle that we are never aware of it. We categorically swear that these are our own independently won opinions, ones no one forced us to have. That is true. And so they sit so deeply that our intellect can no longer argue with them. Had these opinions been forced on us, that would have mobilized all our defiance. But since we have "voluntarily" and unconsciously submitted to the ruling opinions, they govern us in a thoroughly irresistible way. And since children's sexuality in our social order is forbidden, we make tabus with the help of this conscientious inhibition: Hardly one of our contemporaries can reliably remember the details of life occurring before the sixth year of life. Whenever they think they have memories, under examination they always appear as *false* memories. That means they *conceal* the actual occurrences for good, yet unconscious, reasons and substitute them for false memories that better suit their self-image. But just because the actual facts are only *suppressed* and not *forgotten,* all persons can have themselves tested by being able to consult with a trained physician in this field under hypnosis and to record the individual answers on a tape recorder. They would be impressed to discover how much their memory of these years had been censored by their conscience and what a hothouse of rampant childhood sexual desires and sexual fears they would encounter there.

The reason for the suppression is, as we have seen, the tabu against the sexual in our culture. But the suppression is so strong that in most people in our Western world everything nonsexual that occurred before the sixth year also is repressed along with it. We call this process *infantile amnesia.*

Even without hypnosis we can recognize the working of these processes in the adults' individual-specific sexual fears. If adults feel any kind of human sexual inclination or sexual behavior as especially disgusting, diagnostically that means they imagined this tendency or activity with especial passion in their oedipal masturbation fantasies.

Sexual Pathology of the Fifth Year

The fifth year of life shows an increased susceptibility to sleeping disorders, bedwetting, uncontrolled stools, fire igniting, destruction of toys and animals (insects, frogs, earthworms, snails). Speech disorders, muteness, and screaming fits are not rare. Preanancastic ways of behavior (compulsive counting of stairs, pavement stones, cars, etc.), fear syndrome (which can lead to endogenous psychoses), psychogenic physical disorders, neuropathy, exogenous psychosyndrome, depressive symptoms, hebephrenic psychoses, but especially that "schizophrenia" symptom that was once called "adolescent madness" (dementia praecox)—fearfully distorted self-image; obsessions of "dirtiness," of being unwanted, of vulnerability; and a frenzied turning against the external world —all these belong to the behavioral disorders and neuroses.

Many of these disorders are genetically parentogenic, i.e., they originate in the *genes* inherited from the parents. Others, about which we have yet to discuss, are secondary parentogenic, i.e., they have been created by the parents' or caregivers' *behavior.* To this second block belong certain vision defects and paralyses, which were probably caused by the parental prohibition of childhood sexual investigation.

If in the fifth year the children's age-specific curiosity is not only obstructed by parents or educational authorities, but also laden with strong guilt feelings, sooner or later vision defects can appear. We also know that sudden fright paralyzes. Likewise, the sight of forbidden scenes can paralyze. The biblical legend of Lot's wife, who turned around to see the forbidden and promptly hardened into a pillar of salt (Genesis 19:26), is thoroughly convincing medically. One should consider that not the sight of Sodom and Gomorrah, but rather her own conscience caused the paralysis.

It is likewise with the effects of parental prohibition of masturbation. Certainly it does sometimes strike parents that their children, who up until then were happy and talkative, now act taciturn, uncommunicative, and fearful. But parents mostly do not know *why,* and, even when pedologists explain it to them, the parents cannot imagine what that could have to do with the prohibition of masturbation (often not even explicitly expressed by them). In disbelief and in no way convinced, they then sometimes ask whether "this terrible thing" could really make so much fun for the small children after all, that renunciation of it could ruin them completely. The answer is that the problem lies on a different level. Children have just begun to discover themselves with the help of their genitals. They love them because they give them great joy and because the joy is the first proof that they are self-reliant and no longer need the parents for the gratification of their needs. Now they suddenly hear that that which gave them so much joy and pride is "bad" for incomprehensible reasons. With that, their whole, new, carefully developed world image collapses. For some time they no longer understand anything at all, and consider their parents or teachers as bad people who want to hurt them and who can no longer be trusted.

You cannot explain to parents clearly enough that it is not the touching of the genitals which releases joyful mental images in children in this phase, but rather that it is for the most part delightful (but also by this time already suppressed) sexual fantasies that make difficulties for children from the fifth year on, and certainly only *after* the parents or teachers have made it comprehensible to the children that what up until then gave them unlimited joy and great strength of ego is forbidden. Paradoxically, the only possibility of consoling themselves for these new guilt feelings is masturbation.

The naivete of most parents, then, lies in that they see the actual problem in masturbation and not in the desires and fears behind it. Shortsightedness of this kind prevents the understanding that it is the masturbation prohibition that leads to the sexualization of the process. For when parents forbid children to discharge repressive guilt feelings through physical disposal of emotion, children become ill. If they should remain healthy, parents have to accept that masturbation in the fifth year is necessary to help children conquer the difficult problems of the oedipal phase. Sometimes only self-consolation prevents such children from total self-surrender. Self-consolation alone guarantees for them the love of their own body in a time of need and with it the necessary measure of self-esteem.

One of the dangers of oedipal masturbation in girls is the fixation on purely clitoral stimulation. That can lead to frigidity in coitus in adulthood, because on the inside the vagina has no nerve receptors and so can bring about only one sense of the (pleasant or unpleasant) intensity. If girls become accustomed to exclusive clitoral masturbation, they reduce the probability of ever in their life being able to reach orgasm by heterosexual sexual intercourse. So, they later have to be stimulated clitorally by the male or female sex partner, or stay directed to self-gratification their whole life long.

The French child analyst Françoise Dolto says this about childhood masturbation: "The moments in which children indulge in masturbation are in part such in which they are bored, i.e., have nothing else or nothing just as tempting to do . . . but especially whenever they find themselves in a state of physiological excitement (erection of the member, tension of the clitoris). That means that in normal, healthy children masturbation will hardly become public, also not frequent, and that adults should not take any interest in it whatsoever." When adults condemn their children's masturbation, that says something rather more damning about their own sex life than about the children's.

But if any five-year-old children masturbate provocatively in the presence of adults, it is not a matter of normal gratification, but rather of a neurotic reaction to their parents' conduct. It does not reveal licentiousness, but rather fear, a need to punish, and the failure of an emotional bonding to the attendant. Because of lack of care from the mother, father, or caregiver, children compulsively turn to their own body and thereby want to express unconsciously: "If you don't take care of me, I'll have to take care of myself." So, in the oedipal phase the course is set not only into the genital phase but also into neurosis. If the primacy of genitality does not succeed in developing itself, to substitute the oedipal tendencies toward the parents through tendencies toward contemporary partners, the way to neurosis is prescribed. The worst thing that parents could do in this phase is to forbid the children their age-specific sex games.

We already mentioned that the transfer from the parental to contemporary love partner is more difficult for girls than for boys, because girls have the dual task of switching from their first love partner, the mother, to a person of the opposite sex, to the father, and then from a very much older lover to a contemporary one. In addition, the difficulty arises that in the preceding years the five-year-old "woman" still experienced the father as rival for the mother's favors. Now girls have to learn to consider the mother as rival for the father's favors. Both parents have to help them with it. That is difficult for the mother because, in spite of the age difference, she is aware that this is a rival to be taken seriously. And it is difficult for the father because, in spite of the age difference, he is still aware that this is an incestuous situation in the offing and not to be taken lightly.

A regressive aspect of the oedipal wish of five-year-old girls—to sleep with Daddy—is the fear of laceration of inner organs. In adulthood that leads to pleasurable fantasies of the fear of being raped by strange men, but on the other hand, also to frigidity in intercourse with one's own sex partner, because his penis is always felt to be too small in comparison with that of the father. Very similar are the regressions of five-year-old boys, who can never conquer the oedipal competition with the father and so their whole life long suffer under the illusion that their penis is smaller than that of the father, thus too small.

In opposition to Freud's very complicated interpretation of female Oedipus complexes deviating totally from that of the male, today it seems probable that the conquest of the oedipal situation, whenever it succeeds at any time at all, is similar for both sexes. It depends on whether the children break the libidinous tie to the opposite-sex parent and can overcome the jealousy toward the same-sex one. If they suppress their incestuous impulses instead of sublimating them, they remain suspended in the oedipal stage their whole life long and will never be able to love another person. Moreover, this also leads for the most part to a conscience that develops only weakly yet still rigidly and so is as infrequently in the position to catch hold of the libidinous impulses as the aggressive ones. As a result the guilt feelings grow without mitigating the libidinous pressure.

As we have seen, the establishment of the conscience puts an end to the efforts of the Oedipus complex and ushers in the latent period. But in this sense the ego is the successor to the Oedipus complex. If the conscience is developed not at the right time or insufficiently, children will not be done with the Oedipus complex and in addition will tend to de-

velop neuroses. This tendency is reinforced by the narcissistic mortification caused by the children's discovery that
other children are finished with the age-specific frustrations,
while they themselves founder on the unresolved parental
bond. This injury to self-esteem forms one of the sources
of later neurotic inferiority complexes.

In such manner it is explained that the Oedipus complex
is simultaneously the normal high point of childhood sexual
development and the junction of later neuroses. If it appears
at the right time and if it is overcome at the right time,
development proceeds normally and healthily. If it does not
appear or come too early or too late, or if it disappears too
early, too late, or not at all, the development proceeds abnormally and leads to neurosis. So the neurotic disposition
is in no way caused by the Oedipus complex, but only by
the inability to start it at the right time and to conquer it
at the right time.

An initial problem in the conquest, and the nearly simultaneously occurring formation of the conscience, is the fact
that children at this age still do not understand the motives
of the parental prohibition and so internalize only its effects
(for example, pain). So children think that in order to be
considered an "adult" they must cause other children pain.
Result: Children who have never been beaten by their parents
thrash their dolls with murderous cruelty. Children who only
rarely have been forbidden anything behave like despots
toward their younger siblings. Children who were never
threatened with the loss of love threaten other children with
never again in their lives talking to or playing with them.

So parental conduct is not reflected as in a regular mirror
but as in a distorted mirror, because the children definitely
do not act out of reason, but rather under the pressure of
identification, and identification, in opposition to object love,
is an extraordinarily rigid, inexact, and unreliable instrument. Children's object love to parents creates reason. It
enables and motivates children to meet their decisions with

growing insight. In contrast, identification is stubborn and conservative, because it stays at the point at which it started and forces children at this age to hold on to the opinions supported by the parents rigidly and invariably until life's end. But it is also the reason for the compulsive, neurotic, wrongful conduct of many adults.

If apparently insignificant symptoms of compulsion form during the fifth year, in the latent period they can develop into compulsive rituals. Then, in puberty, a regression into the anal-sadistic phase results. The conscience, with whose protestation the new wave of anal-sadistic sexual desires now falls into conflict, will then for its part become incapable of escaping the effects of the regression. It will become sadistic and rage against the anal-sadistic appetites no less than it previously did against the genital ones. But at the same time it will also turn against the descendants of the oedipal desires. The defense system becomes more intolerant and what is to be resisted becomes intolerable—both by the influence of the regression. The result is an acute compulsive neurosis. The continuing war on two fronts can lead to a psychic bleeding to death and to total exhaustion of all psychical resources of the five-year-old.

If parents do not understand the enormous difficulties that children have to fight in the oedipal stage, it can well happen that they now place the children into a frame of mind from which in a decade a manic-depressive situation arises. For, the guilt feelings that form at the age of conscience development are the foundations of later depressions, and the ecstatic gratification, which appears when the children succeed in doing exactly what they experience as the voice of the parents in their own ego, is the foundation of mania.

At the end of the fifth year everything depends on the children's breaking with the oedipal bond. But when parents do not help them with this, they can remain fixated for their whole life long on one or the other parent. In girls at that time it appears in such a way that they feel that every man with the exception of their father is an enemy and that every male attempt to make contact is an insult and proof of men's obsession with sex or the patriarchal claim to power. Every caress is interpreted as rape, every form of manly love for women is a degradation of women to sex object. In contrast, the analogous situation appears thus in boys: provided their mother clings to them instead of releasing them into the arms of a younger woman, in later life they will never try to "seduce" or "conquer" a woman. With the exception of their own mother, all women appear to them as man-crazy maenads whose nymphomania can only be resisted by active participation in an autonomous men's group.

In school, it often comes to the attention of teachers educated in pedology that children founder not because of stupidity or laziness, but because of the unresolved Oedipus complex. The step from rivalry with same-sex parents to identification with them has not been accomplished, and the development of conscience as well as the ability to learn have been wrecked. The many adults for whom our social order blocks entry into psychical maturity and who until their death will never experience the joy of a satisfied thirst for knowledge are in this sense victims of the wrecked sex life of their parents.

In spite of the problems caused by the Oedipus complex, it still represents—at least in our social order—an indispensable transitional phase of sexual ontogenesis. What happens when the social order motivates parents to a behavior that for its part leads to this, that the oedipal stage is skipped, has been shown in the discussion about the preoedipal forms of socialization. In any case, scientists who have concerned themselves with the so-called *narcissistic socialization*, according to whether they have based it on primary or secondary narcissism, have come to different conclusions. Since primary narcissism indicates a normal developmental stage, but the secondary one is considered a regression to the primary one, the effects of a socialization accomplished by secondary narcissism are regressive and possibly pathogenic.

But opinions also divide on the analogous question whether a preoedipal socialization can ever be stable, since it does not orient itself by the parents or other contemporaries, but rather by one's own ego, which is still unstable and has not yet come to terms with reality. A few professionals contest that and consider preoedipal socialization a good thing, because it avoids all those behavioral disorders, neuroses, and psychoses we have described in this and in the previous chapter. They place their hopes in the "new" mother, who neither spoils nor binds the children to her, and in the "new" father, who does not punish his children, but rather furnishes a model for them. The upbringing that is strived for here is in fact worth striving for, but it is the reflection of a social order that, unfortunately, still does not exist today, and therefore also has no possibility of existing in our social order.

Instead, in our pluralistic society we find a pluralistic upbringing that causes pluralistic neuroses. If we compare them with the "classical" neuroses of the nineteenth and early twentieth centuries, the difference between them and the "post-classical" neuroses leaps before our eyes clearly. The most significant "classical" neurosis was hysteria. It develops when an authoritarian father or a mother who is hostile toward the body refuses the children their sexual needs. If five-year-old children's consciences accept the authoritarian, hostile-to-the-body parental conduct as morally just, need and conscience collide and create a psychosomatic disorder of the body parts at which the parental prohibition was directed. Neuroses of this sort, of course, have become rare today, but the "post-classical" disorders already mentioned have taken their place. They can be classified neither as neuroses nor as psychoses, and not even as borderline symptoms. The restrictive, authoritarian father certainly does still terrorize his wife today, but in the face of his children he has become unsure, because he has heard some kind of muttering about modern upbringing. To be sure, he considers all of that as newfangled nonsense, yet he still practices an unsure, subdued style of upbringing that oscillates between roars, beatings, and "comradeship"—a model of pluralistic upbringing by which no more "classical" neuroses can be created.

The "new" mother has heard that children should not be hit, but also remembers that children should not be "spoiled," and out of these contradictory views develops a brittle, inconsistent practice of upbringing that also makes the children just as uncertain as she, the "new" mother, has become uncertain of her husband. As a result, the symbiosis with the mother proves just as unsuccessful for the children as the separation from her. The oedipal coming to terms with the parents is impossible because they do not give themselves up to it.

That leads to a childish subject-formation that reflects the parents' style of upbringing—fragile, inconsistent, uncertain. Since the children have never developed a stable relationship to their parents, they also do not learn to develop stable relationships to others. Since their own ego is fragile, their relationships to the ego of others remain brittle.

The Oedipus complex on which so many children in past decades have run aground at first does not develop at all, because the relationships between parents and children are so weak from the beginning on that they can engender neither love nor hatred, but only indifference. While the classical neuroses were disorders of a developing ego, the post-classical, pluralistic neuroses distinguish themselves in that the ego just does not develop at all and so cannot be disordered, but rather from the beginning on is too unstable to bear the burden of interpersonal relationships.

Pluralistically social people change their personality like their toothpaste, their brand of cigarettes, or their car—depending on just what is modern. One also cannot reproach

them if they put on a show or try to take in their contemporaries. For that would presume that they possessed a
"genuine" ego, a "true" identity that somehow lay hidden
behind a mask. But the mask is no mask, and the ego is
no ego, because the early object relationships upon which
all later relationships indeed unquestioningly rest have not,
as it were, broken down, but were just never formed at all.
The results are "narcissistic disorders," "masked depressions," "vegetative regulatory disorders," and other nonspecific diseases upon which we force empty labels, because
we do not actually know what they are and because therefore
we also cannot cure them.

We cannot "cure" them because in general they are not
grounded in the person of the patients, but rather are
grounded in the behavior of their parents. But the behavior
of these is likewise no subjective blunder, but the objective
outcome of the pluralistic society of our day. Just as the
authoritarian, restrictive, sex-hostile upbringing of the late
nineteenth century had caused unheard-of painful, yet clearly
structured neuroses and psychoses, the pluralistic society
of our day creates pluralistic neuroses that distinguish themselves less by their painfulness than by their lack of emotion.
This is an effect of the sexual revolution of the twentieth
century that had been predicted by none of its fathers or
mothers.

Socially pluralistic children and adolescents are so
spoiled that one can no longer speak at all of socialization
in their case. Since their socialization is preoedipal, their
sexual ideal bases itself neither on the father nor on the
mother, but rather on the creations of the consumer indus-
try—on male and female pop singers, on stars and starlets,
on television personalities, photo models, cover girls, pin-
ups, male and female actors in porno films and porno
magazines.

The paradoxical charm of these subjects of masturbation
is their inaccessibility, their lack of obligation, and their

irresponsibility. If persons conditioned by one of them find themselves confronted for the first time by a living sex partner, for the first time they also feel burdened with responsibility. The other persons have their own desires, become defensive, react peevishly, have other views, contradict, make demands. The preoedipal, the pluralistic socialization has not prepared the young people for all these experiences at all. After the initial blaze of desire for the body of the other person, the libido therefore expires just as quickly as the patience with the idiosyncracies of the other person flags. After the second, third, or fourth experience of this kind they retreat into their shell. Then sexual activities soon reduce themselves to masturbation.

The notion that a pluralistic socialization (because it is supposed to be narcissistic) could make one "more versatile" or "more understanding" (or could even create a "new" sensuality) contradicts all empirical knowledge. On the contrary, it creates paralysis of the power of decision, a decline in emotional and political engagement, indifference, self-pity, shirking—and what is more, even legitimates all that as "sensitivity."

Freud never clearly defined the precise age that is imprinted by primary narcissism. Does it correspond to the cutane phase? That and *only* that would enable a displacement of the early capitalistic developmental process determined by the authoritarian father and fixated on the genitals into the direction of a new sensuality, of a new tenderness, warmth, imaginative activity, and production of desire.

However, if *cutaneous* was equated with preoedipal and not with *preoral*, then the notion of narcissistic socialization loses credibility and can be explained only in a negative sense as a product of a frustrated parent-child relationship on the level of secondary narcissism.

So, to speak of "new sensuality" is sheer self-deception. Socially pluralistic people are much, much less "sensual" than even the most exhausted victims of authoritarian generations, because the latter—their grandparents—at least wasted away in often unsatisfied yearning for the forbidden. In contrast, socially pluralistic people are not consumed in yearning for anybody or anything, but rather sadly lament their fate as victims of society. They do nothing to change this society. The few who are active in the political parties, citizen initiatives, alternative groups, and "criminal organizations" are exactly those who either have been monolinearly socialized at home or, thanks to a great amount of will power, have later conquered their pluralistic socialization in the direction of monolinear activity.

The others suffer from "diffuse images of their condition," "depressive disorders," "anhedonia," "apathy," "lack of initiative," "occupational and contact disorders." The common denominator of all these symptoms is that they are no longer explainable as conflicts between the libido and the prohibiting stages of the ego and superego, but only as conflicts between the ego and reality. They are not resolved by the constitution or the disposition of the individuals, but by their society. That is important, because it moves into the center of the discussion the meaning of reality in the case of symptom formation.

9

Sixth Year
Beginning of Childhood

Compared with the enormous stresses of the fifth year of life, the sixth year, in spite of the serious problem of entry into school, is a year of relative relaxation. The founders of developmental psychology speak about the *end of toddler age* and the *beginning of childhood.* The crisis theoreticians call the sixth year the *fourth phase of rest,* and the adherents of the hypothesis of stress speak about a *third phase of recreation.* Psychoanalysts call the period from the sixth/ seventh years to the twelfth/thirteenth years the *latent period,* because they believe that in this time span the children's sexual development comes to a standstill. As with so many other things in psychoanalysis, that has been proven only partly true. It is a social, not a biological, phenomenon and affects only certain cultures. Even within cultures imprinted by sexual latency there are many children who show no sexual latency between the years of six and thirteen. The somaticists among the developmental psychologists nevertheless agree with psychoanalysts and postulate a *middle childhood* partially concurrent with the latent period that extends from the loss of the first milk teeth to the cutting of the last second teeth (but not yet the wisdom teeth)—the "period of the spongy tooth" (Stone and Church, 1973).

As with almost all phases of rest, the sixth year, too, is a period of slowed growth in height and of increased growth in breadth. Toward the beginning of the year, both sexes are 111 cm (3.64 ft) tall, toward the end 117 cm (3.83 ft). At the beginning of the year, the girl weighs 19 kg (41.88 lb), at the end 21 kg (46.29 lb). At the beginning, the boy weighs .1 kg (3.52 oz) more than the girl, at the end .2 kg (7.05 oz) more. That means that sex difference has hardly any effect on body mass, and that also results in reduced psychosexual stress.

The brain is now twice as large as it was at the end of the first year, and more than four times as large as it was at birth. The need for sleep is still great, approximately ten to twelve hours per night. Dexterity increases, but the haste and unrest of the fifth year decrease. The children's movements have a more harmonious and more controlled effect. Grimacing and face pulling disappear. Girls giggle less, boys no longer bite their nails down to the quick. The quarrelsomeness of both sexes decreases. There is less aggression, less destructiveness, and less brutality in boys. Boasting, showing off, and forcefulness decrease. On the other hand, a certain thick-skinned quality makes itself noticeable, allied with a stronger feeling of reality and a new objectivity, loss of illusions and criticism. They strive for impartiality, and perception of details and the ability for exact observation are valued. A slight variation in friends is felt as stimulating, a greater one as threatening.

In both sexes, solitary sexual activities decrease, brooding disappears, the torment of animals stops. The relations between the sexes are relaxed. Tension increases now more for age- than sex-related reasons. Boys and girls play together and invite each other to birthday parties. On the other hand, with the entry into school something totally new begins—the aggression of the group against the individual person.

Minorities of all kinds are persecuted. Scapegoats are discovered and teased—especially by boys. Girls, on the other hand, discover the "secret" and whisper in groups of two or three, conspiratorily looking over their shoulders and suddenly becoming silent whenever the female teacher walks by. Each dyadic relationship at this age, no matter if it is between girls or boys, appears to be directed against a third party or a group. Herein—and not in the possible sexual character of these relationships—lies the danger, because it can lead to the isolation and traumatization of the excluded children.

Unmistakable signs of the first sublimation are developed. The most aggressive "leaders" of the fifth year become determined peacemakers in the sixth year, tormentors of animals become protectors of animals, master liars become defenders of the truth. On the other hand, the period of conscience development and the beginning of sublimation is also a very discouraging one, because nearly everything that children up until then considered good is now declared bad. Everything that had given them pleasure up until now is called into question. Balint, in her "Psychoanalyse der frühen Lebensjahre" (Psychoanalysis of the early years of life), written more than forty years ago, cites two of the most impressive examples of these difficulties that I know out of all of the professional literature. A six-year-old boy says to his mother, "When I was born, I never thought it was going to be so bad for me." And a seven-year-old girl says to the author of that writing, "Everything that's good is forbidden, and everything that's bad, I have to do." As a sex pedologist, one often asks oneself, when one hears such statements from children at this age, if we are justified to ask such sacrifice from our children, and if the end truly justifies the means.

The main traumatic experience of the sixth year is not just the entry into school, which is easily overcome by children raised in a healthy environment, and is often even experienced with joy ("The game I like best is school"), but rather the recognition, partly caused by the school experience, that the power, intelligence, and the authority of the parents are much, much less than the children had assumed up until then. The discovery that parental omnipotence was illusory is more painful for children than any parental punishment. In the case of the more clever children, it soon follows that even the parental punishments, furious outbursts, and injustices under which they had up until now suffered are a painful expression of parental weakness. Both discoveries are felt to be serious narcissistic mortifications, because in spite of all the conflicts with their parents, children nevertheless do finally identify with them. Children can therefore generally bear all the miseries of childhood in a culture so hostile toward children as our own only because they hope one day to become as strong and powerful themselves as their parents. Now, the parents' strength and power prove illusory, so the children's will to live fades. Everything they had borne up until then now becomes unbearable. Burdens that had been coped with in the fifth year are now considered intolerable, because they have become senseless.

Children can be spared this fate if parents reveal their own vulnerability to the children as soon as possible. The sooner children learn they are similar to the parents, that parents, too, suffer from fears, yearnings, desires, and disappointments, the sooner children learn to love and understand parents. But since most parents try to hide their difficulties from their children and to deny their mistakes, commonalities between the generations can hardly be established in the first place. The same is true about sexuality. Since most parents try to hide their sexual desires and fears from the children, children despair at the incomprehensibility of the parental prohibition of all sexual behavior and learn only when it is too late that the parents also suffer under many self-imposed sexual prohibitions.

If parents were to admit that from the beginning, the

relationship to their children would be an incomparably better one, because children are thoroughly capable of compassion, indeed, even of feeling sympathy with their parents and giving them consolation. But it is just this that many parents fear. They have fits of frenzy when the children's questions force them to the realization that they have imposed senseless demands of renunciation on themselves for their whole life long. Children who understand their parents and who try to console them for their senseless, lackluster lives would be looked upon by such parents as if they were possessed by the devil.

On the other hand, there are many parents who either unscrupulously try to live off of the psychical strength of their children by taking advantage of them, like their domestic animals, as consolation dispensers, and others who are so little aware of their own problems that they thoughtlessly dump them on their children. The tendency of such parents to pass along to their children the unresolved sexual problems of their own childhood, without contemplating or conquering them, also makes them into the most unsuitable sex educators of their children that you could ever imagine. Exactly that which is cited by such parents as reason why they—and only they!—must have the right to teach their children about sex, namely the love between parents and children, is the reason why they must fail this task by the very nature of the matter. For, unfortunately, the love between children and parents in our social order is oedipal, and the Oedipus complex makes the sex education of one's own children all the more difficult the greater the childhood sexual problems of the parents have been.

Psychoanalysts argue that this is inevitable, indeed, even necessary, since children without any oedipal bonds could not reach any understanding of human sexual relations, and without painfully overcoming the Oedipus complex could not form a conscience. The development first of the conscience and of the ability to sublimate makes children ready to learn and ready for school. Sex pedologists accept the correctness of this observation, but are not willing to view it as biologically relevant, and consider the painful conquest of the Oedipus complex a sacrifice that our social order imposes on its children to make them tractable.

We believe that today we can recognize with reasonable certainty the actual conditions under which children produce optimal performance, but, unfortunately, we also know that these conditions can be artificially produced neither by the parents nor by the school. They exist where children of intelligent parents, on whose example children can freely orient themselves, learn how to acquire knowledge and experience out of *curiosity*. If these children are loved and respected by their parents, they need no incitement and no punishment, but develop into independent persons out of the *desire* for learning. The more intelligent they are, the more negative the effects not only of punishment, but also of persuasion or reward.

Learning is not a cognitive process. Learning is an emotional relationship between the learners and certain factors of their environment that works with cognitive instruments. Successful learning needs a strong emotional stimulus. One learns either out of love for teachers or out of love for the theme, or out of hatred for the person or institution that one wants to destroy or eliminate with the help of the knowledge acquired. Such learning has nothing to do with the system of "forced feeding" practiced in our schools, by which one can certainly turn geese into pâté de foie, but not children into adults. Every form of learning in which children have no emotional relationship with the teacher or the topic is condemned to failure and shows its weakness in how quickly all is forgotten. As soon as the children have jumped all the required hurdles—examinations for promotion, graduation, and school-leaving—they promptly rid themselves of all the acquired ballast. School gave them nothing for "life."

The most important things good teachers can rouse in

children—curiosity, craving for knowledge, eagerness to learn—can be created only by mutual affection. Only when children admire, respect, and love the teachers can the children inherit from them that lifelong curiosity that makes learning into a joyful activity. In our overfilled schoolrooms there is almost no possibility for such a relationship between children and teachers. And even if children should one day be given smaller classes because of the decrease in population, it would still contradict all the goals of almost all schools in the West and East. Indeed, we do not want creative people. They could become all too independent and thereby become enemies of the state. We want perfect cogs functioning in a well-oiled machine.

Intellectual curiosity is sublimated sexual curiosity. It is no coincidence that we place our children into schools just when their childhood sexual investigation has passed its high point and so can be sublimated. Even the best teachers can inspire no desire for learning in their children if their underlying sexual curiosity is too little or too great, i.e., when sexual curiosity is still not present or when it is too intense to be able to be sublimated. If the children's sexual curiosity has already been disparaged or choked off at home, not even the best teachers can ever instill the desire for learning.

All teachers know the type of dull pupils lost in daydreams whose intellectual poverty does not originate in inherited stupidity, as it were, but rather is the result of questions about the mystery of life being stifled at home. The "moral" opposition to childhood sexual investigation has in this case led to the children's intellectual stunting.

Teachers take charge of "this burden of the resolved or unresolved conflicts of early childhood sexual development" even in the first year of school: "The healthy or misguided development up until puberty, then, largely determines most of the learning difficulties at school as well as the social problems of the assimilation of the individual pupil" (Brocher).

Even in the first year of the lower grades you can very clearly notice which children have been raised by their parents with patience and informed preparedness and which with impatience and apathy. The difference lies neither in the parents' income, nor intellectual level, nor education, but rather in their attitude about knowledge and learning. Children of the rich are often taken care of less lovingly than many of the poor. Children of factory workers (especially politically active ones) often exhibit greater intellectual curiosity than many of those of middle-class parents. The question whether the mother is working or whether the children are cared for all day by her plays a much smaller role, too, than the question whether she is working for financial reasons or because she is interested in the occupation. We will return to this subject.

Much more important is whether the parents (no matter if "educated" or "uneducated") are willing to answer their children's questions to the best of their knowledge and conscience, and whether they are prepared to give real reasons for their own behavior (for example, for prohibitions). Good parents explain why certain behavior that they desire from their children is also useful to the children. They never stress their own authority and never answer the children's questions with statements such as: "Because I *say* so" or "Because *I* want it that way" or "That's what I *heard*" or "Because that's the way it's *always* been," but rather make the effort to supply children answers that are in accordance with the truth and in a language they can understand. That is also true for all questions of sexuality.

The different measure of openness, joy of living, and security that is already evident to us in six-year-old schoolchildren says much about the parents. Children who have been encouraged to understand from the earliest age (thus even before the onset of speech) behave totally differently as schoolchildren from those who have been raised under prohibitions and orders. Even where the genetic inheritance of intelligence is not above the norm, those of the first group develop almost without exception into above-the-norm persons, while even the most clever of the children socialized by command sooner or later decline in dull accommodation to a hated environment, but one that is felt to be unchangeable.

The relationship of working and nonworking mothers to their children is an extremely complex one, and cannot be presented in the black-and-white pictures of supporters and opponents of maternal employment. No doubt it is of inestimable value when good mothers can devote themselves unhindered to their children. But first of all there are very few good mothers, and secondly, it is also of comparable value when fathers can devote themselves undisturbed to their children. But since our social order assumes it as obvious that fathers, as "breadwinners," remain distant from their children for at least five days a week, it just as systematically suppresses the damage of such conduct from the consciousness of individuals as from that of society. But if we allow economic motives to determine our relationship to our children, no one can criticize mothers if they perceive as right what is fair for fathers.

If mothers take up an occupation not for purely financial reasons, but rather out of conviction, they mostly show higher intelligence than those women uninterested in any occupational activity and so, in spite of their occupation, are mostly in the position of raising their children more sensibly and more intelligently than the latter. The self-confidence of such mothers strengthened by their fought-for equality of rights and proven ability then also always results in strengthened primal confidence, in higher sensitivity, and in superior intelligence in the children, in spite of the little time they spend with their children.

The most severely injured are neither the children of relatively unenlightened and insensitive housewives nor those of enlightened and sensitive mothers with interesting occupations, but rather those children who do not receive sufficient attention from either the father or the mother. And that, sadly, is the overwhelming majority of all children in Western, middle-class society. With them, it makes only a very little difference if the mother is working or not. What is important are interest, affection, communication, sensitivity, and patience. All five abilities are not more developed in homemaker-only mothers than in working mothers. On the contrary, a higher percentage of working mothers included in all tests up until now exhibits, thanks to their broader experience at work, a correspondingly higher measure of understanding for their children. The well-being of the children obviously depends less on the amount of time mothers spend with them than on a second factor that has been rarely treated in the discussions about working mothers, namely, on the relationship to their own mothers and their relationship to their daughters. The better this relationship was, and the more child-friendly the conduct in the previous generation, the greater the chances are that the mother will take good care of her own children, even if she spends much time at work and relatively little time with her children. Conversely, the worse the mothers' relationship to their mothers and the more hostile to children the conduct of the grandmothers, the worse are the chances of the children, even if they were cared for by their mothers all the time.

It is a characteristic aspect of our time-is-money culture that the less time we have for our children, the less time we have for ourselves. Working mothers who love their jobs are also in the main able to care for their children with love and without haste. Homemakers who suffer the entire day from the burdens of never-ending housework, on the other hand, are also seldom able to devote the requisite time to their children. One can recognize this in that the refusal to suckle their children appears, unfortunately, in homemaker-only mothers just as often as in working mothers, and in that the tendency to wean their children as quickly as possible is no less strong, unfortunately, in homemaker-only mothers than in working mothers.

One of the most underrated crises in the life of children grows from the fact that the placement in school acquaints many children, for the first time in their lives, with children of other social classes and other ethnic groups. This experience, which is in contradiction to the experiences in the play groups they "grew up in" in a certain town or on a certain main city street, secures for such children their first glance at the complexity of the environment. The glance does not necessarily lead to insight, because it can quickly form ideas of majorities and minorities, teasing and being teased. If teachers in the classroom notice an unusually aggressive persecution of scapegoats, they can with certainty conclude that in this class there is also great sexual tension that can only be released by sadistic acts against certain pupils or certain minorities.

Those children who have the greatest sexual guilt feelings betray themselves the most by this means, that they seek to release their inner conflicts by external displacement. If they are especially afraid of punishment, they immediately ask for the punishment of scapegoats by telling tales about them. If teachers see through the maneuver by not punishing the one who is told on, an expression of intense frustration often appears on the face of the tattletale—as if the sex partner had withdrawn just at the moment of orgasm. Brocher correctly points to the fact that such observations are of great importance for the required sex education, because in such children's conduct lies the root as well as the explanation of later persecution of minorities. If teachers are not in the position to release children plagued by sexual guilt feelings from their burden, they can become lifelong tormentors of their contemporaries.

Since children's readiness and need to learn do not develop in a straight line and cumulatively, but rather in a series of "critical" or "sensory" phases, it can be useless or downright dangerous when people try to teach children something for which they are still not mature. On the other hand, the children's readiness to learn a certain matter is often already done with if their need to learn is not satisfied at the right time with the right information. But since children are still not totally aware of their own readiness to learn and also cannot define wherein their learning need actually lies, adults can orient themselves only according to the children's reaction to the information offered. If they react with no interest or total resistance, the need is either not yet there or the critical phase is already passed. One can always ascertain the difference only by offering the children an overabundance and not a dearth of learning opportunities.

The mental image of many adults, that one can confuse children through much too many learning opportunities or "trouble" them by "premature" information (for example, in the area of sexuality), is false. At worst, premature information creates boredom, but never alarm. When children show alarm, the information has come too late or was expressed incorrectly, for example, in an anxious or provocative form. In such cases children are not reacting to the content of the information, but rather to the adults' conduct. Adults' uncertainty releases uncertainty in children, no matter how "harmless" the situation may be. Conversely, however, even the "most daring" information creates no uncertainty in children when it is delivered by intrinsically secure adults with a certainty of their knowledge of human nature.

In their communication with children, adults need an especial sensitivity to the emotional feedback of the children: to their facial expressions, to their body language, to the unspoken and to what is held back. In this sense, sex education in school, which has to begin even in the first year of the lower grades, is much more difficult than the one at home, because teachers are just never (or only under special circumstances) alone with one child. In groups, children always behave differently than in private conversations. So sex education in school before an assembled class can develop only from a series of careful questions by the teachers. It is best to avoid a prepared lecture, because of the great difference in the children's sexual development. The class, and not the teachers, should determine the tempo of the progress and the amount of the desired information. Teachers should always be available to individual students for consultation, in case parents so desire and permit.

But all of this is presently possible in only a very few schools because most schools lack the curricula. Many teachers are justifiably anxious about private discussions, because subsequent accusations by children that the teachers verbally or actually "seduced" them are by no means rare and especially feared from children of old-fashioned and sexually disturbed parents.

Sexual Pathology of the Sixth Year

As a transition from the oedipal phase to the so-called latent phase, the beginning of childhood is characterized by anginous heart disorders, balance disorders, headaches, and regressions to early childhood phases. As a year of entry into school, it also imposes difficulties in attention and concentration, and certainly in greater measure with each school year since around 1950. Psychical disorders that can mature to neuroses or psychoses in adulthood exist in approximately a quarter of all male and female pupils of the Federal Republic of Germany, Austria, and Switzerland. There are different opinions about the reasons for this development. The author tends to have the opinion that they are not biological, but rather social in kind, and are closely related to education becoming ever more specialized to career and income. That also results in disorders of the children's psychical and psychosexual development, especially in the pluralistic socialization mentioned at the end of the previous chapter, but also in the reaction effects of acceleration and neoteny described at the outset.

If the children's physical development progresses faster than their mental, they become psychically ill. They most decidedly develop a kind of schizophrenia that Mahler has called *differentiation* and *fragmentation*. The mental immaturity expresses itself in the inability of psychical separation from the mother or caregiver: "Just the fact that the more or less built-in physical maturity progresses while the psychical development does not do this, allows the rudimentary ego to become extremely fragile. . . . This fragmentation can begin at any time from the end of the first year on and in the course of the second year. It can result from a painful, unexpected trauma, but frequently from a seemingly insignificant occurrence such as a short separation or a trifling loss."

But with an especially insidious delayed reaction it can also break out with entry into school. If children show the fear of separation from the mother or caregiver on the first day of school and in the months that follow, it is advisable it speak to them about unresolved fears of separation. Sickness of the mother in subsequent years, but also other family crises that prevent parents from sufficient involvement with their children at this time, belong to the reasons for the regression to the fears of the first and second years. Unwanted children especially often suffer from delayed separation anxiety, but also children of unsure parents, especially when it is a matter of the first child.

Such parents sometimes appear before child psychiatrists and complain about the children's behavior as if the children's fears were based on obstinacy or on a timidity totally unwarranted by the parents. In such cases, as in all other cases of psychical disorders, pediatricians, child psychologists, and child psychiatrists have made it a rule to look behind every complaint by the parents first for wrongful conduct of the accuser. On the other hand, physicians cannot ally themselves with the children against their parents, no matter how wrongfully the parents may have conducted themselves, because as long as children are sheltered under their parents, the parents will act all the more wrongfully the more frightened, troubled, and aware of their guilt they are. Accusing the parents, no matter how justified it may be, is not advising the parents and especially hurts the children. Conversely, prophylactic and preventive advising of the parents, even if it makes the parents insecure, helps the children thoroughly. The book before you was written with this goal.

Yet, unfortunately, from the diagnostic experience of the child specialists it cannot be denied that almost every complaint from parents about their children's fear of school, almost every complaint by mothers about their daughters' sleep, eating, or digestive disorders, almost every father's complaint about the bedwetting or masturbation of his son reveals to the physician's eye what the parents have done to their children. And in some hidden corner of their souls most parents know that also, because the emotionality of their complaints against the children reveals the degree of the repression of their own emotions: The more vehemently they accuse the children, the more clearly they accuse themselves, because the children quite simply are flesh of their flesh and bone of their bone.

So, even in the case of intelligent and enlightened parents, physicians again and again meet with the experience that the parents react to psychical and psychosexual disorders of their children altogether stereotypically, with one of three wrong interpretations:

1. My child is abnormal: She/He *does* not behave normally.
2. My child is sick: He/She *cannot* behave normally.
3. My child is stubborn: She/He does not *want* to behave normally.

The first interpretation is really no interpretation, but rather a capitulation. The second one takes all of the responsibility off of the child. The third one places all of the responsibility onto the child. All three make the suffering worse. The first one mistakes illness for statistics, because normality has just as little to do with health as abnormality with disease. The second one overlooks that it is a self-accusation of the parents. Because if the children *cannot* do otherwise, then they cannot do otherwise because parental inheritance and parental upbringing have made it such as it is. The third one is the worst, because it causes "unconscious guilt feelings in the children on the ground of withdrawal of love and the lack of understanding contained in it" (Dolto).

In all three cases the cause of the children's wrongful behavior lies with the parents. But it probably is less the fault of the intended training measures than the effects of parental problems on children. In the main the intentional, restrictive measures of upbringing hurt the children less than those aspects of parental conduct that originate in their own unresolved sexual problems. So sex pedologists see their most important task as advising educational authorities about the possible effects of their repressed sexual desires and sexual fears on the desires and fears of their children.

Parents can then conquer their own desires and fears only when they succeed in making themselves aware of them. The notion of such parents that they should not speak about their sexual problems with their children, since such a discussion would in the first place just put those "ideas" into their head, ones that would not have been there at all until then, is like advising the police not to take up the fight against crime for goodness' sake, because acquaintance with crime could put the thought to commit a crime into the heads of the innocent police.

So the parents' behavior toward the psychical and psychosexual disorders of their children also depends largely on the quality of their own mental and sexual life. The more satisfied it is, the better they can understand that of their children. The more gratifying it is, the more they also tend to grant to their children that sexual satisfaction that the children must have if they are expected to become stable and intelligent adults.

Conversely, the more unsatisfied the parents are with their own sex life, the more they tend to pass their own sexual problems on to the children and thereby cause those disorders with which they, helplessly, yet full of complaints, run to the pediatrician. The less gratified, the more frustrating their sex life, the more they tend to deny their children sexual satisfaction. That is dangerous, because it can lead to severe regressions to the fantasizing of the first year.

This fantasizing of schoolchildren is a regression into that early-childhood preliminary stage of thought in which a lack of control over motility still prevented thought from being placed into words or actions. If now at school age no behavior develops out of children's thoughts, because the parents or the persons responsible for their upbringing condemn certain behavior, the blocked thinking can intensify into neurosis. For, in a clinical sense, only those fantasies that prepare action are creative. If the environment blocks the action, it operates neurotically. In the case of two "classical" neuroses, hysteria and compulsive neurosis, the neurotic character of the regressive fantasizing can be pursued from early childhood stages onward. "Hysterical persons regress from action to silent daydreaming; their conversion symptoms are a substitute for action. The compulsive character regresses from action to preparation for action through words; their thinking is a kind of incessant preparation for actions that are never carried out" (Fenichel).

If children now tend toward regressive sexual fantasies that lead to intensified stress and cannot be released by the discharge of the pent-up libido because of parental prohibition or out of individual moral convictions, children take the first steps toward neurosis. They cannot do otherwise, because nature did not give children strong sexual desires for nothing. They serve as practice for that precoital tenderness that in adulthood enables the foreplay before coitus. If parents forbid their children the age-specific games and practices that serve this purpose, they condemn the children in their later years to cold, loveless, unprepared sexual intercourse, one that can give neither them nor their sex partner emotional satisfaction.

If children are repeatedly forbidden to do this or that, they often settle on a compromise that permits them to participate in all the "misdeeds" of their playmates, but only passively, as observers, so to speak. When they are called into account by their parents, such children then say truthfully, "But I didn't do anything; I just looked on!" If children remain fixed in this behavior or regress to this stage in the face of later experiences of a similar kind, they become voyeurs. For, voyeurs always have the same infantile excuse before their own conscience: they have done nothing; they have only looked on.

The later turning of the son against his father and the daughter against her mother belongs to the most frequent effects of upbringing in a home where there is hostility toward the body, because the children take an upbringing camouflaged as "morality" all too seriously when it occurs at the age of conscience formation. If parents teach the children that everything sexual is immoral, they should not be surprised when the children feel the parents' sexual intercourse is immoral, too. If sexuality is "bad," then the father is behaving badly if and when he wants to sleep with the mother. He then degrades her by persuading or even forcing her to do it. But then the mother, too, is bad, because she degrades herself by giving herself up to the father. Result: Children never until their lives' end forgive their parents for having gone against their own moral code.

In a similar manner, any criticism of the father against the mother and any of the mother against the father is understood as criticism of the parents' marriage. Any criticism by the mother against "men" is understood as criticism of the father, and any criticism by the father against "women" is borne as criticism of the mother. Through criticism of the other sex parents destroy the children's image of parents.

It was one of the most tragic errors of the nineteenth century to postulate, on the one hand, an antinomy between sensuality and morals, on the other hand, a mutual exclusion of sexuality and intellect. Today we know that morality is built on experienced sensuality and that all intellectual faculties are sublimated forms of sexual abilities. Parents who cut their children off from the joy of sensuality rob them of access to moral judgment. Children whose access to sexual satisfaction has been walled shut often as adults can no longer find the access to intellectual satisfaction. Children traumatized in this way often "fail" even in the first year of school.

Conversely, however, the inability of children to fulfill academic demands can lead to regression to an earlier stage of sexual development. The progress from one attained developmental stage to the next is only possible when it is neither blocked nor made difficult or retrogressive by excessive attraction of the phase overcome. As we have seen, this process is threatened by enormous dangers of ambivalence. So children can regress at any time from disappointed parental love to open parental hate. They then often project this hatred onto academic learning and react aggressively or with total rejection of all learning opportunities. Unsatisfactory lesson work in the first year of school, then, is more often a result of sexual conflict than deficient ability. Without their being aware of it, such children with their refusal to learn express their protest against the parents, against the teachers, or against the subject. Psychogenic stoppage of learning of this kind should never be perceived as a product of conscious obstinacy and be punished as refusal to learn, because the punishment only reinforces the slowdown or projects it onto another facet of childhood behavior.

In children in the first school year chronic fatigue, too, often has psychosexual and no somatic reasons. Neurophysiologists have shown that fatigue depends less on the quantity of the work done than on the psychical condition under which it was accomplished. Children in psychosexual conflict become fatigued more quickly than those who are raised with love and understanding.

The sexual behavior of the male and female teachers, too, is communicated to the children and paradoxically is perceived by them much more clearly the younger they are. That is because of the ability of small children to read adults' body language that we already mentioned. With uncanny precision, children can especially interpret satisfaction, sensual harmony, and pride of the ability of being able to give satisfaction to other people. They perceive sexual frustration, hostility toward the body, and the teachers' sexual fears with equal precision. They naturally cannot express in words what draws them to sexually satisfied adults and repels them from sexually unsatisfied ones, but they react with such positive infallibility toward the sexually balanced and negatively toward sexually imbalanced adults that one can never get over one's surprise.

In didactic terms that means: In addition to the words teachers speak in the classroom, they communicate to the children, unintentionally and unconsciously, a treasure trove of sensual experiences that mean more to the children than verbal instruction.

But that also means: Supplementary to the words that teachers speak in classrooms, they involuntarily and unknowingly secure for the children a powerful store of sensual experiences, which explains more for the children than verbal instruction. Children react less to what teachers say than to what they do. And less to what they do than to what they are.

In pathological terms, the suppressed fears and the repressed desires teachers aim at the pupils are perceived by them. With their finely tuned antennae children pick up the unconsciously sent-out signals, and with their apparatus psychically equipped with a greater degree of sensuality than rationality, they convert the signals into their own desires, their own fears, and into their own physical reactions.

Even in the case of educated career teachers, educational behavior flows according to the principle of unconscious projection. We have been so conditioned by our parents and teachers that every day and every night we suppress and repress an endless sequence of desires and fears. We never become aware of this continuous process of repression—just as little as we become aware of our bloodstream or breathing—but it does occur: Every desire, every fear is first of all defused by repression and then stored, ready to be called up. If at some time later the desire rises into consciousness, then it often is in the changed form of an effective perception that appears to be coming to us from the outside: If I have a bad conscience, I will believe that my pupils have one. If I get angry at pupils, they make me angry. Whatever I project onto my environment, that reflects back to me. The subject presents itself in the mask of the object.

However, the pupils do exactly the same. They often do not learn well not because they are stupid or lazy, but rather because they cannot stand me. Therefore, they often suddenly make great strides not because I have become a better teacher, but because they have learned to love me. But why do they suddenly love me? Because by coincidence I made some gesture that reminded them of the best side of their father. Or of their grandparents with whom they had spent an especially nice vacation. That means: Without being aware of it, they behave according to the principle of projection and counterprojection.

That can create much pain in the first school year— also sexual suffering, when teachers suffer sexual pain.

10

Seventh Year
Middle Childhood

In the seventh year of life, an unmistakable differentiation between the sexes begins, one that for the present time, however, still does not manifest itself in terms of bodily size or weight, but definitely in physical shape. At the beginning of the year girls and boys are equally tall—approximately 1.17 m (3.83 ft) tall. Toward the middle of the year, both have grown approximately 3 cm (1.18 in). At year's end the boy is a scant 2 cm (.78 in) taller than the girl. The comparisons in weight are similar: girls 21 kg (46.29 lb), boys 21.2 kg (46.73 lb) at the beginning of the year; girls 24.7 kg (54.45 lb), boys 25 kg (55.11 lb) around midyear; girls 26.8 kg (59.08 lb), boys 26.9 kg (59.30 lb) at year's end. The numbers may sound similar, but the shapes begin to vary more and more drastically: In girls the hips become more rounded and the pelvis broader; in boys the shoulders become broader and the shape more angular. Secretion of estrogen begins in girls, secretion of testosterone in boys.

The seventh year is also a year of stress. Extreme conflict between the conscious and unconscious levels creates contradictory behavior patterns and symptoms of aggravated adjustment. As in all times of crisis the simultaneous appearance of contradictory feelings and of rapid change between incompatible behaviors becomes noticeable. Extroversion changes with introversion, euphoria with depression, enthusiasm with indifference, interest with lack of interest, ambition with lack of initiative, modesty with immodesty and verbal exhibitionism, guilt feelings with innocence, regret with malice—and all of that inside the shortest periods of time.

On the level of conduct and behavior, a rapid back and forth between the love and torment of animals occurs, between seriousness and evil jokes, attacks of laughter and crying fits, boasting and timidity, bragging and self-doubt, snobbery and self-torment. Talkativeness again increases. Fast talking in girls, loud talking in boys, chattering in both. So the founders of developmental psychology called this phase the *talkative phase,* but when you listen closely you notice that the talkativeness alternates with insensibility, fast talk with silence, roaring with whispering, the need to share with secrecy.

In the relationship to the parents, a certain distancing begins to open. Many children now see their parents very consciously and begin to become ashamed of them. But here, too, the process of contradiction and oscillation between alternative conduct continues. Children demand to be taken seriously by their parents, but make fun of them at the same time. They seek parental affection and yet curtly reject the parents. They swing between dedication and refusal, affection and rejection. They bow obediently to the dictates of reality and at the same time despise the standards of the parents and adults. They fluctuate between sociability and isolation, between courtesy and quarrelsomeness, tractability and aggression, humility and pride, modesty and arrogance.

They dramatize themselves and their environment, change every situation into a situation of conflict, become joyously aware of contradiction, shock their parents with intentional bombardment with "immoral" words, jokes, prose, and verses. According to the parents' standards, they present for view the most peculiar way of walking, the strangest body behavior, and the most provocative facial expressions. They make faces, fool around, imitate the parents, stick out their tongue, put their fingers into their mouth, bite off their nails, and chew on pencils and pens. At school they snap their fingers while raising their hands, jump out of their seat, run away from their place, in between shouting or behaving badly, straddling in their seat.

Children develop daydreams, fantasies about being foundlings, and family fiction. Parents are not at all their true parents; they had been adopted; actually they are descended from very famous people; they had been mixed up in the maternity ward; their true mother is X, the film star; Y, the pop singer, is their true father.

You can hardly believe that this was once the age at which children entered adulthood. If we read reports about the children of the Middle Ages, we notice not only the astounding physical size and the bewilderingly early development of the internal secretions of our children today, but also their psychical retardation. Seven-year-olds of the sixteenth and seventeenth centuries were adults who supported themselves in a normal job. Ours are overindulged, patronized, unbalanced, physically immature, and mentally infantile, but also especially very lonely creatures. They are free of all family and social responsibilities, are artfully isolated from the adult world, and may not do anything except study. But they *must* do that.

It is as if adults had completed a social contract with the children that requires from parents that they release children from every responsibility and finance them up until adulthood. As a return, from the children is demanded that they obey, study, develop no sexual feelings, practice no sexual behavior, and interfere neither in the concerns of the parents nor in that of other contemporaries—a stunting and incapacitating contract, a socially unfavorable agreement.

Placing children in the care of trustees and guardians in the social and sexual areas stands in opposition to the exorbitant demands in the academic area. That has political reasons: The greater the study load, the less the danger of the children finding time for "dumb thoughts." This also deepens the isolation of our children.

Because of the constant increase of street traffic, parents more and more refuse to allow children to play in the street. The ancient children's games, children's verses, and children's songs die out, because children are isolated in their honeycomb homes and in general no longer get together outside of school. When in the following pages we discuss "play groups," it may already be an anachronism in the short time after the publication of this book. Even on the school playground games hardly still take place, because the children have forgotten them. The number of children who never exchange a word with other children during recess is steadily increasing.

We do not know whether the dangerous, growing contact disorders in the lower grades are the cause or effect of this situation. Where street games still do exist, seven-year-olds live on the edge of the "peer group," the group of the older ones they admire, upon whom children now base their role models. In that case, seven-year-olds ascribe higher authority to older children than to parents and obey older children unconditionally.

To hide their fears from the other sex, both sexes at this age develop a certain display behavior. It is expressed in boys in showing off, in boasting, and in cockfighting, which is supposed to establish the pecking order within the classroom or the neighborhood play groups. Belching contests and breaking-wind competitions are harmless regressions to the oral and anal phase. Clearly genital is the fact that girls are sprayed with filled balloons, with water pistols, or even with water-filled condoms. On the other hand, girls try to overtake the boys in school and in their rivalry often develop a thoroughly aggressive zeal for learning.

From the seventh year on, in the school toilet and in every other conceivable room that is not nailed shut, sexual contacts occur—verbal exchange of opinions on sexual intercourse and procreation, exposing genitals, looking over the body of others, and first experiments with the mutual touching of genitals. Parents and teachers who pretend not to know anything about it or believe such practices occur only in the lower classes are closing their eyes to reality and thereby miss the opportunity to help the children in this time of crisis.

It must be repeated here once more that children engage in all these games not as substitute forms of coitus, but as attempts to find their own identity. And it can be found only by defining one's own body from that of another person. But before one can do that one has to get to know others: "I am different from you, so I am I." These attempts begin, at least in large cities, between the seventh and eighth years, thus in the second or third grade. One can partly satisfy children's curiosity through discreetly delivered sexual information. But if children's questions at this age are rejected or if the entire area of child sexuality is omitted from the school curriculum, then children will look for the answers by mutual inspection of their genitals. So, in every school there is a close connection between that which teachers can clarify by verbalization and that which children do when these things are not brought up for discussion. Simply stated: The more open the discussion, the lower the number of active sexual relations between the children. The more hostile to the body the teaching is, the greater the number of childhood "sex offenses."

When adults enter into new surroundings they always try to reestablish the social position they had occupied in the earlier surroundings. Children also try to do this whenever they enter school or come into a new one. They then share their knowledge with the other children and try to find out from them if they know more or less than they themselves do. The results of the individual sexual investigation of each child obviously belong to this exchange of knowledge. Brocher correctly says that this exchange is a part of an "unofficial" yet nevertheless necessary scholastic curriculum.

The already mentioned children's tendency at this age "to make smutty jokes," i.e., to express "forbidden" words in the vernacular, also shows up in school, and certainly especially strongly in the second year of school. All teachers know that, but most are not aware of the fact that in this case unconquered aspects of the oral phase (talkativeness) combine with anal impulses (love of dirt) and urgent questions of the first genital stage. A favorite method of legitimating the forbidden is telling tales: "Sir, Fritz is always saying dirty words!" If teachers then dare to ask, "What kind of dirty words?" most of the time the words are smartly enumerated. If teachers feel certain their principal will cover for them, they can by all means successfully open this safety valve a few times, because once the "unspeakable" is uttered, a part of the urge to repeat is lost. If teachers refuse the unstated desire of the class, they will certainly maintain external order, but hurt the individual pupils, who from now on in secret will each continue making smutty jokes with increased urgency.

For almost a century developmental psychologists conjectured that between ages of six to seven and twelve to thirteen there was a slackening of sexual interest and sexual behavior. To explain this phenomenon, different professionals proposed that a human procreative maturity developed in two thrusts—the first during the "toddler's puberty" of the third to fifth years, the second during actual puberty. Today in humans the first onset comes to an end, that is, it develops the normal desires to couple of mammals able to procreate, but is still not able to procreate, because the boys' semen does not contain any sperm capable of fertilization and the girls' eggs have still not gone on their journey from the ovary into the fallopian tube: Menarche, the age of the release of eggs, has not yet begun.

From this contradictory junction of psychical maturity to mate and somatic immaturity to procreate, several researchers have concluded that in the earliest period in the history of the species, when life expectancy was at best a third of what it is today, humans must have also been mature enough to procreate earlier by a third, thus between the third and fifth years, instead of—as today—between the ninth and fifteenth years.

The archaic memory of this early evolutionary phase of our species, according to this hypothesis, is revealed in the early sexual maturity of children in the third to fifth years and in the "latent period" following it, which is supposed to serve to discharge the tension of the "false" puberty to prepare the organism for the "genuine" puberty.

This theory is probably false, because careful investigations of primitive folk, who impose no prohibition of sexual intercourse for children in the third to fifth years, show, first, that there is no "oedipal" phase there, because when they are able to mate with contemporaries, children do not need to fall back on their own parents as substitute partners; second, that the sexual development between the toddler's "little" puberty and the "big" puberty of adolescents does not proceed in surges, but flows; third, that the psychical phenomena we associate with puberty are lacking. For this very reason in such social orders an artificial barrier must be erected between childhood and adulthood, the barrier of puberty rites. This allows sex pedologists to suppose that the latent period is a phenomenon specific to Western cultures, one that goes back to the sexually restrictive norms of our social order and represents a psychosomatic reaction of the children to the prohibition of sexual activities in the years of the first sexual maturity.

Psychoanalysts who today still cling to the idea of a latent period define it as the "complete overcoming of the oedipal conflict" (Dolto). According to this postulate the latent period releases children from all libidinous impulses. It also proceeds with an emotional separation from the parents. In the separation there is supposedly no protest against the parents, but only development of libidinous energies that had once moreover served to beset the parental love object now given up. The separation is certainly also supposed to be a form of grief over the death of a phase of life, but it is also supposed to be the birth of a present time that is supposed to be equally rich, if not richer, in libidinous gratification. According to this thesis, the latent period expresses itself clinically in behavior characteristic of the successful conquering of the Oedipus complex: in social, familial, playful, and academic behavior that is without instability, without fear, and without nightmares.

According to this theory girls' sexuality is now no longer perceived in the notion of penis envy, but as a secret unknown to boys and reserved for the budding woman. Girls stop seductively considering the father as a sex object to be conquered actively and the mother as an object to be conquered passively. The characteristic of the male latent period, according to this understanding, lies in the analogous resignation of the seven-year-old seductively to pursue the mother as an object to be conquered aggressively and to pursue the father as an object to be conquered passively.

He secretly allows himself to be of a different opinion than his father, without this necessarily meaning that for that reason he seeks to draw punishment on himself by displaying subversive ideas unnecessarily. Inwardly he feels himself free. And especially he shifts the interest applying exclusively to his father or other men of his family to other men and boys and tries either to beat them as rivals—through academic or athletic successes, scuffles—or to admire them objectively as pupils, while he allows himself to pass judgment over them. The effect is that the subjugation of the son in relation to his father is quite naturally acknowledged insofar as it is real, exactly as with any other person, without resulting in the regrowth of aggressive rivalry, painful feelings of inferiority or rejection, to admire him when he deserves it objectively—exactly the opposite. (Françoise Dolto)

Many of the developments described here actually do occur. But in the opinion of psychoanalysts, the thrust of libido, which up until now had been thoroughly irregular, indeed, often simply hectic, now becomes relatively uniform and directs itself toward activities the conscience places at its disposal and has emphasized as simplified. For, in today's practice in the Federal Republic of Germany, Austria, and Switzerland, the latent period is not a phase of sexual stagnation, but rather a period of alternation between longer periods of relative rest and short periods of more intense stress. The age-specific comparison of genitals belongs to the stress periods, which help children to find their sexual identity and thereby release the tension.

Brocher quite correctly argues that the latent period can only exercise its redeeming effect of releasing sexual pressure when infantile sexual investigation has come to a "concrete conclusion," that is, when children have become clearly aware of their sexual identity and the sexual relationship of tension with their parents has relaxed. But since this process of separation from the sexual fascination with the parents and of becoming aware of one's own sexual identity does not completely depend on the children's will power, but is largely shaped by the parents' or caregivers' insight, especially through their ability to act as a model for the children, the process fails all too often—with the result that lower-grade schoolteachers find themselves confronted with many children who are in no way sexually latent and, with that, mature enough for school, but who suffer from great sexual tension and so cannot follow the most simple instruction. They wriggle, fumble with their fingers about their face and other parts of their body, muster neither patience nor attention, and thereby prevent the common progress of the class.

Obviously the latent period in our culture especially serves ego-strengthing. The more successful the socializing efforts of home, school, and children in stabilizing the children's ego at this time, the easier children will be able to deal with the new demands that will be required in the sixth and seventh years by school and in the future years by the drastically intensified sexual needs present in puberty and adolescence. In opposition to the opinion that puberty is the period of sexual decision, the points for the course of puberty are already set by the age of six or seven: "The more authoritarianly the lower and middle grades in school are operated, i.e., the more dependent children at the age between the sixth and twelfth year of life are kept, the worse the chances are for the second phase of sexual development" (Brocher). Conversely: The broader the material offered, the freer the style of education, the greater the demands on the creative development of the children, and the less the obligation of learning by rote and the amount of facts to be memorized, the better the prognosis that the children will learn with joy and resolve the sexual problems of puberty and adolescence with joy.

But parents, too, have to help in conquering of these tasks. When the relationship of the children to the parents is good, sexual activity and sexual "prematurity" also chiefly coincide with intellectual activity and intellectual "prematurity." Sexual "prematurity" (when we use the word in the sense of the theory of evolution) is no symptom of psychical disorder, but either—as the theoreticians of evolution believe—a result of the species-specific dual onset of the human process of maturity or—as we believe—a result of culture-specific demands of our Western social system.

Now, first of all, in our culture clever and sensible people mature just as quickly in a sexual respect as they do intellectually and morally. On the other hand, sexual precocity *without* simultaneous maturity of intelligence and sensibility is mostly an indication of disordered relationships between the children and the persons responsible for them. When parents complain about excessive masturbation or the premature sexual relationships of their children, the complaint mostly falls back on them. For when the children's behavior has no somatic cause and is not a part of a general progress also resulting in intellectual and moral behavior, then the parents or caregivers are to blame for the children's wrongful conduct.

But as we have stressed again and again, this "blaming" of the parents and caregivers in no way means that anyone insinuates they had bad intentions, but only that they need the same help as their children do. First of all, the ability to raise children now is, unfortunately, not an inborn talent for people, but must be learned, and certainly all the more laboriously the further we develop away from our animal ancestors. The fact that most parents dispute this opinion, because they consider it criticism of their intelligence, explains a great part of the rapidly increasing number of psychical disorders in our social order.

Sexual Pathology of the Seventh Year

Hubert Harbauer, holder of the teaching chair in child psychiatry at the University of Frankfurt-on-Main, writes about the first school years in his textbook on child and adolescent psychiatry:

> At this age we encounter an accumulation of behavior difficulties as well as other symptoms of difficult adjustment. . . . The children now becoming noteworthy probably come into the schools already disturbed and "decompensate" owing to the demands of the social community for reasons that reach back into the socialization process of early childhood.

The problem of "already disturbed" children, whose disease symptoms certainly become evident during the schooling period, but were already latent at home, is especially suspicious in the area of psychosexuality. It is the goal of the present book to point to the fact that almost everything that manifests itself as psychical and psychosexual disorders during the school years originates in the preschool period and almost exclusively reverts to *earlier* disorders in the parent-child relationship.

These days the suspicious psychosomatic disorders of the seventh year are colitis ulcerosa and asthma. Among the psychical and psychosexual disorders: wetting oneself and uncontrolled stools, psychogenic anorexia and obesity, eating and sleeping disorders, family neuroses. But weak concentration, fear of school, and school fatigue should also not be disposed of as laziness, but are psychical disorders of school age. Finally, certain forms of stealing, lying, and running away can be understood only as parentogenic disorders.

We quote from Harbauer on the etiology of some of these symptoms.

Colitis ulcerosa: "Earlier experiences and unresolved childhood conflicts are suspected as predisposing. Certain parental conduct, especially that of the mother, should thereby allow no satisfying development of the anal-erotic and anal-sadistic drives. For these reasons the frequently conflict-filled mother-child relationship must be included in the behavioral process."

Bronchial asthma: "With this we meet with fearful, uncertain mothers, occasionally also very domineering personalities. There often is an ambivalence of the children to the mother's personality in the sense that a great dependence as well as aggressive instances against the mother are recognizable. Asthmatic children often show characteristics such as oversensitivity, ambition for achievement, great need for love and affection, egocentricity, and a tendency toward jealousy and rivalry."

Wetting oneself (enuresis): "A conflict with the environment can be considered the most frequent cause for enuresis. But besides this very many rearing behaviors in the social surroundings are factors of disturbance that go back to the first age of children. The fact that a lack of security and safety in early life is essential for the symptomatics is proven from the reports in orphanages and in neglected, unsocialized children who around the time they enter school often still wet themselves as frequently as 60 to 80 percent of the time."

Uncontrolled stools (encopresis): "Etiologically, here, too, the emotionally incorrect relationship between mother and child is of great significance. Mothers with children with uncontrolled stools all too often think in moralistic terms, at times are fearful and self-doubting, or are also characterized by great demands of domination."

Psychogenic thinness (anorexia nervosa): "The relationship to the mother is for the most part depicted negatively. The mothers, too, are often thin personality types, who basically embody what they criticize in their children. Often they are cared-for children from relatively well-integrated families socially. The mother-daughter relationship almost always comes to a crisis."

Psychogenic obesity (nervous hyperexoria): "The most frequent causal characteristic in a family situation with an adipose child and adolescent is for the most part a failed relationship with a domineering mother. Over and above this you will find a 'weak' father who is of little dynamic significance to the family atmosphere. On the part of the mother there is frequently an ambivalent attitude that cramps the children's development by overprotection, that is, by overfeeding. Occasionally there are also mothers of obese children who reject their children and neglect them. But in all of these cases the taking of food represents a leading role in the mother-child relationship."

Eating disorders: "Many psychogenic appetite disorders represent oral symptoms that can be caused by the withdrawal of love or lack of affection. . . . Not eating becomes a weapon in the battle for power with the mother."

Sleeping disorders: "Unresolved emotional conflicts very frequently play a causal role in disorders affecting falling asleep and staying asleep, conflicts that for the most part originate from the family atmosphere. These can be caused especially by fear of separation from the mother (or) by rivalry with siblings."

Family neuroses: "The function of the children's role in the family, the position of their person in the family atmosphere presents an important prerequisite for the development of a psychosomatic disorder. Flight into illness, for example, can be caused by a family neurosis. The sick child supposedly needs it to support the community of the marriage. A symbiotic mother-child neurosis and certain negative sibling relationships are other prerequisites that contribute to a psychosomatic symptom becoming an expression of an unresolved life conflict. Children who have become psychosomatically ill find themselves, in opposition to adults, still in actual altercation with the overwhelmingly traumatizing object, oftentimes the mother. So, it is also almost always necessary to come to terms with the psychical condition of the mothers, although they frequently do not share that opinion."

Stealing: "In so-called symbolic stealing children want to gain emotional affection and love that is not present. For this not small group of children stealing serves as a substitute for love. Such children often lack necessary attention in the family so that the low self-esteem seeks for compensation through the deed."

Lying: "For the most part, children occasionally lie out of fear of punishment from the truly strict and authoritarian parents who raise them. More frequently children also want to avoid confronting their parents with irregularities so that they keep silent about them in order not to irritate or provoke them."

Running away: "The great majority of children at this age run away from home out of fear, out of protest, or, in the sense of a short-circuit reaction, often after harmless conflicts. In the main an authority crisis hides behind this behavior."

So the symptom—whatever it may be—that appears in the seventh year is only the last drop that brings the pot to overflowing. But the first drop is the most important, and especially in disorders of the seventh year it oddly often leads us back to the period of primary narcissism. The reason lies in the fact that the seventh year is the year of the growing need for independence. If parents now try to keep their children away from danger, children perceive this as a deep narcissistic offense. They do not want to be browbeaten. They do not want to be patronized. They do not want to be protected. So the rage of the seven-year-old at the parents' good intentions is often murderous. If this rage devours the children inside, it can then become chronic vindictiveness: "Just as exploited persons spare the exploiter only because they hope one day in turn to become exploiters themselves, sons bear the narcissistic offenses only because they hope one day to inflict the same on their powerful parents" (Wilhelm Reich).

Children's self-respect is determined by the respect their caregivers show to them. In adulthood their respect for others will then depend on their own self-respect. It has gradually become a secret no more to psychologists, psychiatrists, and psychoanalysts that all aggressive, harmful, and destructive behavior of adults originates in the repressed consciousness of their own worthlessness. Thus the fate of humanity is finally determined by the respect or disrespect that we as parents show our children.

These days, everyone knows that children raised without love become loveless adults. Everyone knows that neglected children, ones who were improperly cared for, mature into neglectful adults. Everyone knows that children learn to grasp, walk, and laugh more quickly the more time you spend with them, and that they atrophy mentally as well as physically if from the earliest period on they are not mentally and physically challenged and encouraged. But the most loving and caring parents are often exactly the ones who remove every difficulty from the way of their children and out of fear of the harmful outside world chain the children all too long to themselves and to the parental household.

Such children then suffer from psychical deprivation just as much as the children of loveless parents. They suffer from a lack of experience that can be just as disadvantageous as an absentee mother or the emotional deprivation of many children in orphanages. Every form of spoiling is a type of infantilization, and in the seventh year we have to be especially careful not to divert our children from the progress they so very much want by domineering over and spoiling them.

A certain measure of continuity and cohesion is certainly essential to give children a stable foundation for their development, but the idea of so many parents, that childhood goes all the more successfully the more quietly it runs, is false. Extraordinary creative abilities of adults can almost always be traced back to an extraordinarily wide palette of intellectual, emotional, and sensory stimuli in childhood.

At the same time, we certainly have to distinguish between intellectual *demands* on children and the free choice of *opportunities for experience.* Certainly children can also be overchallenged by excessive psychical stimulation, but for the most part the risk of the *lack of psychical stimulation* is by far greater than that of psychical *oversaturation.*

11

Eighth Year
End of Childhood

Childhood ends at age eight; adolescence begins at age nine. So the first volume of our textbook ends with the eighth year. The second one will deal with the phases of maturation of adolescence.

The eighth year is one of rest, relaxation, and consolidation. Developmental psychologists speak about a *constructive age*, and that truly expresses certain aspects of the patience, creative abilities, and manual dexterity of this phase. The children are now between 1.22 m (4.00 ft) and 1.24 m (4.06 ft) tall and weigh between 23.3 kg (51.36 lb) and 24 kg (52.91 lb). At year's end the girl weighs approximately 26.8 kg (59.08 lb), the boy approximately 26.9 kg (59.30 lb). The girl is 1.29 m (4.23 ft) tall, the boy 1.30 m (4.26 ft).

The agility and self-confidence of the children, but also their curiosity and their learning ability, increase in the course of the year. The children wander around in town and city; they often ride their bicycles so far that they need all their energy for their return home. They inspect forests, fields, and ponds, examine neighboring homes, building sites, garbage dumps, and unoccupied houses. They get into relationships with tramps, the homeless, and other street people. They become acquainted with young prostitutes, who are only a few years older than they are. They climb over fences to find out what is behind them and get into the intimate sphere of strangers. They surprise adolescents and adults who are having sexual intercourse in the forests, gardens, basements, building huts, and on park benches. They commandeer unoccupied summer houses and turn them into "club houses" for the local clique. There, for the immature ones at this age occurs the first experience with sexual intercourse, usually with a friend's sister or brother.

These things must remain hidden from parents. So, in the eighth year, children learn to keep their thoughts and experiences to themselves. Like married people who want to hide an amorous escapade from their spouse, children now learn to lead their parents around by the nose. Of all the phases of childhood, parents know the least about this one. But children do not turn from their parents and to other children for sexual reasons only, but also for ego-boosting. Conscience formation is completed. After the eighth year the superego can no longer be changed. Simultaneously children cease their harmless monologues and begin to weigh their words. That is in no way a result of schooling, because at least until the end of the first year of school almost all children hold a permanent dialogue with themselves while moving, doing homework, and playing. Children ages six to seven who sit still for a longer period of time and hold no conversations with themselves are unusual and can just as well be sick as precocious. But now, in the eighth year, children can sit still for hours, for example, while working at a hobby, sorting stamp collections, or reading, and remain quiet at the same time.

But generally eight-year-olds spend more time with other children than at home. Experiences outside the home become more important than those in the parents' home, strangers more important than the parents and relatives. Eight-year-olds become active members of street cliques, get to know their customs well, and keep to the rules. They stoically and without complaint bear disappointments, rejections, and accidents. They learn to trust their friends and depend on them. Solidarity is the motto of the eighth year. According to adults' standards, that can take on tragicomic proportions. So, for example, eight-year-olds can say, hurtfully, "Everyone in the clique has measles except me."

With regard to their parents, they are sparing with their affections; their love for their contemporaries is unlimited. In both sexes, the highly libidinous friendships of this age can smoothly turn sexual, so imperceptibly that children mostly do not become aware of the difference. Neither parents nor schoolteachers should give a thought to the "homosexuality" of eight-year-olds. In the overwhelming majority of children who at this age mutually masturbate each other or masturbate in the company of others, no vestige of same-sex tendencies stay over into puberty. On the contrary, the transitory homoeroticism of the eighth year probably furthers heterosexual behavior in future years, because the homo-erotic impulses that are planted in all of us discharge once and for all and simultaneously sensitize our bodies for the future joys of adult sex life. Sex pedologists agree on at least this: The earlier heterosexual children's games and homoerotic trial behavior begin, the earlier they also end. This phase is completed at the latest in the thirteenth year in more than 70 percent of all children.

Perhaps it should also be added here that there is a complementary as well as a typologic association between masturbation and the above-mentioned sexual activities. The earlier children enter into active twosome relationships, the earlier they stop masturbating alone. Stated differently: From the eighth year on we can see an unmistakable division of children into introverts and extroverts. The introverts, the uncertain ones, the contact-shy children, continue to masturbate up until adolescence and sometimes into adulthood. The extroverts, the self-assured ones who joyfully make contact, who actively enter relationships with other children at the beginning as well as at the end of the "latent period," mostly stop masturbation once and for all, and return to masturbation temporarily and reluctantly, in a situation of distress.

The traditional observation of the developmental psychologists of yesterday, that separation of the sexes and sexual animosity predominate from the eighth year to the middle of puberty, can no longer be maintained today. Of course, today there are a number of children who in this respect also behave this way, as did their parents and grandparents at age eight, but there are others who at age eight or nine already go to the movies in pairs and smooch.

At the moment, we are living in a transitional period between two very different forms of sex relations. That also manifests itself in children, and certainly so that, as an observer of today's children's scene, one feels like an anthropologist in a strange land who is confronted not with one, single culture, but with two or three races populating the same region and now, surprised, determines that the natives appear to live not according to one unified moral code, but rather according to two or three codes that contradict each other.

Twenty years ago, when our research team began its work among children and adolescents, an exchange of sexual knowledge indeed occurred within the clique of eight-year-olds, but only between girls and only between boys, at least up until the twelfth year. Today, that has totally changed. Most cliques consist of an approximately equal number of boys and girls. Many are led by girls, and their leadership is acknowledged by the boys without hesitation. The traditional monosexual street play group is becoming extinct.

On the other hand, for children, just as for adults, there are two camps fully separated from one another which because of their deep-seated moral differences and view of the world—almost like the ones existing everywhere in Central and Western Europe—can be considered almost like great political camps. There are conservative children who behave much differently than the liberal and socialist ones. Their customs are different, their conduct toward other children is different, their sexual behavior is different: The more conservative the parents, the more intensive the libidinization of the children, the more liberal the parents, the more sublimated the sex life of the children.

Sexual Pathology of the Eighth Year

The sociogenic aspects of human sexuality lead to the reproduction of the existing social order: individual sexuality adjusts to social norms. And since the existing social norm is not always friendly toward sex, the adjustment process often leads to sexual conflicts that begin already at age eight. Many teachers believe that "normal" schoolchildren are free of such, and so consider children who exhibit sexual conflicts as "abnormal." Unfortunately, the opposite is the case. If schoolchildren exhibit no indication of age-specific sexual problems near us, then we can fear that they will later develop much, much more serious problems of a seemingly nonsexual nature.

If we encounter sexual disorders in schoolchildren, these can often be traced back to a lack of experience in the earlier developmental stages. Every one of the sexual transitional stages of childhood must be overcome. If in school or at home children are forced to suppress the problems of any phase instead of conquering them, we then have to consider that these problems will appear later in an encoded, i.e., a seemingly asexual, form and then cause much more harm than in the original developmental stage.

Children frequently attempt to conquer their age-specific sexual problems by replacing their repressed desire with libidinously beset, compulsively performed, but seemingly nongenital behavior. When we observe that a certain child on the way to school compulsively avoids a certain stone on the street pavement or walks back as if directed to take the same steps again by an invisible hand, then we can be sure that this child has problems with the overcoming of age-specific sexual problems.

A characteristic of girls at age eight is the revival of the twosome that was formed around a common "secret" in the sixth year. The "secret" is never an active sexual one, but at closer observation it is always revealed as an individually encoded sexual symbol. Through the libidinous character of their relationship, both girls test their later relationship to their sex partner, and with the discretion demanded by the "secret," they practice the intimacy of this later relationship. Much of what can occur positively and negatively in a later marriage is worked through in a similar manner: love and hate, affection and jealousy, sympathy and rivalry, care and negligence.

Brocher very cleverly pointed to the reasons that make inadvisable an adult's indiscreet invasion into such a relationship:

Each painful, exact question by the teacher about the content of the secret or the hunting out of this form of relationship would be educationally a mistake, especially on the part of male teachers, because:
1. no answer can result,
2. distress of conscience arises in relation to the girl-friend concerned,
3. the feeling of violent invasion from the outside and with it the loss of an existing, magical protection is experienced.

The fear that behind the "secret" there is, perhaps, a direct sexual activity is almost without exception unjustified in girls. Problematic situations can occasionally occur when a girl who acts too strongly in the boy's role leads a group of passive girls. In such associations, the practicable activities of such an active leading girl most certainly take place outside of school, but they can have repercussions in class. It is mostly a question of a passive interest of children who were denied sex education at home. These children, otherwise regarded as "well-behaved," want to make up for the missed infantile sexual investigation. The corresponding sexualized inquiries are often mostly limited to somewhat embarrassed inspection of the genital region.

What has been repeatedly suggested in the course of this book should be summarized yet again as a reminder at the end of this latest contribution to the field of sexual pathology of children:

1. The sex life of children is all the more complicated the earlier we enter into their developmental history. It becomes all the more simple and understandable the older the children become. So the first chapters of this textbook are longer than the later ones.

2. The general public's notion that children generally have no sexuality and that sex begins at the earliest with puberty is false for several reasons: On the one hand, because it equates sexuality with genitality; on the other hand, because it equates sex life with coitus. But since human sex life differs from that of animals in that the greater part occurs in fantasy, for that very reason children's sex life has very much more in common with adult sex life than that of adult persons with that of anthropoid apes.

3. Since human sexual intercourse does not confine itself to touching the primary sex organs, but rather occurs also through sight, touch, and kissing as well as the use

of all other sense organs, the notion that when there is no coitus, there also is no sexual intercourse, is erroneous.

4. Human sex life consists mainly of *desires* and *mental images* of which the conscious ones in turn make up only the smallest part. In comparison with the amount of time spent on these desires and their effect on our romantic behavior, our sexual *acts* ("contacts," as Alfred Kinsey so nicely called it) take up only a minimal part of our life.

5. In all of these important precoital and noncoital aspects of our sex life, children, from birth on, play a major role. No aspect of adult sex life, not even the apparently most simple, can be understood if we do not consider it from the perspective of sexual ontogenesis. That is also true for all of the psychosexual disorders and all of adults' sexual "deviations."

6. To the extent in which human sex life expresses itself in *actions*, it will be very much easier to understand and describe. It is problematic only when it *cannot* be expressed in actions. Then, and only then, do sexual problems arise for children *and* adults.

Afterword

This book began as an answer to the question whether there are precise ages at which children need and can cope with certain sexual information. For several years the question has been directed to us, the few sex researchers active in the area of pedology, by parents and teachers, by pediatricians and child psychologists, by child analysts and child psychiatrists.

The answer is difficult, because it is a highly charged, emotional question. In this conclusion I want to play devil's advocate and discuss a few of the protests against the opinions rendered in this book:

1. Premature and involuntary confrontation with sexual subjects harms the children's natural development and causes moral injury to the psyche.

2. Sex education in school violates the parents' rights of custody as well as the special protection under which marriage and family stand in most Western countries.

3. Sex education in school is an implicit criticism of those parents who have foregone sex education at home out

of moral and religious convictions. When through sex education in school children are made aware that parents have neglected to set a family basis for this education, parental authority is undermined and the cohesion of the family destroyed.

4. Sex education in school is supported mainly by leftist teachers, leftist parties, and leftist governments. So it is to be rated as intentional usurpation of parental authority, as a weapon against parents loyal to tradition.

5. Sex education in school outside of religious instruction does not distinguish between the loving sexual intercourse of religious, trusting married people being of service to the procreation of a Christian next generation, and the loveless sexual intercourse of the unmarried, or even minors, that only serves the gratification of the senses.

No matter where one stands politically, these objections are pedologically untenable. For the concept of a "natural" development of children endangered by external (e.g., from school) influences is just as unreal and uninformed as that of an upbringing accompanied by the fewest possible "disorders." It asserts, without being aware of the implications of the postulate, that at the time of birth people are "better" than at some later time in their life. And it implies that all influential external forces endanger the goodness in the children's minds.

In this case, "good" means three things:

1. free of sexual impulses;
2. free of doubts about the parents, their view of the world, and their methods of upbringing;
3. free of opposition to the parents, their view of the world, and their methods of upbringing.

With that, parents declare their children in their bondage. Their children's rights to an autonomous development independent of parental influences are denied. Upbringing is no longer oriented toward the children's interest, but toward those of the parents. Children should not do what they want, but what the parents want. It is not important what is best for the children, but what brings satisfaction to the parents. That is psychic exploitation of the children by their parents—the total opposite of just what such parents think to do for the good of their children, when they deny them the right to a scholastic counterweight to the parental home.

These parents mostly argue with a revealing proprietary claim to the body and soul of their children—as if the children were consumer products for which parents have paid full price because they were willing to feed them since birth. They argue that these, indeed, are "their" children, that they know more about "their" children than all "strangers," and that "strangers" (e.g., schoolteachers) could indeed never "love" and "understand" the children as much as their "real" parents.

They have to be told that we have to complete an apprenticeship before we may practice the simplest professional activity; that before we may ever use the roads we have to be able to prove our ability to drive a car; that female kindergarten and elementary schoolteachers have to complete their education before they may even dare to teach children the a-b-c's or the multiplication tables; and that actually only parents already enjoy a freedom of fools bordering on the criminal in the education of "their" children.

The conception, birth, education, and death of all people influence not only their next of kin, but also all members of the society in which they live and die. So society not only has the right, but also the duty of "involvement" in the fate of the individual. If we basically accept this by making laws, electing a government, and financing an administration, then we ourselves cannot also avoid granting society the right to the education of "our" children. This is also true for the sexual as well as for the moral and intellectual education of children. Strange to say, the greatest responsibility that our society can really delegate to individual members—the right to produce and raise children—remains to this day without any duty in the Eastern as well as in the Western world. The results of this educational contradiction stare us in the face everywhere. For the notion that we know "by nature" how one does what is "best" for children, unfortunately, is false. Everything that we know about the nature of higher primates speaks against it. If we do not learn to give our children better models than our parents gave to us, the serious danger exists that each generation will be less able to survive than the preceding one.

In the case of anthropoid apes, which are directed at least halfway by inherited patterns of behavior, the raising of the young still only just barely occurs. In zoos, where young animals have at their disposal an insufficient number of attending animals from which to select a suitable model, they fare just as badly as in the human small family, in which children at best have two alternative models to which they are relinquished for better or for worse. In the case of rural large families, where children often had grandparents and other relatives in addition to their parents, but especially had models in the form of farmhands, the chance was far better to be able to move up to an alternative attendant at the parents' failure. So, exactly in the age of the small family there is the great danger to the success of the children, because under certain circumstances parents are not in a position to give them more than an improvised model.

This means that the education in the family must be learned all the more carefully and all the more laboriously than that in school. Parents who imagine they are somehow born with the talent to educate their children suffer from severe megalomania, from pathological deception of grandeur. Parents who consider the school as the enemy of the family and schoolteachers as feared rivals for the favors of their children implant schizophrenia in the psyche of the next generation. That is true for sex education in school in exactly the same way as for the gym lesson or music instruction. Either we leave the responsibility for the academic instruction of our children to the teachers trained for it—and then we have to do that in the area of sexology exactly as in that of mathematics—or we deny the school the right to education, and then that must be done equally consistently for the German lesson as for sex education.

The psyche of children is laid out such that the influences of school and of other nonfamily factors feared by many parents are indispensable for children to get accustomed to their environment and for their sexual development to adjust to the demands of their social order. These extrafamilial influences also include those of the "street," of "pornography," and of the "corrupter of children." In the history of children's development, these factors play the role of a prophylactic, a kind of psychic immunization against the pathogenic effects of similar influences in later life. For, contrary to the opinion still held today by a large segment of the general public— that children are especially endangered when such influences have an effect on the children's psyche "prematurely"—children are on this account shielded against these factors exactly *because* they affect them early and only *when* they play their role *before* sexual maturity. If children are familiar with them before their psychic receptivity is mature for them, then the negative influence ricochets away. If children are *not* prepared for them, they can leave traumatic consequences behind at the age of sexual maturity.

Exactly what many parents consider an especially harmful "disorder" of sexual development often proves itself a useful preventive process that makes possible the children's psychical and sexual maturity in the first place. If parents try to keep these extrafamilial influences away from the

children, they mostly prevent the healthy development of
their children, instead of furthering it.

The same thing goes for the "premature" influence of sex
education in school. In this case, the sexual pedological research has revealed that children react to all sexual influences
in the same way—thus, to sex education exactly as to pornography or seduction: If the children are mature enough
for a given stimulus, they then react with interest and care;
if they are not yet mature, all influences rebound from their
indifference. It is impossible that children who are loved
by and secure in the mutual sexual affection of their parents
can be troubled by "pornography," "seduction," or "premature" sex education. In every single case in which such uncertainty could be proven, it was a matter of children of
loveless parents, but especially of abandoned ones or of
children raised in orphanages. In their devotion to older sex
partners they seek that love and safety they missed in their
own parents' home or at the orphanage; thus they are more
likely "seducers" than "seduced." On the other hand, those
children just as harmed by pornography as by biological
sex education are those who have been raised to equate
sexuality with sin and so have never learned from their
parents that sexual love is the greatest joy that people can
share with each other. Such children belong to the few who
can be even more troubled by a purely biological sex
education than they already are.

So here we find ourselves confronted with the instructive
experience that those parents who turn against the school
sex education of their children are often identical to those
parents who have already run their children so far to the
ground by lovelessness and hostility toward the body that
sex education in school could actually be harmful to them.

Bibliography

Since the original list of sources for this book had to be drastically reduced because of the lack of space, we concentrated our bibliographical data on literary high points and so in the following suggest a source list of our theme's crucial points according to chapter. At the same time, we also have registered a few pioneer works on all the themes discussed, works we today, unfortunately, all too often pass over.

Preface

Child Sexuality

Abraham, K. "Über die Sexualität des Kindes." *Archiv für Frauenkunde, Sexualwissenschaftliches Beiheft* 6 (1920): 278ff.

Bönheim, C. "Über die Sexualität des Kindes." *Nervenarzt* 4 (1931): 663.

Borneman, E. "Sexualität" in *Kritische Stichwörter zur Kinderkultur*, edited by K. W. Bauer and H. Hengst. Munich, 1978, pp. 292–305.

Broderick, C. B. *Kinder- und Jugendsexualität.* Reinbek, 1970.

Burchard, E. *Das Geschlechtsleben des Kindes.* Berlin, 1913.

De sexuele ontwikkeling van het kind. Niederländisches Institut für socialsexologische Untersuchungen NISSO. Zeist, 1972.

Erikson, E. H. "Die Theorie der infantilen Sexualität." In E. H. Erikson, *Kindheit und Gesellschaft.* Stuttgart, 1961, pp. 30–84.

Frank, R. L. "Childhood Sexuality." In *Psychosexual Development in Health and Disease,* edited by P. H. Hoch and J. Zubin. New York, 1949, pp. 143–58.

Freud, A. "Sex in Childhood." *Health Education Journal* 2 (1944): 2–6.

Freud, S. "Die infantile Sexualität." *Gesammelte Werke* 5 (1905): 73–107.

———. "Die infantile Genitalorganisation." *Gesammelte Werke* 13 (1923): 293–98.

Friedjung, J. K. *Die kindliche Sexualität und ihre Bedeutung für Erziehung und ärztliche Praxis.* Berlin, 1923.

Frijling-Schreuder, E. "Sexuele ontwikkeling van het kind." *Huisarts en wetenschap* 6 (1963).

Grassel, H., and K. R. Bach. *Kinder und Jugendsexualität.* Berlin, 1979.

Groves, E. R., and G. H. Groves. *Sex in Childhood.* New York, 1933.

Guyon, R. "The Child and Sexual Activity." *International Journal of Sexology* 2 (1948): 26–34.

Harnik, J. "Ein Beitrag zum Thema Infantile Sexualität." *Zentralblatt f. Psychoanalyse u. Psychotherapie* 2 (1912): 37–38.

Heggli, J. *Kinder- und Jugendsexualität in der Krise.* 4 vols. Zurich, 1976–79.

Jelliffe, S. E. "The Sexual Life of the Child." In *The System of Pediatrics,* edited by I. A. Abt. Philadelphia, 1925, pp. 796–854.

Jennebach, N. *Die leiblich-seelische Geschlechtsentwicklung des Kindes und Jugendlichen und ihre Stellung in Familie, Schule und Gericht.* Leipzig & Berlin, 1937.

"Kindersexualität." *Betrifft Erziehung,* special issue 6. Weinheim, 1976.

Kläsi, J. "Beitrag zur Frage der kindlichen Sexualität." *Zeitschr. f. ges. Neurol. u. Psychiat.* 74, nos. 1–3 (1922): 362–78.

Klein, M. "Die Sexualbetätigung des Kindes." *Almanach* (1933): 138–51.

Lewis, M. "Psychosexual Development and Sexual Behavior in Children." *Conn. Med.* 32 (1968): 437–43.

London, L. S. "Psychosexual Psychology of the Child." *Urological Review* 35 (1931): 764–69.

Löwenfeld, L. "Über die Sexualität im Kindesalter." *Sexualprobleme* 7 (1911): 444–54, 516–34.

Marcus, E. "Zur infantilen Sexualität." *Zentralblatt f. Psychoanalyse u. Psychotherapie* 3 (1913): 363.

Moll, A. *Das Sexualleben des Kindes.* Berlin, 1909.

Monagues, J. "Esquema de l'evolucio sexual de l'infant." *Rev. Psicol. Pedag.* 2 (1934): 117–19.

Money, J. "Progress of Knowledge and Revision of the Theory of Infantile Sexuality." *International Journal of Psychiatry* 4 (1967): 50–54.

Newbauer, P. B. "Infantile Sexuality and the Developmental Point of View." *International Journal of Psychiatry* 4 (1967): 54–56.

Pacharzina, K., and K. Albrecht-Désirat, eds. *Konfliktfeld Kindersexualität.* Frankfurt-on-Main, 1978.

Raalte, F. v. "Äußerungen der Sexualität bei Kindern." *Intern. Zeitschr. f. ärztl. Psychoanalyse* 5 (1919): 103–8.

Rambert, M. L. "L'évolution de l'amour de l'enfance à l'âge adulte." *Revue Française de Psychoanalyse* 12 (1948): 457–73.

Rank, O. "Ein Beitrag zur infantilen Sexualität." *Intern. Zeitschr. f. ärztl. Psychoanalyse* 1 (1913): 366–71.

Rascovsky, A. "Consideraciones psicosomáticas sobre la evolución sexual del niño. *Rev. Psicoanál* 1 (Buenos Aires, 1943): 182–229.

Reevy, W. R. "Child Sexuality." In *Encyclopedia of Sexual Behavior,* edited by A. Ellis and A. Abarbanel. New York, 1961, pp. 258–67.

Rubin, I., and L. A. Kirkendall, eds. *Sex in the Childhood Years.* New York, 1970.

Sadger, J. "Sexualität und Erotik im Kindesalter." *Mod. Med.* 6, no. 2 (1915): 3.

Schérer, R., and G. Hocquenghem. *Kinderträume—Kindersexualität.* Munich, 1977.

Schmeer, G. *Das sinnliche Kind.* Stuttgart, 1975.

Schnorr, H. "Beiträge zur infantilen Sexualität." *Zentralblatt f. Psychoanalyse u. Psychotherapie* 4 (1913): 101–2.

Stekel, W. "Das Geschlechtsleben des Kindes." In W. Stekel, *Psychosexueller Infantilismus.* Berlin & Vienna, 1922, pp. 39–63.

Stockert, F.-G. v. *Die Sexualität des Kindes.* Stuttgart, 1956.

Strain, F. *The Normal Sex Interests of Children from Infancy to Adolescence.* New York, 1948.

Tamm, A. "Om sexualitet i barnalderen." *Hjälpskolan* 3 (1934): 16.

——. "Om barnete sexualitet." *Svenska Läkartiden* 33 (1936): 1831–43.

Tausk, V. "Zur Psychologie der Kindersexualität." *Intern. Zeitschr. f. ärztl. Psychoanalyse* 1 (1913): 444–58.

Thompson, E. "Sexualität im Kindesalter." In *Mensch, Geschlecht, Gesellschaft,* edited by H. Giese, vol. 1. Munich (no year), pp. 217–24.

Tordjman, G. *Réalités et problèmes de la vie sexuelle de l'enfance à l'âge adulte.* Paris, 1975.

Toussieng, P. W. "Psychosexual Development in Childhood and Adolescence." *Journal Sch. Health* 35 (1965): 158–65.

Weiss, K. "Aus dem kindlichen Sexualleben." *Zeitschr. f. Sexualw.* 7 (1920): 32–33.

Winnicott, D. W. "The Child and Sex." *The Practitioner* (April 1947): 158ff.

Witt, A. "Ein Beitrag zum Thema Sexuelle Eindrücke beim Kinde." *Zentralblatt f. Psychoanalyse u. Psychotherapie* 1 (1911): 165–66.

Zulliger, H. "Elternbeobachtungen über die Sexualität kleiner Kinder." *Imago* 15 (1929): 111–34.

Introduction

Relationships Between Inherited and Acquired Aspects of Sexuality

Burns, G. W. "Inheritance Related to Sex." In *The Science of Genetics.* New York, 1969.

Freytag, W. *Sex, Umwelt und Vererbung.* Cologne, 1978.

Pechstein, J. *Umweltabhängigkeit der frühkindlichen zentralnervösen Entwicklung.* Stuttgart, 1974.

Spitz, R. A. "The Role of Ecological Factors in Emotional Development in Infancy." *Child Development* 10 (1949): 145–55.
Winnicott, D. W. *Reifungsprozesse und fördernde Umwelt.* Munich, 1974.

Acceleration and Neoteny

Backmann, G. "Die beschleunigte Entwicklung der Jugend. Verfrühte Menarche, verspätete Menopause, verlängerte Lebensdauer." *Acta Anatomica* 4 (1948): 421–80.
Laslett, P. "Age at Sexual Maturity Since the Middle Ages." In P. Laslett, *Family Life and Illicit Love in Earlier Generations.* Cambridge, 1977.
Lenz, W. "Ursachen des gesteigerten Wachstums der heutigen Jugend. Akzeleration und Ernährung." *Deutsche Ges. f. Ernährung.* Darmstadt, 1959.
Paschlau, R., and G. Paschlau. "Beitrag zur Frage des Verhältnisses der körperlichen Entwicklungsbeschleunigung unserer Jugend zu ihrer Leistungsfähigkeit in der Schule." *Öff. Gesundh.-Dienst* 25 (1963): 63ff.

Sexual Developmental Psychology

Borneman, E. "Zur Frage eines Lehrbuchs der sexuellen Entwicklungspsychologie." *Sexualpädagogik* 3 (1979): 28–30.
———. "Entwicklung der Sexualität." In *50 Stichwörter zur Sexualerziehung in der Schule,* edited by F. Koch and K.-H. Lutzmann. Hamburg, 1981.
Brocher, T. *Psychosexuelle Grundlagen der Entwicklung.* Opladen, 1971.
Bühler, Ch. "Zum Problem der sexuellen Entwicklung." *Zeitschr. f. Kinderheilkunde* 51 (1931): 612–42.
Erikson, E. H. "Psychosexual Development." In *Discussions in Child Development,* vol. 4. New York, 1960.
Ramsey, G. V. "The Sexual Development of Boys." *Am. Journal Orthopsychiat.* 13 (1943): 347ff.

Chapter 1: From Conception to Birth

Human Genetics

Becker, P., ed. *Humangenetik.* 5 vols. Stuttgart, 1964–76.
Murken, J. D., and H. Cleve. *Humangenetik.* 2d ed. Stuttgart, 1979.
Stengel, H. *Humangenetik.* 3rd ed. Heidelberg, 1979.
Vogel, F. *Lehrbuch der allgemeinen Humangenetik.* Berlin, 1961.

Proportions of the Sexes

Huerkovay, O., et al. "Prenatal Sex Ratio in Man." *Acta Univ. Carol. Med.* 18 (Prague, 1964): 109ff.
Ludwig, W., and Ch. Boost. "Über das Geschlechtsverhältnis beim Menschen." *Zeitschr. f. Naturw.* 94 (1940): 1ff., 37ff.; *Biol. generalis* 16 (1942): 160ff.
Rauber, A. *Der Überschuß der Knabengeburten und seine biologische Bedeutung.* Leipzig, 1900.
Vosgerau, H. *Morphologische und statistische Untersuchungen zur Frage der intrauterinen Übersterblichkeit des männlichen Geschlechts.* Med. diss. Heidelberg, 1958.

Embryology

Blechschmidt, E. *Die vorgeburtlichen Entwicklungsstadien des Menschen.* Basel, 1961.
———. *Die pränatalen Organsysteme des Menschen.* Stuttgart, 1973.
Schumacher, G.-H. *Embryonale Entwicklung des Menschen.* Berlin, 1974.

Prenatal Determinants of Later Sexual Behavior

Loewit, K. "Neuropsyicoendocrinologia prenatale. Le determinanti prenatali del comportamento sessuale." Ed. Borla, 4, Rome, 1980, 10–18.

Influence of the Mother's Psychical Problems on the Fetus

Ottinger, D. R., and J. E. Simmons. "Maternal Anxiety during Gestation and Neonate Behavior." *Rec. Adv. Biol. Psychiat.* 5 (1963): 7–12.

Rottmann, G. *Die vorgeburtliche Mutter-Kind-Beziehung.* Diss. Saltzburg, 1974.

Simmons, J. E., and D. Ottinger. "Behavior of Human Neonates and Prenatal Maternal Anxiety." *Psychol. Rep.* 14 (1964): 391–94.

Turner, E. K. "The Syndrome in the Infant Resulting from Maternal Emotional Tension during Pregnancy." *Medical Journal Australia* 1 (1956): 221–22.

Birth Trauma

Bernfeld, S. "Traumen und Versagung." In S. Bernfeld, *Psychologie des Säuglings.* Berlin, 1925, pp. 183–228.

Garley, D. "Über den Schock des Geborenwerdens und seine möglichen Nachwirkungen." *Intern. Zeitschr. f. Psychoanalyse* 10 (1924): 134–63.

Krapf, E. E. "A propos de la signification psychologique de la régulation de l'oxigène chez le foetus." *Archive suisse de Neurologie et de Psychiatrie* 65 (1950): 108–115.

Rank, O. *Das Trauma der Geburt.* Vienna, 1924.

Winnicott, D. W. "Birth Memories, Birth Trauma and Anxiety." In D. W. Winnicott, *Collected Papers.* London and New York, 1958, pp. 174–93.

Pathology: Disordered Parental Relations in the Children's Prenatal Stage and their Influence on Postnatal Sexual Behavior

Lukesch, M. *Psychogene Faktoren der Schwangerschaft, mit einer Untersuchung über die Bedeutung der Partnerbeziehung für die Einstellung der Mutter zur Schwangerschaft.* Diss. Salzburg, 1975.

Ward, J. "Prenatal Stress Feminizes and Demasculinizes the Behavior of Males." *Science* 175 (1972): 82–84.

Pathology: Chromosomal Disorders

Danon, M. "The Sex Chromosomes and the Development of Human Intersexes." In *Symposium on Nuclear Sex,* edited by D. R. Smith and W. M. Davidson. London, 1958, 55ff.

Koch, G., and G. Neuhäuser. *Das Klinefelter-Syndrom und seine Varianten XXY und XXXY.* Stuttgart, 1978.

Valentine, G. H. *The Chromosomal Disorders.* 2d ed. London, 1970.

Pathology: Endocrine Disorders

Jones, H. W., Jr., and W. W. Scott. *Hermaphroditism, Genital Anomalies and Related Endocrine Disorders.* Baltimore, 1958.

Overzier, C. *Endokrinologische Fragen des Hermaphroditismus.* Berlin, Göttingen, Heidelberg, 1956.

Rumphorst, K., and H. H. Stange. "Über Geschlechtsbestimmungen bei Keimdrüsenfehlbildungen und Hermaphroditen." *Med. Monatsschr.* (1956): 1296ff.

Sebaoun-Zucman, M. *Les états intersexuels d'origine gonadique.* Diss. Paris, 1958.

Young, H. H. *Genital Abnormalities, Hermaphroditism and Related Adrenal Disease.* Baltimore, 1937.

Pathology: Incorrect Sex Assignments of Newborns

Dost, F. H. "Grundsätze beim ärztlichen Entscheid über die rechtliche Geschlechtszuordnung neugeborener Intersexe." *Mün. med. Wochenschr.* (1957): 1051ff.

Keller, R. *Das Gutachten über die Geschlechtszugehörigkeit.* Stuttgart, 1980.

Taylor, A. I. "Ambiguous Sex and Sex Chromatin in the Newborn." *Lancet* 2 (1962): 1059ff.

Pathology: Psychosexual Differentiation in the First Year

Dannhauer, H. *Geschlecht und Persönlichkeit. Eine Untersuchung zur psychischen Geschlechtsdifferenzierung in der Ontogenese.* Berlin, 1973.
Henseler, H. "Die Entwicklung der menschlichen Sexualität." In *Psychoanalytische Entwicklungspsychologie,* edited by D. Ohlmeier. Freiburg, 1973.
Money, J. "Determinanten der geschlechtsspezifischen Identität und des Sexualverhaltens." In *Handbuch der Ehe- Familien- und Gruppentherapie,* vol. 2. Munich, 1973, pp. 718–47.
Schein, M. W., and E. B. Hale. "A Hypothetical Model Clarifying the Effect of Early Social Experience on Sexual Behavior." *Anatomical Record* 134 (1959): 634.

Chapter 2: First Month

Development of the Newborn's Sexuality

Harnik, J. "Die postnatale Entwicklungsstufe der Libido." *Intern. Zeitschr. f. Psychoanalyse* 19 (1933): 147–51.
Harris, G. W., and S. Levine. "Sexual Differentiation of the Brain and its Experimental Control." *Journal Physiol.* 181 (1965): 379–400.
Sherfey, M. J. "Introductory Theory of Primary Sexual Differentiation." *Journal Am. Psychoanal. Assoc.* 4 (1966).
Singer, J. E., M. Westphal, and K. R. Niswander. "Sex Differences in the Incidence of Neonatal Abnormal Performance in Early Childhood." *Child Development* 39 (1968): 103–12.

Erections in Newborns

Jovanovic, U. J. "Erectionen im Schlaf bei Säuglingen." In U. J. Jovanovic, *Sexuelle Reaktionen und Schlafperiodik des Menschen.* Stuttgart, 1972, pp. 115–21.

Narcissism

Freud, S. "Zur Einführung des Narzißmus." *Gesammelte Werke* 10 (1914): 138-70.

Cutaneous Phase

Borneman, E. "Die kutane Phase." In E. Borneman, *Lexikon der Liebe* (1978), 2: 763-65.
———. "Die polymorph-perverse Phase." In E. Borneman, *Lexikon der Liebe* (1978), 3: 1103-4.
———. "Die präorale Phase." In E. Borneman, *Lexikon der Liebe* (1978), 3: 1117.
———. "Die Zärtlichkeit des Kindes." *Neue Sammlung* 1, no. 21 (Jan.-Feb. 1981): 36-44.
Lacombe, P. "Du rôle de la peau dans l'attachement mère-enfant." *Revue Française de Psychoanalyse* 23 (1959): 83-101.
Montagu, M. F. A. *Körperkontakt. Die Bedeutung der Haut für die Entwicklung des Menschen.* 1971. 2d ed. Stuttgart, 1974.

Perception of the Primary Love Object

Handelsman, I. "The Effect of Early Object Relationships on Sexual Development." *The Psychoanalytic Study of the Child* 20 (1965): 367-83.
Rodrigué, E. "El objeto de amor primario—una revisión." *Rev. Psicoanál.* 12 (1955): 3.
Spitz, R. "Die Entstehung der ersten Objektbeziehungen." *Direkte Beobachtungen an Säuglingen des ersten Lebensjahres.* 2d ed. Stuttgart, 1960.

Oral Phase

Eissler, K. R. "Zur genaueren Kenntnis des Geschehens an der Mundzone Neugeborener." *Zeitschr. f. Kinderpsychiat.* 5 (1938): 81-85.

Hetzer, H., et al. "Frühes Lernen des Säuglings in der Ernährungs-situation." *Int. Zeitschr. f. Psychoanalyse* 16 (1930): 118ff.

Spitz, R. "Die Urhöhle. Zur Genese der Wahrnehmung und ihrer Rolle in der psychoanalytischen Theorie." *Psyche* 9 (1956): 641-67.

Pathology: Effects of Sex Role Assignment

Brackmann, M. *Geschlechtsspezifische Sozialisation in der Familie.* Diss. Berlin, 1972.

Bub, B. *Familienstruktur und geschlechtsspezifische Sozialisationsvorgänge.* Diss. Frankfurt-on-Main, 1968.

Eckert, Ch., and S. Kontos. *Der Identifikationsbegriff in den Theorien des Geschlechtsrollenerwerbs.* Diss. Frankfurt-on-Main, 1971-72.

Grundmann, H. "Bermerkungen zur Entwicklung der Geschlechtsidentität und Geschlechtrolle im frühen Kindesalter." In *Zur Situation und Kreativität der Frau. Forum für aktuelle Kunst.* Innsbruck, 1976.

Kagan, J. "The Acquisition and Significance of Sex Typing and Sex Role Identity." In *Review of Child Development Research,* edited by M. L. Hoffman and L. W. Hoffman, vol. 1. New York, 1964, pp. 137-67.

Pathology: Sexual Differentiation of the Boy

Brown, D. G. "Masculinity-Femininity Development in Children." *Journal Consult. Psychol.* 21 (1957): 197-202.

Pathology: Later Effects of Incorrect Parental Behavior in the Newborn

Deming, J. "Problems Presented by Children of Parents Forced to Marry." *Am. Journal Orthopsychiat.* 2 (1932): 70-81.

Ferenczi, S. "Das unwillkommene Kind und sein Todestrieb." *Intern. Zeitschr. f. Psychoanalyse* 15 (1929): 149-53.

———. "Die grundlegende traumatische Wirkung des Mutterhasses oder der Lieblosigkeit." In S. Ferenczi, *Bausteine zur psycho-analyse,* vol. 4. Bern, 1939, pp. 228–29.

Mahler, M. S., and R. Rabinovitch. "The Effects of Marital Conflict on Child Development." In *Neurotic Interaction in Marriage,* edited by V. W. Eisenstein. New York, 1956, pp. 44–56.

Spitz, R. *Somatic Consequences of Emotional Starvation in Infants.* 16 mm film. New York, 1948.

Pathology: Unintentional Parental Influence
on the Newborn's Later Sex Life

Strauss, A. "The Influence of Parent-Image upon Marital Choice." *Am. Sociol. Rev.* 11 (1946): 554–59.

Chapter 3: Second to Sixth Month

Sexuality

Galant, S. "Sexualleben im Säuglings- und Kindesalter." *Neurol. Zentralbl.* 38 (1919): 652ff.

Hammer, W. "Liebesleben im ersten Lebensjahr." In W. Hammer, *Psychopathia Sexualis* (no date), pp. 35–41.

Klein, M. "Some Theoretical Conclusions Regarding the Emotional Life of the Infant." In *Developments in Psychoanalysis,* edited by J. Riviere. London, 1952, pp. 198–236.

Infant Masturbation

Freud, S. *Gesammelte Werke* 5: 74, 81, 86–94, 121, 153; 7: 260, 263, 424; 8: 46, 336; 11: 336–37; 14: 418.

Breast Feeding Versus Bottle Feeding

Goldman-Eisler, F. "Breastfeeding and Character Formation." *Journal of Personality* 17 (1948): 82–103.

———. "Breastfeeding and Character Formation." *Journal of Per-*

sonality 19 (1950): 189-96.

McKinney, B. M. "The Sexual Aspects of Breast Feeding." *Child-Fam. Dig.* 13 (1955): 45-57.

Newton, N. "Interrelationships between Sexual Responsiveness, Birth and Breast Feeding." In *Contemporary Sexual Behavior*, edited by J. Zubin and J. Money. Baltimore and London, 1973, pp. 77-98.

Winter, S. K. "Fantasies at Breast Feeding Time." *Psychology Today* 3, no. 8 (1970): 30-32, 56.

Orgasmic Potency

Kentler, H. "Orgasmus beim weiblichen Kleinkind." In H. Kentler, *Texte zur Sozio-Sexualität.* Opladen, 1973, pp. 66-67.

Kinsey, A. C. "Orgasmus beim männlichen Kleinkind." In *Texte zur Sozio-Sexualität*, edited by H. Kentler. Opladen, 1973, pp. 63-65.

Kramer, P. "Early Capacity for Orgastic Discharge and Character Formation." *Study of the Child* 9 (1954): 128-41.

Lewis, W. C. "Coital Movements in the First Year of Life." *Intern. Journal Psychoanalysis* 46 (1965): 372-74.

More on the Oral Phase

Abraham, K. *Beiträge der Oralerotik zur Characterbildung.* Leipzig, Vienna, Zurich, 1925.

Ferenczi, S. "Die Oralerotik in der Kindererziehung." In S. Ferenczi, *Bausteine zur Psychoanalyse*, vol. 4. Berne, 1939, pp. 218-19.

Leitch, M. "A Commentary on the Oral Phase of Psycho-sexual Development." *Bulletin of the Menninger Clinic* 12 (1948): 117-25.

Papousek, H. "Experimental Studies of Appetitional Behavior in Human Newborns and Infants." In *Early Behavior*, edited by Wh. H. Stevenson and H. L. Rheingold. New York, 1967, pp. 249-99.

Ribble, M. A. "The Significance of Infantile Sucking for the Psychic Development of the Individual." *Journal Nervous Mental Dis.* 90 (1939): 455-63.

Ripin, R., and H. Hetzer. "A Study of the Infant's Feeding Reaction during the First Six Months of Life." *Arch. Psychol.* 18 (1930).

Sameroff, A. J. "The Components of Sucking in the Human Newborn." *Journal Child Psychol.* 6 (1968): 607–23.

Pathology: Autoerotic Regressions to Early Infancy

Kris, E. "Einige Gedanken und Beobachtungen über den frühkindlichen Autoerotismus." *Psyche* 24 (1970): 270–91.

——. "Frühe autoerotische Aktivität. Beobachtungen und Erläuterungen." In E. Kris, *Psychoanalytische Kinderpsychologie.* Frankfurt-on-Main, 1979.

Nagera, H. "Autoerotism, Autoerotic Activities, and Ego Development." *The Psychoanalytic Study of the Child* 19 (1964): 240–55.

Spitz, R., and K. M. Wolf. "Autoerotism. Some Empirical Findings and Hypotheses on Three of its Manifestations in the First Year of Life." *The Psychoanalytic Study of the Child* 3/4 (1949): 85–120.

——. "Ein Nachtrag zum Problem des Autoerotismus; frühe sexuelle Verhaltensmuster und ihre Bedeutung für die Persönlichkeitsbildung." *Psyche* 18 (1964): 241–72.

Chapter 4: Seventh to Twelfth Month

Sexual Origins of Thinking and Learning

Bornstein, B. "Beziehungen zwischen Sexual- und Intellekentwicklung." *Zeitschr. f. psychoanalyt. Päd.* 4 (1930): 446–54.

Gagnon, J. H. "Sexuality and Sexual Learning of the Child." *Psychiatry* 28 (1965): 212–28.

Hermann, I. "Organlibido und Begabung." *Intern. Zeitschr. f. Psychoanalyse* 9 (1923): 297–310.

Salzman, L. "The Role of Sexuality in the Formation of Ideas." *Journal Ind. Psych.* 17 (1961): 108–9.

Pathology: Oral and Oral-Sadistic Regressions to Late Infancy

Abraham, K. Über sadistische Phantasien im Kindesalter. Berlin,
  1910.
Rascovsky, M. W. "Imágines del pecho materno." Rev. Psicoanál.
  13 (1956): 66–69.
Sterba, E. "Homesickness and the Mother's Breast." Psychiat.
  Quarterly 14 (1940): 701–8.
Sterba, R. "Vom oralen Ursprung des Neides." Zeitschr. f. psy-
  choanalyt. Päd. 3 (1929): 472–73.

Pathology: Effects of the Frustration of Infantile Sexual Discovery

Landauer, K. "Zur psychosexuellen Genese der Dummheit."
  Zeitschr. f. Sexualwissensch. 16 (1929): 87–96.

Chapter 5: Second Year

Sexual Development

Adler, A. "Das Zärtlichkeitsbedürfnis des Kindes." Monatshefte
  f. päd. Schulpolitik 1 (1908).
Balint, A. "Zwei Notizen über die erotische Komponente der Ich-
  Triebe." Intern. Zeitschr. f. Psychoanalyse 19 (1933): 428–33.
Deutsch, H. "Der erste Liebeskummer eines zweijährigen Knaben."
  Intern. Zeitschr. f. Psychoanalyse 5 (1919): 111–15.
Flandrin, J.-L. "L'attitude à l'égard du petit enfant et les conduites
  sexuelles dans la civilisation occidentale: structures anciennes
  et évolution." Annales de démographie historique, 1973, 143–
  210.
Fried, E. "Some Connections between Sexuality and Ego Organiza-
  tion." Am. Journal Orthopsychiat. 29 (1959): 391–401.
Ziebeil-Luttner, F. C. Frühkindliche Sexualität und Sexualerziehung. Munich, 1972.

Discovery of Sex Differences

Bells, E. K., and P. B. Neubauer. "Sex Differences and Symptom Patterns in Early Childhood." *Journal Child Psychiat.* 2 (1963): 417–33.

Cramer, B. "Sex Differences in Early Childhood." *Child Psychiat. and Human Dev.* 1 (1971).

Levy, D. M. "Contra-Situation Studies of Children's Responses to the Difference in Genitalia." *Am. Journal Orthopsychiat.* 10 (1940): 755–63.

Lewis, M. "Culture and Gender Roles: There Is no Unisex in the Nursery." *Psychol. Today* 5 (1972): 54–57.

——. "Early Sex Differences in the Human." In *New Directions in Sex Research,* edited by E. A. Rubenstein et al. New York, 1975, pp. 7–14.

Searl, M. N. "A Note on the Relation between Physical and Psychical Differences in Boys and Girls." *Int. Journal Psychoanalysis* 19 (1938): 50–62.

Terzian, A. S. "An Early Recognition of Sex Differences." *Bull. Phila. Psychoanal. Assn.* 5 (1955): 56ff.

Penis Envy Theory

Barnett, M. C. "Vaginal Awareness in the Infancy and Childhood of Girls." *Journal Am. Psychoanal. Assn.* 14 (1966): 129–51.

Greenacre, Ph. "Penis Awe and its Relation to Penis Envy." In *Drives, Affects, Behavior,* edited by R. M. Loewenstein. New York, 1953, pp. 176–90.

Müller-Braunschweig, K. "Die erste Objektbesetzung des Mädchens in ihrer Bedeutung für Penisneid und Weiblichkeit." *Psyche* 13, no. 1 (1959).

Thompson, C. "Penis Envy in Women." *Psychiatry* 6 (1943): 123ff.

First Sexual Games

Adler, A. "Erotische Kinderspiele." *Anthropophyteia* 8 (1911): 256–58.

Peller, L. "Das Spiel als Spiegel der Libidoentwicklung." In *Handbuch der Kinderpsychotherapie*, edited by G. Biermann. Munich, 1969, pp. 45–53.

Pfeifer, S. "Äußerungen infantil-erotischer Triebe im Spiel." *Imago* 5 (1919): 243–82.

Sadger, I. "Aus dem Sexualleben eines Jungen vom vierten bis achtzehnten Lebensmonat." *Zeitschr. f. psychoanal. Päd.* 3 (1929): 127–30.

Roots of the Anal Character

Abraham, K. "Ergänzungen zur Lehre vom Analcharakter." *Intern. Zeitschr. f. Psychoanalyse* 9 (1921): 27–47.

Brill, A. A. "Anal Eroticism and Character." *Journal Abn. Psychol.* 7 (1912): 196–203.

Finney, J. C. "Material Influences on Anal or Compulsive Character in Children." *Journal Genet. Psychol.* 103 (1963): 351–67.

Freud, S. "Charakter und Analerotik" (1908). *Gesammelte Werke* 7 (1941): 103–209.

Hetherington, E. M., and Y. Brackbill. "Etiology and Covariations of Obstinacy, Orderliness and Parsimony in Young Children." *Child Dev.* 34 (1963): 919–43.

Jones, E. "Über analerotische Charakterzüge." *Intern. Zeitschr. f. Psychoanal.* 5 (1919): 69–92.

Landauer, K. "Some Remarks on the Formation of the Anal-Erotic Character." *Intern. Journal Psychoanal.* 20 (1939): 418–25.

Menninger, W. C. "Characterological and Symptomatic Expressions Related to the Anal Phase of Psychosexual Development." *Psychoanalytic Quarterly* 12 (1943): 161–95.

Sadger, I. "Analerotik und Analcharakter." *Die Heilkunde*, 1910.

Pathology: Anal Regressions and Psychoses

Arlow, J. "Anal Sensations and Feelings of Persecution." *Psychoanalytic Quarterly* 18 (1949): 79–84.

Bender, L. "The Anal Component in Persecutory Delusions." *Psychoanalytic Review* 21 (1934): 75–85.

Berkeley-Hill, O. "The Anal Complex and its Relation to Delusion and Persecution." *Ind. Med. Gazette* 56 (1921): 255ff.
Ferenczi, S. "Reizungen der analen Zone als auslösende Ursache der Paranoia." *Intern. Zeitschr. f. ärztliche Psychoanalyse* 1 (1911): 557–59.
Hitschmann, E. "Paranoia, Homosexualität und Analerotik." *Intern. Zeitschr. f. Psychoanalyse* 1 (1913): 251–54.

Pathology: Dangers of the Prohibition of Masturbation

Freud, S. *Gesammelte Werke* 5: 89; 7: 179; 9: 156; 13: 396–97; 14: 21–22, 525; 15: 93, 132–33; 17: 61, 77, 117.
Reich, W. "Über die Spezifität der Onanieformen." *Intern. Zeitschr. f. Psychoanalyse* 8 (1922): 333–37.
———. "Über die Onanie im Kindesalter." *Zeitschr. f. psychoanal. Päd.* 2 (1927): 149–52.

Pathology: Transsexual Motivations

Sigusch, V., B. Meyenburg, and R. Reiche. "Transsexualität." In *Sexualität und Medizin,* edited by V. Sigusch. Cologne, 1979, pp. 249–311.
Stoller, R. J. "Parental Influences in Male Transsexualism." In *Transsexualism and Sex Reassignment,* edited by R. Green and J. Money. Baltimore, 1969, pp. 153–69.

Pathology: Dangers of the Prohibition of Childhood Sexual Investigation

Galenson, E., and H. Rolphe. "The Impact of Early Sexual Discovery on Mood, Defensive Organization and Symbolization." *The Psychoanalytic Study of the Child* 26 (1972).
Montagu, M. F. A. "The Acquisition of Sexual Knowledge in Children." *Am. Journal Orthopsychiat.* 15 (1945): 290–300.

Pathology: Danger of Fixation on the Prohibited

Berge, A. "Le sentiment de culpabilité." In *Le Coupable, est-il un Malade ou un Pécheur?* Paris, 1951.
Bretschneider, A. "Sexualität und Schuldgefühl beim Kleinkind." *Psychoanalytische Praxis* 3 (1933): 186–87.

Chapter 6: Third Year

Kindergarten Age

Biller, B. "Father Absence, Maternal Encouragement and Sex Role Development in Kindergarten-Age Boys." *Child Development* 40 (1969): 539–46.
Fling, S., and M. Manosevitz. "Sex Typing in Nursery Schools." *Developmental Psychology* 7 (1972): 146–52.

"Forbidden" Rhymes and Fascination with "Obscene" Words

Borneman, E. "Kindersprüche." In *Kritische Stichwörter zur Kinderkultur*, edited by K. W. Bauer and H. Hengst. Munich, 1978, pp. 199–205.
——. "Oben und Unten im Kinder- und Jugendreim." *Jahrbuch f. Volksliedforschung* 23 (1978): 151–64.
——. *Unsere Kinder im Spiegel ihrer Lieder, Reime, Verse und Rätsel.* Olten, 1973; Berlin 1979.
——. *Die Umwelt des Kindes im Spiegel seiner "verbotenen" Lieder, Reime, Verse und Rätsel.* Olten, 1974; Berlin, 1980.
——. " 'Verbotene' Kinderreime und das Geschlechtsleben des Kindes." In *Kindersexualität.* Sonderdruck 6 der Zeitschrift *Betrifft Erziehung.* Weinheim, 1976, pp. 20–24.
——. *Die Welt der Erwachsenen in den "verbotenen" Reimen deutschsprachiger Stadtkinder.* Olten, 1976; Berlin, 1981.

The So-Called Primal Scene

Borneman, E. *Die Urszene.* Frankfurt-on-Main, 1977, 1980.

Freud, S. "Aus der Geschichte einer infantilen Neurose" (1918). *Gesammelte Werke* 12: 29–157.

Graber, G. H. "Urszene, Spiel und Schicksal." In G. H. Graber, *Seelenspiegel des Kindes*. Zurich, 1946, pp. 100–118.

Sex Discovery in Infancy

Freud, S. "Über infantile Sexualtheorien" (1908). *Gesammelte Werke* 7: 171–88.

Hattendorf, K. W. "A Study of the Questions of Young Children Concerning Sex." *Journal of Social Psychol.* 3 (1932): 37–65.

Schneider, E. "Zur Sexualforschung des Kindes." *Zeitschr. f. psychoanal. Päd.* 1 (1926/27): 203–23.

Development of Female Sexuality

Chodoff, P. "Feminine Psychology and Infant Sexuality." In *Science and Psychoanalysis*, edited by J. H. Masserman, vol. 10. New York, 1966, pp. 28–42.

Fenichel, O. "Weiteres zur präödipalen Phase der Mädchen." *Intern. Zeitschr. f. Psychoanalyse* 20 (1934): 151–90.

Fleiss, R. "Female and Preoedipal Sexuality—A Historical Survey." In R. Fleiss, *The Psychoanalytic Reader*. New York, 1948, pp. 158–91.

Freud, S. "Einige psychische Folgen des anatomischen Geschlechtsunterschieds" (1925). *Gesammelte Werke* 14: 19–30.

Greenacre, Ph. "Special Problems of Early Female Sexual Development." *The Psychoanalytic Study of the Child* 5 (1950): 122–26.

Jones, E. "Die erste Entwicklung der weiblichen Sexualität." *Intern. Zeitschr. f. Psychoanalyse* 14 (1928): 11–25.

———. "Über die Frühstadien der weiblichen Sexualentwicklung." *Intern. Zeitschr. f. Psychoanalyse* 21 (1935): 331–41.

Kayton, E. C. "Development of Sexual Identity in a Little Girl." *Psychoanalysis and the Psychoanalytic Review* 47, no. 1 (1960): 116ff.

Weber, A. "Zur Entwicklung der weiblichen Sexualität in der frühen Kindheit." *Nervenarzt* 9 (1936): 615–20.

Masturbation

Freud, S. *Gesammelte Werke* 5: 89–91, 136, 241–43; 13: 375; 14: 63; 17: 117.

Schmidt, V. "Onanie bei kleinen Kindern." *Zeitschr. f. psychoanal. Päd.* 2 (1927/28): 153–55.

Development of Sexual Identity

Hartup, W. W., and E. A. Zook. "Sex-Role Preferences in Three- and Four-Year-Old Children." *Journal Consult. Psychol.* 24 (1960): 420–26.

Masochism

Dinard, C. "A propos du masochisme chez l'enfant." *Bull. Assn. psychoanalytique Française* 4 (1968): 103–8.

Doneth, J. "Ideeller Masochismus im zarten Kindesalter." *Deutsche Zeitschr. f. Nervenheilkunde* (1921): 68–69.

Federn, P. "Die infantilen Bedingungen des Masochismus." *Protokolle der Wiener psychoanalytischen Vereinigung* 2 (1977): 405–11.

Urethral Toilet Training

Coriat, I. H. "The Character Traits of Urethral Eroticism." *Psychoanalytic Review* 11 (1924): 426–34.

Hitschmann, E. "Urethralerotik und Zwangsneurose." *Intern. Zeitschr. f. Psychoanalyse* 6 (1920): 263–64.

Jones, E. "Urethralerotik und Ehrgeiz." *Intern. Zeitschr. f. Psychoanalyse* 3 (1915): 156–57.

Sadger, I. "Über Harnerotik." *Protokolle der Wiener psychoanalytischen Vereinigung* 2 (1977): 529–38.

———. "Über Urethralerotik." *Jahrbuch für psychoanalytische Forschung* 2 (1910): 409–50.

Pathology: Perversions as Psychosexual Infantilisms
and Acts of Revenge

Carp, E. A. D. E. "Die Rolle der Prägenitalen Libidofixierungen in der Perversion." *Intern. Zeitschr. f. Psychoanalyse* 10 (1924): 258–56.
Stoller, R. A. *Perversion—die erotische Form von Haß.* Reinbek, 1979.

Chapter 7: Fourth Year

Advances in Childhood Sexual Investigation

Arnold-Carey, L. *Und sie erkannten, daß sie nackt waren . . . Geschlechtswahrnehmung und kindliche Entwicklung.* Göttingen, 1971.
Sands, R. "The Sexual Curiosity of Preschoolers." *Offspring* 8 (1966): 1.

Development of Sexual Identity

Brown, D. G. "Masculinity-Femininity Development in Children." *Journal Consult. Psychol.* 21 (1957): 197–202.
Green, R. *Sexual Identity Conflict in Children and Adults.* New York, 1974.
Neuendorff, B. *Geschlechtliche Identität und Strukturierung der Person-Umwelt-Aktion.* Frankfurt-on-Main, 1977.
Smith, S. "Age and Sex Differences in Children's Opinions Concerning Sex Differences." *Journal Genetic Psychol.* 54 (1939): 17–25.

Sexual Games

Avery, C. E. "The Problem of Children's 'Sex Play.' " In *Guide to Sexology.* New York, 1965, pp. 238–40.
Erikson, E. H. "Sex and its Role in Play." In *Reflexes to Intelligence,*

edited by S. V. Beck and H. B. Molisch. Glencoe, 1959, pp. 290-99.

Simmel, E. "Doktorspiel, Kranksein und Ärzteberuf." *Intern. Zeitschr. f. Psychoanalyse* 12 (1926): 528-39.

Sex Theories

Boyer, L. B. "An Unusual Childhood Theory of Pregnancy." *Journal Hills. Hosp.* 8 (1959): 279-83.

Graber, G. H. "Zeugung und Geburt in der Vorstellung des Kindes." *Zeitschr. f. psychoan. Päd.* 1 (1926/27): 244-54.

Mannheim, M. J. "Zur infantilen Geburtstheorie." *Zeitschr. f. psychoan. Päd.* 2 (1927/28): 234-35.

Nagy, M. H. "Children's Birth Theories." *Journal Genet. Psychol.* 83 (1953): 217-26.

Ruben, H. E. "Some Meanings of the 'Belly Button' to Children." *Bull. Phila. Assn. Psychoanalysis* 4 (1954): 98-100.

On the Phallic Phase

Freedman, A. "Observations in the Phallic Stage." *Bull. Phila. Assn. Psychoanalysis* 4 (1954): 38ff.

Jones, E. "Die phallische Phase." *Intern. Zeitschr. f. Psychoanalyse* 19 (1933): 322-57.

Mittelman, M. "Les differentes phases du stade phallique chez l'enfant et leur répercussion individuelle et sociale." *Revue de Neuropsychiatrie infantile* 14 (1966): 687-94.

First Love

Brenner, M. "Kinderfreundschaften." In *Kinderkultur,* edited by K. W. Bauer and H. Hengst. Munich, 1978, pp. 127-37.

Hammer, W. "Das Liebesleben des kleinen Kindes." In W. Hammer, *Psychopathia Sexualis.* Berlin (no date), pp. 42-52.

Stekel, W. "Kinderfreundschaften." In W. Stekel, *Was im Grund der Seele ruht.* Vienna (no date), pp. 22-28.

Wolffheim, N. "Erotisch gefärbte Freundschaften in der frühen

Kindheit." *Zeitschr. f. psychoanalytische Päd.* 2 (1927/28): 264–74.

Oedipal Patterns of Behavior

Benjamin, E. "The Oedipus Complex in Childhood." *Nervous Child* 2 (1942): 47–54.

Fenichel, O. "Zur Prägenitalen Vorgeschichte des Ödipuskomplexes." *Intern. Zeitschr. f. Psychoanalyse* 16 (1930): 319–42.

Granjet, L. S. "La sexualidad infantil y el complejo de Edipo." *Acta pediatr. esp.* 8 (1950): 763–85.

Klein, M. "Frühstadien des Ödipuskonflikts." *Intern. Zeitschr. f. Psychoanalyse* 14 (1928): 65–77.

Lampl de Groot, J. "Re-Evaluation of the Role of the Oedipus Complex." *Intern. Journal Psychoanalysis* 33 (1952): 335–42.

Mandler, G. "Parent and Child in the Development of the Oedipus Complex." *Journal Nervous Mental Diseases* 136 (1963): 227–35.

Rangell, L. "The Role of the Parent in the Oedipus Complex." *British Medical Journal* 19 (1955): 9–15.

Roheim, G. "The Oedipus Complex and Infantile Sexuality." *Psychoanalytic Quarterly* 15 (1946): 190–508.

Spielrein, S. "Die Äußerungen des Ödipuskomplexes im Kindesalter." *Intern. Zeitschr. f. ärztliche Psychoanalyse* 4 (1916): 44–48.

Widlöcher, D. "Fonction paternelle, complexe d'Oedipe et formation de la personnalité." *Revue de Neuropsychiatrie infantile* 13 (1965): 777–81.

On the So-Called Breast Envy

Bergler, E., and L. Eidelberg. "Der Mammakomplex des Mannes." *Intern. Zeitschr. f. Psychoanalyse* 19 (1933): 547–83.

Grinstein, A. "Some Comments on Breast Envy in Women." *Journal Hills. Hosp.* 11 (1962): 171–77.

On the So-Called Castration Complex

Alexander, F. "The Castration Complex in the Formation of Character." *Intern. Journal Psychoanalysis* 6 (1923): 11–42.
————. "Zur Genese des Kastrationskomplexes." *Intern. Zeitschr. f. Psychoanalyse* 16 (1930): 349–52.
Baudouin, Ch. "Der Kastrationskomplex beim Kind." *Zeitschr. f. psychoan. Päd.* 1 (1926/27): 75–77.
Oberndorf, C. P. "The Castration Complex in the Nursery." *Intern. Journal Psychoanal.* 6 (1925): 324–25; 9 (1928): 359–60.
Zulliger, H. "Über den Kastrationskomplex und den Penisneid bei normalen Kindern." *Psyche* 12 (1958): 199–210.

Carnal Pleasure as Overcoming the Fear of Separation

Balint, A. *Angstlust und Regression.* Stuttgart, 1960; Reinbek, 1972.
Dunn, J. *Lust und Unbehagen bei Kleinkindern.* Stuttgart, 1978.
Lincke, H. "Über Angstlust und infantile Sexualität." *Psyche* 8 (1954): 427–49.

On Girls' Phallic-Oedipal Phase

Bibring-Lehner, G. "Über die phallische Phase und ihre Störungen beim Mädchen." *Zeitschr. f. psychoan. Päd.* 7 (1933): 145–52.
Lampl de Groot, J. "Zur Entwicklungsgeschichte des Ödipuskomplexes der Frau." *Psyche* 19 (1965): 402–16.
Nagera, H. *Female Sexuality and the Oedipus Complex.* New York, 1975.
Sterba, R. F. "Über den Ödipuskomplex beim Mädchen." *Zeitschr. f. psychoan. Päd.* 7 (1933): 334–48.

Pathology: Influence of Parental Sexual Behavior on That of the Child

Berge, A. "Les relations sentimentales et sexuelles des parents." *Les Conférences sentimentales des Parents* 3 (Jan. 1951).
Mussen, P., and E. Rutherford. "Parent-Child Relations and Par-

ental Personality in Relation to Young Children's Sex-Role Preferences." *Child Development* 34 (1963): 589–607.

Pathology: Unconscious Seduction of Children by Their Parents

Graber, G. H. *Vater-Mutter-Sohn.* Zurich, 1965.

Hug-Hellmuth, H. v. "Mutter-Sohn, Vater-Tochter." *Imago* 5 (1917): 129–31.

Kaplan, L. "Parent Erotism." *Journal Sexol. Psychoanal.* 2 (1924): 577–84.

Pathology: Dangers of Masturbation at Oedipal Age

Blanchard, Ph. "Masturbation Fantasies of Children and Adolescents." *Bull. Phila. Assn. Psychoanalysis* 3 (1953): 25–38.

Gardner, R. A. "Sexual Fantasies in Childhood." *Medical Aspects of Human Sexuality* (Oct. 1969): 121–34.

Hodann, M. "Die sexuelle Phantasie der Kinder." *Monatsschr. f. Harnkrankheiten und sexuelle Hygiene* 1 (1927): 78–84.

Pathology: On the Female Castration Complex and its Consequences

Abraham, K. "Äußerungsformen des weiblichen Kastrationskomplexes." *Intern. Zeitschr. f. Psychoanalyse* 7 (1920/21): 422–52. [Also E. Jones, ibid., 8 (1922): 329–30.]

Bieber, I., and M. Drellich. "The Female Castration Complex." *Journal Nerv. Ment. Dis.* 129 (1959): 235–42.

Bousfield, E. P. "The Castration Complex in Women." *Psychoanalytic Review* 11 (1924): 121–43.

Hayward, E. P. "Types of Female Castration Reaction." *Psychoanalytic Quarterly* 12 (1943): 45–66.

Horney, K. "Flucht aus der Weiblichkeit." *Intern. Zeitschr. f. Psychoanalyse* 12 (1926): 360–74.

———. "Die Verleugnung der Vagina." *Intern. Zeitschr. f. Psychoanalyse* 19 (1933): 372–84.

———. "Zur Genese des weiblichen Kastrationskomplexes." *Intern. Zeitschr. f. Psychoanalyse* 9 (1923): 12–26.

Rado, S. *Die Kastrationsangst des Weibes.* Vienna, 1934.

Wulff, M. "Mutter-Kind-Beziehungen als Äußerungsformen des weiblichen Kastrationskomplexes." *Intern. Zeitschr. f. Psychoanalyse* 18 (1932): 104–9.

Chapter 8: Fifth Year

Preschool Sexuality

Angrilli, A. F. "Psychosexual Identification of Pre-School Boys." *Journal Genet. Psychol.* 97 (1960): 329–40.

Bauersfeld, K.-H. "Heterosexuelle Beziehungen zwischen kleinen Mädchen und Knaben in der Präpubertät." In *Sexuelle Fehlhaltungen*, edited by R. Bang. Munich and Basel, 1968, pp. 113–14.

Dwelly, A. B. "Sex Interests of the Pre-School Child." In *Guide to Sexology.* New York, 1965, pp. 235–38.

Erikson, E. H. "Sex Differences in the Play Configurations of Pre-Adolescents." *Am. Journal Orthopsychiatry* 21 (1951): 667–92.

Fagot, B. I., and G. R. Patterson. "An in vivo Analysis of Reinforcing Contingencies for Sex-Role Behavior in the Pre-School Child." *Developmental Psychol.* 1 (1969): 563–68.

McCandless, B. R., and H. R. Marschall. "Sex Differences in Social Acceptance and Participation of Pre-School Children." *Child Development* 28 (1957): 421–25.

Mussen, P. H., J. C. Conger, and J. Kagen. "Sexuelle Motive und Neugier (des Vorschulkindes)." In P. H. Mussen, J. C. Conger, and J. Kagen, *Lehrbuch der Kinderpsychologie.* Stuttgart, 1976, pp. 379–80.

Veneer, A. M., and C. A. Snyder. "The Preschool Child's Awareness and Anticipation of Adult Sex Roles." *Sociology* 29 (1966): 159–68.

On the Negative Oedipus Complex

Bakwin, H. "Deviant Gender Role Behavior in Children." *Pediatrics* 41 (1968): 620-29.

Green, R. S. "Childhood Cross-Gender Identification." *Journal Nerv. Ment. Diseases* 147 (1968): 500-509.

———. "The Significance of Cross-Gender Behavior during Childhood." *Proceedings of the 4th World Congress of Psychiatry* 1966, 3043-44.

———. "Sissies and Tomboys." In *Sexual Problems,* edited by C. W. Wahl. New York, 1967, pp. 89-114.

Kelly, G. F. "Bisexuality and the Youth Culture." *Homosexual Counseling* 1 (1974): 16-25.

Stern, H. "Der Ödipuskomplex einer Fünfjährigen." *Zeitschr. f. psychoanal. Päd.* 1 (1926/27): 305.

Parental Influences on Later Sex Life

Bells, R. R. "Parent-Child Conflict in Sexual Values." *Journal Social Issues* 22 (1966): 34-44.

Richter, H. E. "Die narzißtischen Projektionen der Eltern auf das Kind." *Jahrbuch der Psychoanalyse* 1 (1960): 62-81.

Stoller, R. J. "Effects of Parents' Attitudes on Core Gender Identity." *Intern. Journal Psychiat.* 4 (1967): 57-60.

On Overcoming the Oedipus Complex

Dalmau, C. J. "Post-Oedipal Psychodynamics." *Psychoanalytic Review* 44 (1957): 1-9.

Freud, S. "Der Untergang des Ödipuskomplexes" (1924): *Gesammelte Werke* 13: 395-402.

Friedman, D. B. "Toward a Unitary Theory of the Passing of the Oedipal Conflict." *Psychoanalytic Review* 53 (1966): 38-48.

Reich, W. "Die charakterologische Überwindung des Ödipuskomplexes." *Intern. Zeitschr. f. Psychoanalyse* 17 (1931): 55-71.

On the So-Called Latent Phase

Hermann, I. "Die sexuelle Latenzperiode des menschlichen Kindes."
Zeitschr. f. Kinderpsychiat. 8 (1941): 97-102; 1942, 129-37.
Kaplan, S. "Report on the Panel 'The Latency Period.' " *Journal
of the Am. Psychoanalytic Assn.* 5 (1957): 525-38.

On the Formation of Conscience, Superego, and Character

Greenacre, Ph. "Anatomical Structure and Super-Ego Development." *Am. Journal Orthopsychiat.* 18 (1948) 636-48.
Nass, M. L. "The Super-Ego and Moral Development in the
Theories of Freud and Piaget." *The Psychoanalytic Study of
the Child* 21 (1966): 51-68.
Wittels, F. "Das Überich in der Geschlechtserziehung." *Almanach*
(1933): 131-37.

Pathology: Psychopathology

Freud, S. "Analyse der Phobie eines fünfjährigen Knaben" (1909).
Gesammelte Werke 7: 243-377.
Müller-Küpers, M. "Fehlhaltungen transitorischen Charakters.
Psychiatrische Gesichtspunkte der sexuellen Entwicklung und
Reifung." *Sexualmedizin* 9 (1976): 617-23. [Also R. Rosen, ibid.,
2 (1977): 148.]
Nissen, G., and P. Strunk. *Seelische Fehlentwicklungen im Kindes-
alter und Gesellschaftsstruktur.* Neuwied, 1975.

Pathology: Narcissistic and Pluralized Forms of Socialization

Borneman, E. "Am narzißtischen Wesen soll die Welt genesen."
Neue Sammlung 3 (1981).
———. "Warnung vor Illusionen. Statement zum Komplex 'Neue
Sinnlichkeit und Narzißmus.' " *Westermanns Pädagogische
Beiträge* 11 (1980): 452-54.
Federn, P. "Zur Unterscheidung des gesunden und krankhaften
Narzißmus." *Imago* 22 (1936): 5-39.

Kernberg, O. *Borderline Störungen und pathologischer Narzißmus.* Frankfurt-on-Main, 1977.

Kohut, H. *Narzißmus. Eine Theorie der psychoanalytischen Behandlung narzißtischer Persönlichkeitsstörungen.* Frankfurt-on-Main, 1975.

Ziehe, Th. *Pubertät und Narzimus.* Frankfurt-on-Main, 1975.

Chapter 9: Sixth Year

On the Psychology of Joyful Learning

Chadwick, M. "Über die Wurzeln der Wißbegierde." *Intern. Zeitschr. f. Psychoanalyse* 11 (1926): 54–68.

Piaget, J. *Les relations entre l'affectivitée et l'intelligence dans le développement de l'enfant.* Paris, 1954.

Pathology: Sexual Problems of Elementary School Age

Allendy, R. *Le problème sexuel à l'école.* Paris, 1938.

Mechler, H.-J. "Schülersexualität und Doppelmoral." *Österr. Z. f. Soziologie* 1 (1976): 25–36.

Perkins, G. L. "The Emotional Conflicts of the School-Age Child." In *Understanding Your Patient,* edited by S. Liebman. Philadelphia, 1957, pp. 65–76.

Pathology: Effects of Disordered Child Sexuality on Academic Learning

Jacobson, E. "Lernstörungen beim Schulkind durch masochistische Mechanismen." *Intern. Zeitschr. f. Psychoanalyse* 18 (1932): 242–51.

Klein, M. "Die Rolle der Schule in der libidinösen Entwicklung des Kindes." *Intern. Zeitschr. f. Psychoanalyse* 9 (1929): 323–44.

Lessler, K., and M. T. Erickson. "Response to Sexual Symbols by Elementary School Children." *Journal Consult. Psycho.* 32 (1968): 473–78.

Chapter 10: Seventh Year

Sex-Specific Behavior

Argelander, A. "Geschlechtsunterschiede in Leistung und Persönlichkeit des Schulkindes." *Zeitschr. f. päd. Psychol.* 32 (1931): 1.

Knoche, W. *Jungen, Mädchen, Lehrer und Schüler im Zensurenvergleich.* Weinheim, 1969.

Krug, H. "Geschlechtsspezifische Schulleistungen." *Staatsarbeit f. d. Lehramt an berufsbildenden Schulen.* Aachen, 1973.

Otto, K. H. "Geschlechtsspezifische Unterschiede im Disziplinverhalten von Schülerinnen und Schülern." In *Psychologie als gesellschaftliche Produktivkraft.* Berlin, 1965, pp. 356–65.

Reimann-Hunziker, R. "Über die Sexualität des 5. bis 7. Lebensjahres." *Praxis* 49 (1960): 1105–7.

Sexual Play

Stekel, W. "Koitus im Kindesalter." *Wiener medizinische Blätter,* Apr. 4, 1896.

Sex Education in the Lower Grades

Aibauer, R., et al. *Sexualpädagogik der Volksschule.* Freiburg, 1967.

Hartmann, G. H. *Geschlechtserziehung in der Grundschule.* Vienna, 1976.

Neugebauer, L. *Sexualerziehung im Sachunterricht der Grundschule.* Braunschweig, 1973.

Ockel, G., H. C. Gobbin, and I. Bauer. *Sexualerziehung im Grundschulalter.* Frankfurt-on-Main, 1969, 1970.

Rockstroh, U., and H. Vergin. *Curriculum zur Sexualerziehung in der Grundschule.* Bielefeld, 1975.

Smidt, E., and Th. Smidt. *Sexualerziehung in der Grundschule.* Starnberg, 1974.

"Smutty Jokes"

Bittner, G. *Sprache und affektive Entwicklung.* Stuttgart, 1969.
Jones, R. M. "Psychosexuality in Speech Development." *Percept. Mot. Skills* 19 (1964): 390ff.
Meerlo, J. A. M. "Koprolalia, the Child's Urge to Use Indecent Words." *Child-Fam. Digest* 17, no. 5 (1958): 19-20.
Müller, R., et al. "Sexualität und Sprache." In *Betrifft Sexualität.* Braunschweig, 1977, pp. 57-64.

On the Question of a Biological Latency in Childhood

Levy-Suhl, M. "Über die frühkindliche Sexualität des Menschen im Vergleich mit der Geschlechtsreife bei Säugetieren." *Imago* 19 (1933): 27-33.
Szekely, L. "On the Origin of Man and the Latency Period." *Intern. Journal Psychoanalysis* 38 (1957): 98-104.
Yazmajian, R. V. "Biological Aspects of Infantile Sexuality and the Latency Period." *Psychoanalytical Quarterly* 36 (1967): 203-229.

Associations Between Psychosexual and Intellectual Maturity

Alexander, F. "Emotional Maturity." In *The Adolescent,* edited by J. M. Seidman. New York, 1954, pp. 754-62.
Jones, M. C. "The Later Careers of Boys Who Were Early or Late Maturing." *Child Development* 28 (1957): 113-28.
Kubie, L. K. "Education and the Process of Maturation." *Associates of Bank Street College of Education,* New York, 1957, pp. 7-18.
Winnicott, D. W. *Reifungsprozesse und fördernde Umwelt.* Munich, 1974.

Sex Education of the Parents

Heckmann, L. "Die Einbeziehung der Eltern in die schulische Sexualerziehung." *Sexualpädagogik* 2 (1977): 21-22.

Hinrichs, W. *Sexualerziehung im Elternabend.* Ratingen, 1972.

Kentler, H. *Eltern lernen Sexualerziehung.* Reinbek, 1975.

Knecht, I. "Möglichkeiten der Zusammenarbeit von Elternhaus und Schule im Bereich der Sexualerziehung." *Lebendige Schule* no. 6 (1974).

Pathology: Parental Responsibility for Psychical, Psychosomatic, and Psychosexual Disorders of their Children

Langenmayr, A. *Familienkonstellation, Persönlichkeitsentwicklung, Neurosenentstehung.* Göttingen, 1978.

Richter, H. E. *Eltern, Kind und Neurose.* Stuttgart, 1967; Reinbek, 1969.

Spitz, R. "Familienneurose und neurotische Familie." *Intern. Zeitschr. f. Psychoanalyse* 23 (1937): 548-60.

Szurek, S. A. "Concerning the Sexual Disorders of Parents and Their Children." *Journal Nervous Mental Diseases* 120 (1954): 369-78.

Chapter 11: Eighth Year

Sexuality

Kulemeyer, W. "An Straßen und Zäunen. Ein Beitrag zum Problem der infantilen Sexualität." *Zeitschr. f. psychoan. Päd.* 6 (1932): 37-39.

Mende, J. *Schülersexualität.* Frankfurt-on-Main, 1971.

Müller, R., et al. "Sexualität in der Schule." In *Betrifft Sexualität.* Braunschweig, 1977, pp. 49-56.

Sigusch, V., and G. Schmidt. "Sexualpraxis und Sexualmoral der Schüler. Ergebnisse einer empirischen Untersuchung an 602 Mädchen und Jungen." *Sexualmedizin* 2 (1973): 240-44. [Also H. Scarbath in *Katechetische Blätter* 98, no. 10 (1973): 603-17.]

Weissenberg, S. "Die geschlechtlichen Interresen der Schulkinder." *Zeitschr. f. Sexualw.* 12 (1925): 22-27.

Zulliger, H. "Schulkinder und Sexualität." In Mensch-Geschlecht-Gesellschaft, edited by H. Giese. Frankfurt-on-Main, 1954.

Homoeroticism

Bakwin, H., and R. Bakwin. "Homosexual Behavior in Children." Journal Pediatrics 43 (1953): 108–11.

Bender, L., and S. Paster. "Homosexual Trends in Children." Am. Journal Orthopsychiatry 11 (1941): 730–43.

Kirkendall, L. A. "Does Homosexuality Threaten a Child?" In Guide to Sexology. New York, 1965, pp. 246–48.

Manosevitz, M. "Early Sexual Behavior in Adult Homosexual and Heterosexual Males." Journal Abn. Psychol. 76 (1970): 396–402.

Ollendorf, R. Juvenile Homosexual Experience and Its Effect on Adult Sexuality. New York, 1966.

Thompson, U. L., et al. "Parent-Child-Relationships and Sexual Identity in Male and Female Homosexuals and Heterosexuals." Journal Consult. Clin. Psychol. 41 (1973): 120–27.

Masturbation

Bornstein, B. "Masturbation in the Latency Period." The Psychoanalytic Study of the Child 8 (1953): 65–78.

Freud, S. Gesammelte Werke 14: 144–46.

Hulse, W. C. "The Impact of the Environment on Masturbation in Children." Verhandlungen der deutschen Gesellschaft für Kinderheilkunde in Dresden 1931. Berlin, 1932, 420ff.

Zulliger, H. "Schule und Onanie." Zeitschr. f. psychoanal. Päd. 2 (1927/28): 135–43.

Different Forms of Sexual Socialization

Barry, H., et al. "A Cross-Cultural Survey of Some Sex Differences in Socialisation." Journal Abn. Soc. Psychol. 67 (1963): 527–34.

Kürthy, T. Geschlechtsspezifische Sozialisation. 2 vols. Paderborn, 1978. [Also E. Borneman in Das Argument, no. 79, 119–20.]

Lehr, U. "Das Problem der Sozialisation geschlechtsspezifischer Verhaltensweisen." In *Forschungsbereiche der Psychologie,* edited by C. F. Graumann. Göttingen, 1972, pp. 886–954.

Pathology: Sexual Problems

Moses, J. "Konstitution und Erlebnis in der Sexualpsychologie und -pathologie des Kindesalters." *Zeitschr. f. Sexualw.* 8 (1922): 305–19.

The "Secret" of the Eight-Year-Old Girl

Harley, M. "A Secret in Prepuberty." *New York Psychoanalytic Society,* Mar. 26, 1963.

Hermann, I. "Geheime Gesellschaften der Kinder und die Sexualität." *Sexualw. Beiheft, Archiv f. Frauenkunde und Eugenetik* 8 (1922) 175–77.

Zulliger, H. "Das 'Geheimnis' pubertierender Mädchen." *Psyche* 9 (1955): 498–512.

Sex Education in the Schools

Fippinger, F. *Schule und Geschlechtererziehung. Eine empirische Untersuchung zur Einstellung der Lehrer und Lehrerinnen.* Basel, 1969.

Kamratowski, J., and R. Heitmann. *Sexualerziehung in der Reifezeit.* Munich and Basel, 1970.

Loch, W. *Die Verleugnung des Kindes in der evangelischen Pädagogik.* Essen, 1977.

Winkler, B. "Können Lehrer lieben lehren lernen?" *Erziehung heute* 20, no. 7 (1976): 11.

Afterword

Sex Education at Home

Freud, S. "Zur sexuellen Aufklärung der Kinder" (1907). *Gesammelte Werke* 7: 19–27.

Heinrich, H. *Sexualerziehung und Aufklärung im Elternhaus, Kindergarten und Schule.* Kevelaer, 1971.

Hufen, Fr. "Elternrecht—Schranke und Maßstab staatlicher Sexualpädagogik?" In *Konfliktfeld Kindersexualität,* edited by K. Pacharzina and K. Albrecht-Désirat. Frankfurt-on-Main, 1978, pp. 69–90.

Ostermeyer, H. "Das Recht des Kindes auf eine ungestörte Sexualerziehung." In *Konfliktfeld Kindersexualität,* edited by K. Albrecht-Désirat. Frankfurt-on-Main, 1978, pp. 122–28.

Rost, D. *Vom ersten Tag an. Geschlechtserziehung im Vorschulalter.* Limburg, 1973.

Schuh-Gademann, L. *Vorschulische Geschlechtserziehung und ihre Praxis im Kindergarten.* Heidelberg, 1972.

Verch, K. *Sexualerziehung. Lehrmappe zum Unterricht in der Familie.* St. Augustin, 1970.

Zulliger, H. "Eltern, Schule und sexuelle Aufklärung." *Zeitschr. f. psychoan. Päd.* 1 (1926/27): 228–39.

On the Dangers of the Limitation of Sex Education to Biology

Beiler, A. *Biologisches Sachwissen und Geschlechtserziehung.* Ratingen, 1966.

Mechler, H.-J. "Der Auftrag an die Schule—Der Biologismus schulischer Sexualerziehung." *Erziehung heute* 20, no. 7 (1976): 8–10.

Other Works Cited

Besides the works mentioned above, the following writings were cited in the text:

Abraham, Karl. *Psychoanalytische Studien.* 2 vols. Frankfurt-on-Main, 1969, 1971.

Balint, Alice. *Psychoanalyse der frühen Lebensjahre.* Munich and Basel, 1966.

Bloom, Benjamin S. *Stability and Change in Human Characteristics.* New York, 1964.

Brunet, O., and E. Lézine. *Le développment psychologique de la première enfance.* Paris, 1951.

Dolto, Françoise. *Psychoanalyse und Kinderheilkunde.* Frankfurt-on-Main, 1973.

Fenichel, Otto. *Psychoanalytische Neurosenlehre.* 3 vols. Olten and Freiburg, 1974–77.

Ferenczi, Sandor. *Schriften zur Psychoanalyse.* 2 vols. Frankfurt-on-Main, 1970, 1972.

Fornari, Franco. *Psychoanalyse des ersten Lebensjahres.* Frankfurt-on-Main, 1970.

Freud, Sigmund. *Gesammelte Werke in 17 Bänden.* Frankfurt-on-Main, 1964ff.

Gesell, Arnold. *Säugling und Kleinkind in der Kultur der Gegenwart.* 4th ed. Bad Nauheim, 1962.

Harbauer, Hubert. *Kinder- und Jugendpsychiatrie.* 2d ed. Cologne and Lövenich, 1979.

Kierkegaard, Sören. *Werkausgabe in 2 Bänden,* translated by E. Hirsch and H. Gerde. Cologne, 1971.

Lacey, J. I. "The Evaluation of Autonomic Responses." *N. Y. Ac. Sciences* 67 (1956): 123–64.

Mahler, Margaret S., Fred Pine, and Anni Bergman. *Die psychische Geburt des Menschen.* Frankfurt-on-Main, 1978.

Peters, Uwe Henrik. *Anna Freud.* Munich, 1979.

Reich, Wilhelm. *Verbatim-Niederschrift aus dem Jahre 1932.*

Rosenbauer, Karlheinz A. *Genitalorgane—Anatomie und Physiologie.* Reinbek, 1969.

Spitz, René. *Vom Säugling zum Kleinkind. Naturgeschichte der Mutter-Kind-Beziehungen im ersten Lebensjahr.* 4th ed. Stuttgart, 1974.

Stone, Joseph L., and Joseph Church. *Kindheit und Jugend. Einführung in die Entwicklungspsychologie.* 2 vols. Munich, 1978.

Addendum: Translator's Note

Translators, Goethe believed, are to be regarded as meddle-some matchmakers who speak to us in radiant terms of a half-cloaked beauty: they awaken a relentless desire for the original. The origin of this translation, *Childhood Phases of Maturity: Sexual Developmental Psychology*, is Ernest Borneman's *Reifungsphasen der Kindheit: Sexuelle Entwicklungspsychologie*, published in Vienna in 1981.

For the opportunity to make insights and participate in Borneman's singular writing, I now wish to thank friends and associates who provided for and helped facilitate this translation: Distinguished Professor Vern L. Bullough, and at Prometheus Books, Paul Kurtz, Steven Mitchell, Mark G. Hall, Eugene O'Connor, and Lynette Nisbet. Paul J. Nash, Denis Nash, Hajo Gottwald, and Hanne Kaiser-Gottwald, thank you, too.

Michael Lombardi-Nash
Jacksonville, Florida
May 13, 1994

Index

Abortion, 46
Abraham, Karl, 173
Adler, Alfred, 97
Analingus, 115, 130, 135
Androgyne, 45
Asexual (-ity), 7, 213
Autoerotism, 55
Autopedophilia, 116

Bach, Johann Sebastian, 25
Balint, Alice, 131, 194, 233
Bandura, Albert, 49
Bedwetting (bedwetters), 162, 173f., 193f., 200, 217, 145
Bergman, Anni, 102
Bernfeld, Siegfried, 41, 43
Bisexual (-ity), 37, 47, 170
Bloom, Benjamin, 182
Bonaparte, Napoleon, 168
Bond (-ing), 84, 103, 146, 220, 222f., 235, 279
Borneman, Ernest, 17
Bottle (-fed; -feeding), 72, 103, 107f., 110, 116
Bowlby, John, 17
Brain, 129
Breast-feeding, 102f.
Brocher, Tobias, 7, 13, 135, 237, 241, 258, 261f., 274
Broderick, Carlfred, 25
Brody, Sylvia, 104
Brunet, O., 17, 68
Bühler, Charlotte, 17
Bullough, Vern L., 11
Busemann, Adolf, 22

Caesar, Julius, 168
Castration (complex), 81, 109, 137, 157, 191, 200ff., 212
Church, Joseph, 50, 126, 161, 165, 207, 232
Clara, Max, 37
Contrary psychosexuality, 87
Cunnilingus, 115

Daltroff, W., 102

Defiance, 143
Deviancies (deviation), 87, 135
Differentiation, 138, 244
Dolto, Françoise, 152, 219, 246, 260f.

Ego, 81, 84, 86, 122f., 133, 139, 145, 156, 178, 195, 215f., 223, 229, 244, 270
Erikson, Erik, 12
Exhibitionism, 169, 201

Fellatio, 115
Fenichel, Otto, 106, 184, 196, 247
Ferenczi, Sandor, 71, 76, 174
Fixation, 31, 64, 134f.
Fornari, Franco, 91
Fragmentation, 138, 244
Freud, Anna, 75, 160
Freud, Sigmund, 43, 55, 63, 106, 128, 148, 161, 169, 184, 187, 192, 201, 221, 228
Frigidity, 114

Gesell, Arnold, 12, 17, 155, 160
Goslinger, Bertram, 86
Greenacre, Phyllis, 43, 93
Gross, I. H., 102

Harbauer, Hubert, 263f.
Hartmann, Hans, 23
Hermaphrodite, 45ff.
Heterosexuality, 107, 152f., 271
Hetzer, Hildegard, 17
Hirschfeld, Magnus, 175
Hitler, Adolf, 168
Homesickness, 64
Homoerotic (-ism), 208, 210, 271

Homosexuality, 48, 97, 152f., 209, 212, 271

Jungian, 147

Karyotype, 45
Kestenberg, Judith, 102
Kielleutner, L., 176
Kierkegaard, Sören, 93f.
Kinsey, Alfred, 11, 276
Klein, Melanie, 59, 64, 136
Kohlberg, Lawrence, 49
Kollmann, Julius, 24
Kris, Ernst, 17, 23

Lacey, J. I., 164
Latent (period; phase; -cy), 21, 30, 37, 137, 213, 221, 223, 231, 243, 259ff., 272
Lebovici, Sege, 17
Leboyer, Frédéric, 58
Lesbian (-ism), 48, 116
Lézine, I., 17
Libido, 56, 229
Loewenstein, Rudolph, M. 23

Mahler, Margaret S., 17, 76, 86, 90, 92f., 102, 123, 125, 128, 137f., 244
Malinowski, Bronislaw, 7
Marriage, 185, 201, 274
Martinson, Floyd, 11, 12n.
Masochism (-istic), 117, 131, 138, 157, 159, 172, 196f.
Masturbation, 70, 75, 81f., 90, 110, 117, 128, 130, 135, 139, 151f., 154, 162, 168f., 174ff., 190f., 199f., 208, 213, 217,

219, 227f., 245, 263, 271f.
Misogyny, 175
Moll, Albert, 56

Näcke, Paul, 55
Narcissism, 55
Neuroses, 31, 225
Nonheterosexuality, 43

Obscene language, 135

Paschlau, G., 21
Paschlau, R., 21
Pedophilia (pedophile), 11, 116
Persecution, 241
Perversion, 31, 64, 135, 153, 176f.
Piaget, Jean, 12, 17
Pine, Fred, 102
Prostitutes, 116
Psychoses, 135

Rank, Otto, 41
Regression, 31, 64, 134, 171
Reich, Wilhelm, 7, 267
Rett, Andreas, 148
Rosenbauer, Karlheinz, A. 51

Sadism (sadistic), 110, 131, 133, 138, 156, 169, 171f., 174, 200, 208, 223, 241, 264

Sadomasochism, 175
Schilder, Paul, 106
Sperber, Hans, 148
Spitz, René, 7, 17, 23, 53f., 57ff., 72f., 90ff., 104f., 112, 117, 132f., 163
Stoller, Robert J., 84, 97f.
Stone, Joseph L., 50, 126, 207, 232
Stuttering, 175
Superego, 124, 215, 229, 270
Symbiosis (symbotic phase), 76f., 80, 84, 86f., 90, 97ff., 104, 108, 113, 226, 266

Toilet training, 107, 121, 124, 133, 137, 154ff., 159, 163ff., 167, 172, 184, 191
Transsexuality, 87, 96f., 139, 153

Voyeurs, 248

Wallon, Henri, 17
Walters, R. H., 49
Winnicott, D. W., 17
Wolf, Katherine M., 17
Women's movement, 98

Zazzo, René, 17